APPRECIATIONS OF POETRY

APPRECIATIONS
OF POETRY

BY

LAFCADIO HEARN

SELECTED AND EDITED WITH
AN INTRODUCTION BY

JOHN ERSKINE

Essay Index Reprint Series

 BOOKS FOR LIBRARIES PRESS
FREEPORT, NEW YORK

PR
593
H4
1969

STANDARD BOOK NUMBER

8369-0044-8

LIBRARY OF CONGRESS CATALOG CARD NUMBER

68-58794

PRINTED IN THE UNITED STATES OF AMERICA

CONTENTS

INTRODUCTION

I

THIS volume contains a second selection from the lectures which Lafcadio Hearn delivered at the University of Tokyo between 1896 and 1902. An account of these lectures and of the remarkable student notes in which they were preserved, is given in the Introduction to the first selection, "Interpretations of Literature," 1915. The reader of the present volume should be reminded at least that Lafcadio Hearn lectured without notes, but very slowly, choosing simple words and constructions, in order to make the foreign language as easy as possible to his Japanese students; and some of his students managed to take down many of his lectures word for word. From their notes the present volume, like the "Interpretations of Literature," is selected.

The fact that the lectures come to us indirectly, in places perhaps inaccurately, without Hearn's revision and therefore without the exquisite surface of his style, may give us at first a sense of loss; but second thoughts suggest rather our good fortune in having the lectures as they are. The best of Hearn's style, the man himself, is perhaps more clearly revealed here than in any of his finished work. His letters indicate that had he come back to lecture in the United States, as in 1902 he thought of doing, he would have used the substance of some of these classroom talks; and he apparently thought of writing them out and publishing them. He had made no beginning on them, however, when he died. Even if he had lived to publish a volume or two, it is not likely that he could have come before the public as a critic with the same lack of self-consciousness with which he addressed his classes, for he modestly undervalued his wide and profound knowledge of the essentials of literature, and he was aware of the fault-finding abilities of professional scholarship. It is doubtful also whether we should have suspected from carefully written lectures his extraordinary genius as an interpreter of the West to the East, since he would have been writing for us rather than for the Japanese. The complete range of his powers could have been recorded only in a faithful report of what he said in his classroom; and this his students have provided for us in their notes.

It is perhaps unnecessary to say that with few exceptions these chapters were not composed in the order in which they are here grouped. In fact, it is impossible to tell, save in one case, just when the lectures were delivered. From a date at the end of the Browning notes, it appears that the course on Tennyson, Rossetti, Swinburne, and Browning was brought to a close in May, 1899. Since the notes of the Tennyson lecture were hopelessly inadequate, a fragment on that poet from a single, more elementary lecture on Victorian literature is substituted. The editor believes that this lecture gives in substance Hearn's interpretation of Tennyson, though without the brilliant illustrations of the elaborate study.

It seemed wise to omit from most of these chapters a number of paraphrases, which Hearn employed to clarify the English poems for his Japanese students, but which are superfluous for the English reader. It also seemed best to omit a sentence here and there, where the notes were hopelessly tangled; if the reader detects an occasional abruptness, he may attribute it to such an omission, and be thankful that he was not invited to decipher the original. Such places, however, are not many, and the lectures are sufficiently coherent to encourage the hope that nothing important has been thrown overboard. No attempt has been made to reconcile an occasional contradiction, as when

Hearn seems to say, at different times, that Tennyson is the greatest artist of the Victorian era, and so is Rossetti, and so is Swinburne. The editor believes that such variations of mood, so natural to all lecturers, and especially to lovers of poetry, should stand untouched. He has imposed his personal tastes upon Lafcadio Hearn only in the choice of passages for publication. The further task he set himself has been merely mechanical—the correction of spelling and of punctuation, and the verification of facts, dates, and quotations. In preparing this volume, as in preparing the "Interpretations of Literature," he has enjoyed the advice and the assistance of Pay Director Mitchell McDonald, U. S. N., Lafcadio Hearn's friend and literary executor.

II

In the Introduction to "Interpretations of Literature" the editor stressed the significance of those lectures as interpretations of the Western mind to the Eastern. Hearn's published works taught us to understand something of Japan; in his classroom he performed a service as remarkable, in helping the young men who now mould some part of Japanese opinion, to think intelligently and kindly of our civilisation. The unique position in world culture which he thereby won for himself, appeals easily to the imagination, and it is not surprising that the first two volumes of his lectures were accepted promptly and cordially as the documents of this portion of his fame. In the same Introduction, however, the editor tried to stress also what seems to him Lafcadio Hearn's very great genius as an interpretative critic. He is glad of this opportunity to make the attempt again, for a number of reviewers stumbled somewhat over his praise, denouncing it as extravagant and as likely to react to Hearn's disadvantage. The editor persists in thinking that what he said was not extravagant; if it is, however, he wishes to turn it plainly to his own discredit rather than to Hearn's.

The passage that bothered the reviewers was this: "In substance if not in form they [the lectures] are criticism of the finest kind, unmatched in English unless we return to the best of Coleridge, and in some ways unequalled by anything in Coleridge." The sentences immediately following were intended to make clear what the editor meant by "criticism of the finest kind": "Most literary criticism discusses other things than the one matter in which the writer and the reader are interested—that is, the effect of the writing upon the reader. It is hardly too severe to say that most critics talk around a poem or a story or a play, without risking a judgment on the centre of their subject; or else, like even Coleridge at times, they tell you what you ought to read into a given work, instead of showing you what is waiting there to be seen. Lafcadio Hearn is remarkable among critics for throwing a clear light on genuine literary experience—on the emotions which the books under discussion actually give us."

Some of the objections to this praise of Hearn doubtless were simply the expression of surprise that the great name of Coleridge should be brought into comparison with any contemporary name. Against those who think that to be great a writer must have been dead a long time, the editor is not eager to defend himself. He did not mean to suggest that in creative genius Lafcadio Hearn is the equal of Samuel Taylor Coleridge at his best. He did have in mind, however, the fact that in his critical writings Coleridge for the most part discusses philosophical principles rather than particular books; that his criticism is studied chiefly for those abstract discussions of poetry; and that he left us all too few examples of the ability he undoubtedly had, the ability which Lafcadio Hearn's lectures exhibit on so vast a scale—the ability to explain to us our own feelings about books, why we like this or are perplexed by that, and what else there is in the book to fascinate or perplex us. This kind of interpretation, though it looks simple, is extraordinarily rare; it is possible only to the critic who understands human nature, and who approaches books from the poetic or creative point of view. Coleridge had the knowledge of human nature, and in dealing with the poetry of his own school or age he had creative sympathy of the finest kind. But he left us no evidence that his sympathy extended much outside of the romantic period; what would he have said of Zola or of de Maupassant or of Kipling or of Masefield? Later English critics, following Coleridge in their smaller way, have discussed general principles of art, and in most cases have shown creative sympathy with their own particular kind of art—the limits of their sympathy, it would seem, becoming narrower and narrower, until in Arnold and in Pater we find a certain estrangement even from the best writers of their own day. The remarkable fact about Lafcadio Hearn is that though his professed creed was a somewhat narrow romanticism, he exhibits again and again the most acute understanding of writers whose temperament, training, and environment differed widely from his.

The point may be made more plainly. From Aristotle down, the academic tradition of criticism has dealt with principles which, if valid, would afford a basis for judging literature, for classifying it, for deciding what is bad and what is good. Fascinating, amusing, or distressing as the tradition may be as a record of large ambition and of human mistakes, it has often been a source of grief to creative writers, since it can be carried on—it sometimes has been carried on—with authority by men who knew little about writing and cared less, and it has therefore tended frequently to degenerate into formulas of technique. A more radical objection, however, is that the principles in this tradition are drawn from observations of established literature—a great many plays, for example, being taken as the phenomena

from which the definitions of drama are deduced.   In this
process criticism has never found a method to distinguish
safely between what is local and what is universal in the
phenomena before it, and the definitions so made have had
to be revised continually in a hopeless attempt to keep up
with a living and growing art.   It would be more profitable
to examine the original terms on which art lives, studying,
for example, the effect of the play upon the audience, rather
than the theory of the action on the stage.   If our logic is
resolute, we must come to that at last; for when we examine
all the great plays of our time, as Aristotle did, to determine
what a great play is, an earlier verdict has already decided
for us which are the great plays; the most that our criticism
can hope to accomplish is a belated and elaborate restate-
ment of our own premises.   Meanwhile there are curious
pitfalls for even the best of theoretical critics.   Arnold, for
example, looking over the poems generally recognised as
great, concluded that they were so recognised because they
had the grand style; the grand style makes a poem great.
If there were any connection between poetic greatness and
the grand style, Arnold might have enjoyed peace of mind
thenceforth, knowing that the grand style would bring
about an automatic recognition of poetic greatness.   But he
proceeded to preach the recognition of the grand style as a
cultured obligation rather than as a scientific fact, and we
cannot take his word for it that his own verse in the grand
style is greater poetry than some other verse we like better.
    Over against the traditional criticism there has always
been the practical science, the shop-talk, of the artists themselves.   The best critic of a wagon is probably the wagon-
builder, as the immortal shoe-maker was the best critic of
the shoe in the Greek picture.   When he ventured to criticise the painting further, the shoe-maker was told to stick
to his last.   The creative artist might repeat the invitation
to the merely academic critic who cannot himself create.
The creator is not greatly concerned with pigeon-holing

his art; he is interested in the work before him for what it is intended to accomplish, and he draws on his practical experience for an opinion as to whether it will accomplish its purpose. Therefore he is not afraid to give an opinion about an entirely new work of art; he recognises immediately its essential usefulness, as Emerson foresaw at once the great career of Walt Whitman's poetry. Traditional criticism, on the contrary, is often unwilling to readjust itself to new genius. If it is thought that the shop-talk of artists would naturally be impressionistic or haphazard, it should be remembered that they alone among critics work out the illustrations of their principles, as the wagon maker illustrates his idea of a wagon. The basis of a real science is here; these critics try to understand in order to practise the art.

In literature, as distinguished from other arts, the wisest talk of the creator has to do with life, with human nature; for these are the materials he works in, and for his knowledge of these his readers are best equipped to judge him. In the letters and the memoirs of expert writers, what incomparable criticism we often find! Witness the various penetrating remarks of Tennyson recorded in his memoirs, the superb insights of Charles Lamb in his letters, especially to Wordsworth, and the equally remarkable observations in the journals of Emerson and of Hawthorne. This wisdom shows no sign of deserting the contemporary writer. A Broadway playwright remarks that nowadays you cannot let your hero and heroine, in anything but a farce, fall in love at first sight, because most of your audience have fallen in love by the more deliberate modern process. Professor Santayana expresses the same truth when he says that wherever the sexes have been jealously guarded from each other, with few opportunities for meeting, they have fallen in love at first sight, since fall in love they must. Similar knowledge of life, together with the creative observation of that which lies under our eyes, but which the average reader and the theoretical critic often do not see, might be illustrated in several passages from Professor Santayana's too inaccessible study of "Hamlet." He says in effect, for example, that no one ever feels that Hamlet is mad, but everybody feels that he is irrational. Though we cannot all of us explain why we feel he is irrational, our impression is correct. The impression is produced by such episodes as the performance of the play before the king. Hamlet had no doubt that his uncle murdered his father; his question was whether he should avenge the murder by assassination. To clear his doubts, he set a trap which merely confirmed the king's guilt, but gave no advice as to taking revenge. To those of us who have felt Hamlet's irrationality, without perceiving the slip in his logic, this kind of criticism brings intelligence in understanding our old impressions, and increases our susceptibility to new ones.

This is what the editor meant by "criticism of the finest kind"—the discussion of art by those who know how to create it, the interpretation of books which opens our eyes to life, which sets no gulf between the problem of how to read and the problem of how to write. For this kind of criticism, the editor believes, Lafcadio Hearn's lectures have a unique place in English literature, unmatched in quality by any but the best of Coleridge, and in quantity quite without parallel.

APPRECIATIONS OF POETRY

CHAPTER I

ON LOVE IN ENGLISH POETRY

I OFTEN imagine that the longer he studies English literature the more the Japanese student must be astonished at
the extraordinary predominance given to the passion of love
both in fiction and in poetry. Indeed, by this time I have
begun to feel a little astonished at it myself. Of course,
before I came to this country it seemed to me quite natural
that love should be the chief subject of literature; because
I did not know anything about any other kind of society except Western society. But to-day it really seems to me a
little strange. If it seems strange to me, how much more
ought it to seem strange to you! Of course, the simple explanation of the fact is that marriage is the most important
act of man's life in Europe or America, and that everything
depends upon it. It is quite different on this side of the
world. But the simple explanation of the difference is not
enough. There are many things to be explained. Why
should not only the novel writers but all the poets make love
the principal subject of their work? I never knew, because
I never thought, how much English literature was saturated
with the subject of love until I attempted to make selections
of poetry and prose for class use—naturally endeavouring to
select such pages or poems as related to other subjects than
passion. Instead of finding a good deal of what I was
looking for, I could find scarcely anything. The great prose
writers, outside of the essay or history, are nearly all famous as tellers of love stories. And it is almost impossible
to select half a dozen stanzas of classic verse from Tennyson
or Rossetti or Browning or Shelley or Byron, which do not
contain anything about kissing, embracing, or longing for
some imaginary or real beloved. Wordsworth, indeed, is

something of an exception; and Coleridge is most famous for a poem which contains nothing at all about love. But exceptions do not affect the general rule that love is the theme of English poetry, as it is also of French, Italian, Spanish, or German poetry. It is the dominant motive.

So with the English novelists. There have been here also a few exceptions—such as the late Robert Louis Stevenson, most of whose novels contain little about women; they are chiefly novels or romances of adventure. But the exceptions are very few. At the present time there are produced almost every year in England about a thousand new novels, and all of these or nearly all are love stories. To write a novel without a woman in it would be a dangerous undertaking; in ninety-nine cases out of a hundred the book would not sell.

Of course all this means that the English people throughout the world, as readers, are chiefly interested in the subject under discussion. When you find a whole race interested more in one thing than in anything else, you may be sure that it is so because the subject is of paramount importance in the life of the average person. You must try to imagine then, a society in which every man must choose his wife, and every woman must choose her husband, independent of all outside help, and not only choose but obtain if possible. The great principle of Western society is that competition rules here as it rules in everything else. The best man—that is to say, the strongest and cleverest— is likely to get the best woman, in the sense of the most beautiful person. The weak, the feeble, the poor, and the ugly have little chance of being able to marry at all. Tens of thousands of men and women cannot possibly marry. I am speaking of the upper and middle classes. The working people, the peasants, the labourers, these marry young; but the competition there is just the same — just as difficult, and only a little rougher. So it may be said that every man has a struggle of some kind in order to marry, and that there is a kind of fight or contest for the possession of every woman worth having. Taking this view of Western society, not only in England but throughout all Europe, you will easily be able to see why the Western public have reason to be more interested in literature which treats of love than in any other kind of literature.

But although the conditions that I have been describing are about the same in all Western countries, the tone of the literature which deals with love is not at all the same. There are very great differences. In prose they are much more serious than in poetry; because in all countries a man is allowed, by public opinion, more freedom in verse than in prose. Now these differences in the way of treating the subject in different countries really indicate national differences of character. Northern love stories and Northern poetry about love are very serious; and these authors are kept within fixed limits. Certain subjects are generally forbidden. For example, the English public wants novels about love, but the love must be the love of a girl who is to become somebody's wife. The rule in the English novel is to describe the pains, fears, and struggles of the period before marriage—the contest in the world for the right of marriage. A man must not write a novel about any other point of love. Of course there are plenty of authors who have broken this rule, but the rule still exists. A man may represent a contest between two women, one good and one bad, but if the bad woman is allowed to conquer in the story, the public will growl. This English fashion has existed since the eighteenth century, since the time of Richardson, and is likely to last for generations to come.

Now this is not the rule at all which governs the making of novels in France. French novels generally treat of the relations of women to the world and to lovers, after marriage; consequently there is a great deal in French novels about adultery, about improper relations between the sexes, about many things which the English public would

not allow.   This does not mean that the English are morally a better people than the French or other Southern races.
But it does mean that there are great differences in the social
conditions.   One such difference can be very briefly expressed.   An English girl, an American girl, a Norwegian,
a Dane, a Swede, is allowed all possible liberty before marriage.   The girl is told, "You must be able to take care of
yourself, and not do wrong."   After marriage there is no
more such liberty.   After marriage in all Northern countries a woman's conduct is strictly watched.   But in France,
and in Southern countries, the young girl has no liberty before marriage.   She is always under the guard of her
brother, her father, her mother, or some experienced relation.   She is accompanied wherever she walks.   She is not
allowed to see her betrothed except in the presence of witnesses.   But after marriage her liberty begins.   Then she is
told for the first time that she must take care of herself.
Well, you will see that the conditions which inspire the
novels, in treating of the subject of love and marriage, are
very different in Northern and in Southern Europe.   For
this reason alone the character of the novel produced in
France and of the novel produced in England could not be
the same.

You must remember, however, that there are many other
reasons for this difference—reasons of literary sentiment.
The Southern or Latin races have been civilised for a much
longer time than the Northern races; they have inherited
the feelings of the ancient world, the old Greek and Roman
world, and they think still about the relation of the sexes
in very much the same way that the ancient poets and romance writers used to think.   And they can do things which
English writers cannot do, because their language has power
of more delicate expression.

We may say that the Latin writers still speak of love in
very much the same way that it was considered before Christianity.   But when I speak of Christianity I am only refer-

ring to an historical date. Before Christianity the Northern races also thought about love very much in the same way
that their best poets do at this day. The ancient Scandinavian literature would show this. The Viking, the old
sea-pirate, felt very much as Tennyson or as Meredith
would feel upon this subject; he thought of only one kind
of love as real—that which ends in marriage, the affection
between husband and wife. Anything else was to him mere
folly and weakness. Christianity did not change his sentiment on this subject. The modern Englishman, Swede,
Dane, Norwegian, or German regards love in exactly that
deep, serious, noble way that his pagan ancestors did. I
think we can say that different races have differences of feeling on sexual relations, which differences are very much
older than any written history. They are in the blood and
soul of a people, and neither religion nor civilisation can
utterly change them.

So far I have been speaking particularly about the differences in English and French novels; and a novel is especially a reflection of national life, a kind of dramatic narration of truth, in the form of a story. But in poetry, which
is the highest form of literature, the difference is much more
observable. We find the Latin poets of to-day writing just
as freely on the subject of love as the old Latin poets of
the age of Augustus, while Northern poets observe with few
exceptions great restraint when treating of this theme.
Now where is the line to be drawn? Are the Latins right?
Are the English right? How are we to make a sharp distinction between what is moral and good and what is immoral and bad in treating love-subjects?

Some definition must be attempted.

What is meant by love? As used by Latin writers the
word has a range of meanings, from that of the sexual relation between insects or animals up to the highest form of
religious emotion, called "The love of God." I need
scarcely say that this definition is too loose for our use. The

English word, by general consent, means both sexual passion and deep friendship. This again is a meaning too wide for our purpose. By putting the adjective "true" before love, some definition is attempted in ordinary conversation. When an Englishman speaks of "true love," he usually means something that has no passion at all; he means a perfect friendship which grows up between man and wife and which has nothing to do with the passion which brought the pair together. But when the English poet speaks of love, he generally means passion, not friendship. I am only stating very general rules. You see how confusing the subject is, how difficult to define the matter. Let us leave the definition alone for a moment, and consider the matter philosophically.

Some very foolish persons have attempted even within recent years to make a classification of different kinds of love—love between the sexes. They talk about romantic love, and other such things. All that is utter nonsense. In the meaning of sexual affection there is only one kind of love, the natural attraction of one sex for the other; and the only difference in the highest form of this attraction and the lowest is this, that in the nobler nature a vast number of moral, æsthetic, and ethical sentiments are related to the passion, and that in lower natures those sentiments are absent. Therefore we may say that even in the highest forms of the sentiment there is only one dominant feeling, complex though it be, the desire for possession. What follows the possession we may call love if we please; but it might better be called perfect friendship and sympathy. It is altogether a different thing. The love that is the theme of poets in all countries is really love, not the friendship that grows out of it.

I suppose you know that the etymological meaning of "passion" is "a state of suffering." In regard to love, the word has particular signification to the Western mind, for it refers to the time of struggle and doubt and longing before the object is attained. Now how much of this passion is a legitimate subject of literary art?

The difficulty may, I think, be met by remembering the extraordinary character of the mental phenomena which manifest themselves in the time of passion. There is during that time a strange illusion, an illusion so wonderful that it has engaged the attention of great philosophers for thousands of years; Plato, you know, tried to explain it in a very famous theory. I mean the illusion that seems to change, or rather, actually does change the senses of a man at a certain time. To his eye a certain face has suddenly become the most beautiful object in the world. To his ears the accents of one voice become the sweetest of all music. Reason has nothing to do with this, and reason has no power against the enchantment. Out of Nature's mystery, somehow or other, this strange magic suddenly illuminates the senses of a man; then vanishes again, as noiselessly as it came. It is a very ghostly thing, and cannot be explained by any theory not of a very ghostly kind. Even Herbert Spencer has devoted his reasoning to a new theory about it. I need not go further in this particular than to tell you that in a certain way passion is now thought to have something to do with other lives than the present; in short, it is a kind of organic memory of relations that existed in thousands and tens of thousands of former states of being. Right or wrong though the theories may be, this mysterious moment of love, the period of this illusion, is properly the subject of high poetry, simply because it is the most beautiful and the most wonderful experience of a human life. And why?

Because in the brief time of such passion the very highest and finest emotions of which human nature is capable are brought into play. In that time more than at any other hour in life do men become unselfish, unselfish at least toward one human being. Not only unselfishness but self-sacrifice is a desire peculiar to the period. The young man in love is not merely willing to give away everything that he possesses to the person beloved; he wishes to suffer pain, to meet danger, to risk his life for her sake. Therefore Tennyson, in speaking of that time, beautifully said:

Love took up the harp of Life, and smote on all the chords with might,
Smote the chord of Self, that, trembling, pass'd in music out of sight.

Unselfishness is, of course, a very noble feeling, independently of the cause. But this is only one of the emotions of a higher class when powerfully aroused. There is pity, tenderness—the same kind of tenderness that one feels toward a child—the love of the helpless, the desire to protect. And a third sentiment felt at such a time more strongly than at any other, is the sentiment of duty; responsibilities moral and social are then comprehended in a totally new way. Surely none can dispute these facts nor the beauty of them.

Moral sentiments are the highest of all; but next to them the sentiment of beauty in itself, the artistic feeling, is also a very high form of intellectual and even of secondary moral experience. Scientifically there is a relation between the beautiful and the good, between the physically perfect and the ethically perfect. Of course it is not absolute. There is nothing absolute in this world. But the relation exists. Whoever can comprehend the highest form of one kind of beauty must be able to comprehend something of the other. I know very well that the ideal of the love-season is an illusion; in nine hundred and ninety-nine cases out of the thousand the beauty of the woman is only imagined. But does that make any possible difference? I do not think that it does. To imagine beauty is really to see it—not objectively, perhaps, but subjectively beyond all possibility of doubt. Though you see the beauty only in your mind, in your mind it is; and in your mind its ethical influence must operate. During the time that a man worships even imaginary bodily beauty, he receives some secret glimpse of a higher kind of beauty—beauty of heart and mind. Was there ever in this world a real lover who did not believe the woman of his choice to be not only the most beautiful of mortals, but also the best in a moral sense? I do not think that there ever was.

The moral and the ethical sentiments of a being thus aroused call into sudden action all the finer energies of the man—the capacities for effort, for heroism, for high pressure work of any sort, mental or physical, for all that requires quickness in thought and exactitude in act. There is for the time being a sense of new power. Anything that makes strong appeal to the best exercise of one's faculties is beneficent and, in most cases, worthy of reverence. Indeed, it is in the short season of which I am speaking that we always discover the best of everything in the character of woman or of man. In that period the evil qualities, the ungenerous side, is usually kept as much out of sight as possible.

Now for all these suggested reasons, as for many others which might be suggested, the period of illusion in love is really the period which poets and writers of romance are naturally justified in describing. Can they go beyond it with safety, with propriety? That depends very much upon whether they go up or down. By going up I mean keeping within the region of moral idealism. By going down I mean descending to the level of merely animal realism. In this realism there is nothing deserving the highest effort of art of any sort.

What is the object of art? Is it not, or should it not be, to make us imagine better conditions than that which at present exist in the world, and by so imagining to prepare the way for the coming of such conditions? I think that all great art has done this. Do you remember the old story about Greek mothers keeping in their rooms the statue of a god or a man, more beautiful than anything real, so that their imagination might be constantly influenced by the sight of beauty, and that they might perhaps be able to bring more beautiful children into the world? Among the Arabs, mothers also do something of this kind, only, as they have no art of imagery, they go to nature herself for the living image. Black luminous eyes are beautiful, and wives keep in their tents a little deer, the gazelle, which is famous for the brilliancy and beauty of its eyes. By constantly looking at this charming pet the Arab wife hopes to bring into the world some day a child with eyes as beautiful as the eyes of the gazelle. Well, the highest function of art ought to do for us, or at least for the world, what the statue and the gazelle were expected to do for Grecian and Arab mothers—to make possible higher conditions than the existing ones.

So much being said, consider again the place and the meaning of the passion of love in any human life. It is essentially a period of idealism, of imagining better things and conditions than are possible in this world. For everybody who has been in love has imagined something higher than the possible and the present. Any idealism is a proper subject for art. It is not at all the same in the case of realism. Grant that all this passion, imagination, and fine sentiment is based upon a very simple animal impulse. That does not make the least difference in the value of the highest results of that passion. We might say the very same thing about any human emotion; every emotion can be evolutionally traced back to simple and selfish impulses shared by man with the lower animals. But because an apple tree or a pear tree happens to have its roots in the ground, does that mean that its fruits are not beautiful and wholesome? Most assuredly we must not judge the fruit of the tree from the unseen roots; but what about turning up the ground to look at the roots? What becomes of the beauty of the tree when you do that? The realist—at least the French realist—likes to do that. He likes to bring back the attention of his reader to the lowest rather than to the highest, to that which should be kept hidden, for the very same reason that the roots of a tree should be kept underground if the tree is to live.

The time of illusion, then, is the beautiful moment of passion; it represents the artistic zone in which the poet or romance writer ought to be free to do the very best that he can. He may go beyond that zone; but then he has only two directions in which he can travel. Above it there is religion, and an artist may, like Dante, succeed in transforming love into a sentiment of religious ecstasy. I do not think that any artist could do that to-day; this is not an age of religious ecstasy. But upwards there is no other way to go. Downwards the artist may travel until he finds himself in hell. Between the zone of idealism and the brutality of realism there are no doubt many gradations. I am only indicating what I think to be an absolute truth, that in treating of love the literary master should keep to the period of illusion, and that to go below it is a dangerous undertaking. And now, having tried to make what are believed to be proper distinctions between great literature on this subject and all that is not great, we may begin to study a few examples. I am going to select at random passages from English poets and others, illustrating my meaning.

Tennyson is perhaps the most familiar to you among poets of our own time; and he has given a few exquisite examples of the ideal sentiment in passion. One is a concluding verse in the beautiful song that occurs in the monodrama of "Maud," where the lover, listening in the garden, hears the steps of his beloved approaching.

She is coming, my own, my sweet,
  Were it ever so airy a tread,
My heart would hear her and beat,
  Were it earth in an earthy bed;
My dust would hear her and beat,
  Had I lain for a century dead;
Would start and tremble under her feet,
  And blossom in purple and red.

This is a very fine instance of the purely ideal emotion—
extravagant, if you like, in the force of the imagery used,
but absolutely sincere and true; for the imagination of love
is necessarily extravagant.   It would be quite useless to ask
whether the sound of a girl's footsteps could really waken
a dead man; we know that love can fancy such things quite
naturally, not in one country only but everywhere.   An
Arabian poem written long before the time of Mohammed
contains exactly the same thought in simpler words; and I
think that there are some old Japanese songs containing
something similar.   All that the statement really means is
that the voice, the look, the touch, even the footstep of the
woman beloved have come to possess for the lover a significance as great as life and death.   For the moment he knows
no other divinity; she is his god, in the sense that her power
over him has become infinite and irresistible.

The second example may be furnished from another part
of the same composition—the little song of exaltation after
the promise to marry has been given.

> O let the solid ground
>   Not fail beneath my feet
> Before my life has found
>   What some have found so sweet;
> Then let come what come may,
> What matter if I go mad,
> I shall have had my day.
>
> Let the sweet heavens endure,
>   Not close and darken above me
> Before I am quite, quite sure
>   That there is one to love me;
> Then let come what come may
> To a life that has been so sad,
> I shall have had my day.

The feeling of the lover is that no matter what happens
afterwards, the winning of the woman is enough to pay for
life, death, pain, or anything else.   One of the most re-

markable phenomena of the illusion is the supreme indifference to consequences—at least to any consequences which
would not signify moral shame or loss of honour. Of
course the poet is supposed to consider the emotion only in
generous natures. But the subject of this splendid indifference has been more wonderfully treated by Victor Hugo
than by Tennyson—as we shall see later on, when considering another phase of the emotion. Before doing that, I
want to call your attention to a very charming treatment of
love's romance by an American. It is one of the most delicate of modern compositions, and it is likely to become a
classic, as it has already been printed in four or five different
anthologies. The title is "Atalanta's Race."

First let me tell you the story of Atalanta, so that you
will be better able to see the fine symbolism of the poem.
Atalanta, the daughter of a Greek king, was not only the
most beautiful of maidens, but the swiftest runner in the
world. She passed her time in hunting, and did not wish
to marry. But as many men wanted to marry her, a law
was passed that any one who desired to win her must run
a race with her. If he could beat her in running, then she
promised to marry him, but if he lost the race, he was to be
killed. Some say that the man was allowed to run first,
and that the girl followed with a spear in her hand and
killed him when she overtook him. There are different accounts of the contest. Many suitors lost the race and were
killed. But finally a young man called Hippomenes obtained from the Goddess of Love three golden apples, and
he was told that if he dropped these apples while running,
the girl would stop to pick them up, and that in this way
he might be able to win the race. So he ran, and when he
found himself about to be beaten, he dropped one apple.
She stopped to pick it up and thus he gained a little. In
this way he won the race and married Atalanta. Greek
mythology says that afterwards she and her husband were
turned into lions because they offended the gods; however,

that need not concern us here.   There is a very beautiful moral in the old Greek story, and the merit of the American composition is that its author, Maurice Thompson, perceived this moral and used it to illustrate a great philosophical truth.

> When Spring grows old, and sleepy winds
>   Set from the South with odours sweet,
> I see my love, in green, cool groves,
>   Speed down dusk aisles on shining feet.
>
> She throws a kiss and bids me run,
>   In whispers sweet as roses' breath;
> I know I cannot win the race,
>   And at the end, I know, is death.
>
> But joyfully I bare my limbs,
>   Anoint me with the tropic breeze,
> And feel through every sinew run
>   The vigour of Hippomenes.
>
> O race of love! we all have run
>   Thy happy course through groves of Spring,
> And cared not, when at last we lost,
>   For life or death, or anything!

There are a few thoughts here requiring a little comment. You know that the Greek games and athletic contests were held in the fairest season, and that the contestants were stripped.   They were also anointed with oil, partly to protect the skin against sun and temperature and partly to make the body more supple.   The poet speaks of the young man as being anointed by the warm wind of Spring, the tropic season of life.   It is a very pretty fancy.   What he is really telling us is this:

"There are no more Greek games, but the race of love is still run to-day as in times gone by; youth is the season, and the atmosphere of youth is the anointing of the contestant."

But the moral of the piece is its great charm, the poetical statement of a beautiful and a wonderful fact.   In almost **every** life there is a time when we care for only one person, and suffer much for that person's sake; yet in that period we do not care whether we suffer or die, and in after life, when we look back at those hours of youth, we wonder at the way in which we then felt.   In European life of to-day the old Greek fable is still true; almost everybody must run Atalanta's race and abide by the result.

One of the delightful phases of the illusion of love is the sense of old acquaintance, the feeling as if the person loved had been known and loved long ago in some time and place forgotten.   I think you must have observed, many of you, that when the senses of sight and hearing happen to be strongly stirred by some new and most pleasurable experience, the feeling of novelty is absent, or almost absent. You do not feel as if you were seeing or hearing something new, but as if you saw or heard something that you knew all about very long ago.   I remember once travelling with a Japanese boy into a charming little country town in Shikoku—and scarcely had we entered the main street, than he cried out: "Oh, I have seen this place before!"   Of course he had not seen it before; he was from Osaka and had never left the great city until then.   But the pleasure of his new experience had given him this feeling of familiarity with the unfamiliar.   I do not pretend to explain this familiarity with the new—it is a great mystery still, just as it was a great mystery to the Roman Cicero.   But almost everybody that has been in love has probably had the same feeling during a moment or two—the feeling "I have known that woman before," though the where and the when are mysteries.   Some of the modern poets have beautifully treated this feeling.   The best example that I can give you is the exquisite lyric by Rossetti entitled "Sudden Light."

I have been here before,
　　But when or how I cannot tell:
I know the grass beyond the door,
　　The sweet keen smell,
The sighing sound, the lights around the shore.

And the dream of the earliest day
Brought back to the desolate heart.

It was knowledge of all that had been
In the thought, in the soul unseen;
'Twas the word which the lips could not say
To redeem or recover the past.
It was more than was taken away
Which the heart got back at the last.

The passion that lost its spell,
The rose that died where it fell,
The look that was look'd in vain,
The prayer that seemed lost evermore,
They were found in the heart again,
With all that the heart would restore.

Put into less mystical language the legend is this: A
young man and a young woman loved each other for a time;
then they were separated by some great wrong—we may
suppose the woman was untrue. The man always loved
her memory, in spite of this wrong which she had done.
The two died and were buried; hundreds and hundreds of
years they remained buried, and the dust of them mixed
with the dust of the earth. But in the perpetual order of
things, a pure love never can die, though bodies may die
and pass away. So after many generations the pure love
which this man had for a bad woman was born again in the
heart of another man—the same, yet not the same. And
the spirit of the woman that long ago had done the wrong,
also found incarnation again; and the two meeting, are
drawn to each other by what people call love, but what is
really Greater Memory, the recollection of past lives. But
now all is happiness for them, because the weaker and worse
part of each has really died and has been left hundreds of
years behind, and only the higher nature has been born
again. All that ought not to have been is not; but all that
ought to be now is. This is really an evolutionary teaching, but it is also poetical license, for the immoral side of

mankind does not by any means die so quickly as the poet supposes. It is perhaps a question of many tens of thousands of years to get rid of a few of our simpler faults. Anyway, the fancy charms us and tempts us really to hope that these things might be so.

While the poets of our time so extend the history of a love backwards beyond this life, we might expect them to do the very same thing in the other direction. I do not refer to reunion in heaven, or anything of that sort, but simply to affection continued after death. There are some very pretty fancies of the kind. But they cannot prove to you quite so interesting as the poems which treat the recollection of past life. When we consider the past imaginatively, we have some ground to stand on. The past has been—there is no doubt about that. The fact that we are at this moment alive makes it seem sufficiently true that we were alive thousands or millions of years ago. But when we turn to the future for poetical inspiration, the case is very different. There we must imagine without having anything to stand upon in the way of experience. Of course if born again into a body we could imagine many things; but there is the ghostly interval between death and birth which nobody is able to tell us about. Here the poet depends upon dream experiences, and it is of such an experience that Christina Rossetti speaks in her beautiful poem entitled "A Pause."

> They made the chamber sweet with flowers and leaves,
>   And the bed sweet with flowers on which I lay,
>   While my soul, love-bound, loitered on its way.
> I did not hear the birds about the eaves,
> Nor hear the reapers talk among the sheaves:
>   Only my soul kept watch from day to day,
>   My thirsty soul kept watch for one away:—
> Perhaps he loves, I thought, remembers, grieves.
>
> At length there came the step upon the stair,
>   Upon the lock the old familiar hand:

> Then first my spirit seemed to scent the air
> Of Paradise; then first the tardy sand
> Of time ran golden; and I felt my hair
> Put on a glory, and my soul expand.

The woman is dead.   In the room where her body died, flowers have been placed, offerings to the dead.   Also there are flowers upon the bed.   The ghost of the woman observes all this, but she does not feel either glad or sad because of it; she is thinking only of the living lover, who was not there when she died, but far away.   She wants to know whether he really loved her, whether he will really be sorry to hear that she is dead.   Outside the room of death the birds are singing; in the fields beyond the windows peasants are working, and talking as they work.   But the ghost does not listen to these sounds.   The ghost remains in the room only for love's sake; she cannot go away until the lover comes.   At last she hears him coming.   She knows the sound of the step; she knows the touch of the hand upon the lock of the door.   And instantly, before she sees him at all, she first feels delight.   Already it seems to her that she can smell the perfume of the flowers of heaven; it then seems to her that about her head, as about the head of an angel, a circle of glory is shaping itself, and the real heaven, the Heaven of Love, is at hand.

How very beautiful this is.   There is still one line which requires a separate explanation — I mean the sentence about " the sands of time running golden."   Perhaps you may remember the same simile in Tennyson's "Locksley Hall":

Love took up the glass of Time, and turn'd it in his glowing hands;
Every moment, lightly shaken, ran itself in golden sands.

Here time is identified with the sand of the hour glass, and the verb "to run" is used because this verb commonly expresses the trickling of the sand from the upper part of the glass into the lower.   In other words, fine sand "runs" just like water.   To say that the "sands of time ran golden," or become changed into gold, is only a poetical way of stating that the time becomes more than happy—almost heavenly or divine. And now you will see how very beautiful the comparison becomes in this little poem about the ghost of the woman waiting for the coming step of her lover.

Several other aspects of the emotion may now be considered separately. One of these, an especially beautiful one, is memory. Of course, there are many aspects of love's memories, some all happiness, others intensely sorrowful—the memory of a walk, a meeting, a moment of good-bye. Such memories occupy a very large place in the treasure house of English love poems. I am going to give three examples only, but each of a different kind. The first poet that I am going to mention is Coventry Patmore. He wrote two curious books of poetry, respectively called "The Angel in the House" and "The Unknown Eros." In the first of these books he wrote the whole history of his courtship and marriage—a very dangerous thing for a poet to do, but he did it successfully. The second volume is miscellaneous, and contains some very beautiful things. I am going to quote only a few lines from the piece called "Amelia." This piece is the story of an evening spent with a sweetheart, and the lines which I am quoting refer to the moment of taking the girl home. They are now rather famous:

> . . . To the dim street
> I led her sacred feet;
> And so the Daughter gave,
> Soft, moth-like, sweet,
> Showy as damask-rose and shy as musk,
> Back to her Mother, anxious in the dusk.
> And now "Good Night!"

Why should the poet speak of the girl in this way? Why does he call her feet sacred? She has just promised to marry him; and now she seems to him quite divine. But he discovers very plain words with which to communicate his finer feelings to the reader.   The street is "dim" because it is night; and in the night the beautifully dressed maiden seems like a splendid moth—the name given to night butter-flies in England.   In England the moths are much more beautiful than the true butterflies; they have wings of scar-let and purple and brown and gold.   So the comparison, though peculiarly English, is very fine.   Also there is a suggestion of the soundlessness of the moth's flight.   Now "showy as damask rose" is a striking simile only because the damask-rose is a wonderfully splendid flower—richest in colour of all roses in English gardens.   "Shy as musk" is rather a daring simile.   "Musk" is a perfume used by English as well as Japanese ladies, but there is no perfume which must be used with more discretion, carefulness.   If you use ever so little too much, the effect is not pleasant. But if you use exactly the proper quantity, and no more, there is no perfume which is more lovely.   "Shy as musk" thus refers to that kind of girlish modesty which never com-mits a fault even by the measure of a grain—a beautiful shyness incapable of being anything but beautiful.   Never-theless the comparison must be confessed one which should be felt rather than explained.

The second of the three promised quotations shall be from Robert Browning.   There is one feeling, not often touched upon by poets, yet peculiar to lovers, that is here treated —the desire when you are very happy or when you are look-ing at anything attractive to share the pleasure of the moment with the beloved.   But it seldom happens that the wish and the conditions really meet.   Referring to this longing Browning made a short lyric that is now a classic; it is among the most dainty things of the century.

> Never the time and the place
>   And the loved one all together!
> This path—how soft to pace!
> This May—what magic weather!

Where is the loved one's face?
In a dream that loved one's face meets mine
But the house is narrow, the place is bleak,
Where, outside, rain and wind combine
With a furtive ear, if I try to speak,
With a hostile eye at my flushing cheek
With a malice that marks each word, each sign!

Never can we have things the way we wish in this world
—a beautiful day, a beautiful place, and the presence of
the beloved all at the same time.   Something is always
missing; if the place be beautiful, the weather perhaps is
bad.   Or if the weather and the place both happen to be
perfect, the woman is absent.   So the poet finding himself
in some very beautiful place, and remembering this, remembers also the last time that he met the woman beloved.   It
was a small dark house and chilly; outside there was rain
and storm; and the sounds of the wind and of the rain
were as the sounds of people secretly listening, or sounds
of people trying to look in secretly through the windows.
Evidently it was necessary that the meeting should be
secret, and it was not altogether as happy as could have
been wished.

The third example is a very beautiful poem; we must
content ourselves with an extract from it.   It is the memory
of a betrothal day, and the poet is Frederick Tennyson.   I
suppose you know that there were three Tennysons, and
although Alfred happened to be the greatest, all of them
were good poets.

It is a golden morning of the spring,
   My cheek is pale, and hers is warm with bloom,
   And we are left in that old cavern room
And she begins to sing.

The open casement quivers in the breeze,
   And one large musk-rose leans its dewy grace
   Into the chamber like a happy face,
And round it swim the bees.

    ·   ·   ·   ·   ·   ·   ·   ·

I know not what I said;—what she replied
  Lives, like eternal sunshine, in my heart;
  And then I murmured, Oh! we never part,
My love, my life, my bride!

And silence o'er us, after that great bliss,
  Fell like a welcome shadow; and I heard
  The far woods sighing, and a summer bird
Singing amid the trees.

The sweet bird's happy song that streamed around,
  The murmur of the woods, the azure skies,
  Were graven on my heart, though ears and eyes
Marked neither sight nor sound.

She sleeps in peace beneath the chancel stone,
  But ah! so clearly is the vision seen,
  The dead seem raised, or Death has never been,
Were I not here alone.

This is great art in its power of picturing a memory of the heart. Let us notice some of the beauties. The lover is pale because he is afraid, anxious; he is going to ask a question and he does not know how she may answer him. All this was long ago, years and years ago, but the strong emotions of that morning leave their every detail painted in remembrance, with strange vividness. After all those years the man still recollects the appearance of the room, the sunshine entering, and the crimson rose looking into the room from the garden, with bees humming round it. Then after the question had been asked and happily answered, neither could speak for joy; and because of the silence all the sounds of nature outside became almost painfully distinct. Now he remembers how he heard in that room the sound of the wind in far away trees, the singing of a bird—he also remembers all the colours and the lights of the day. But it was very, very long ago, and she is dead. Still, the memory is so clear and bright in his heart that it is as if time had stood still, or as if she had come back from

the grave. Only one thing assures him that it is but a
memory—he is alone.

Returning now to the subject of love's illusion in itself,
let me remind you that the illusion does not always pass
away—not at all. It passes away in every case of happy
union, when it has become no longer necessary to the great
purposes of nature. But in case of disappointment, loss,
failure to win the maiden desired, it often happens that the
ideal image never fades away, but persistently haunts the
mind through life, and is capable thus of making even the
most successful life unhappy. Sometimes the result of such
disappointment may be to change all a man's ideas about
the world, about life, about religion; and everything remains
darkened for him. Many a young person disappointed in
love begins to lose religious feeling from that moment, for
it seems to him, simply because he happens to be unfortunate, that the universe is all wrong. On the other hand
the successful lover thinks that the universe is all right; he
utters his thanks to the gods, and feels his faith in religion
and human nature greater than before. I do not at this
moment remember any striking English poem illustrating
this fact; but there is a pretty little poem in French by
Victor Hugo showing well the relation between successful
love and religious feeling in simple minds. Here is an
English translation of it. The subject is simply a walk
at night, the girl-bride leaning upon the arm of her husband;
and his memory of the evening is thus expressed:

> The trembling arm I pressed
> Fondly; our thoughts confessed
> Love's conquest tender;
> God filled the vast sweet night,
> Love filled our hearts; the light
> Of stars made splendour.
>
> Even as we walked and dreamed,
> 'Twixt heaven and earth, it seemed

Our souls were speaking;
The stars looked on thy face;
Thine eyes through violet space
The stars were seeking.

And from the astral light
Feeling the soft sweet night
  Thrill to thy soul,
Thou saidst: "O God of Bliss
Lord of the Blue Abyss,
  Thou madest the whole!"

And the stars whispered low
To the God of Space, "We know,
  God of Eternity,
Dear Lord, all Love is Thine,
Even by Love's Light we shine!
  Thou madest Beauty!"

Of course here the religious feeling itself is part of the
illusion, but it serves to give great depth and beauty to
simple feeling.   Besides, the poem illustrates one truth very
forcibly—namely, that when we are perfectly happy all the
universe appears to be divine and divinely beautiful; in
other words, we are in heaven.   On the contrary, when we
are very unhappy the universe appears to be a kind of hell,
in which there is no hope, no joy, and no gods to pray to.
   But the special reason I wished to call attention to
Victor Hugo's lyric is that it has that particular quality
called by philosophical critics "cosmic emotion."   Cosmic
emotion means the highest quality of human emotion.
The word "cosmos" signifies the universe—not simply this
world, but all the hundred millions of suns and worlds in
the known heaven.   And the adjective "cosmic," means,
of course, "related to the whole universe."   Ordinary
emotion may be more than individual in its relations.   I
mean that your feelings may be moved by the thought or
the perception of something relating not only to your own
life but also to the lives of many others.   The largest form

of such ordinary emotion is what would be called national feeling, the feeling of your own relation to the whole nation or the whole race.   But there is higher emotion even than that.   When you think of yourself emotionally not only in relation to your own country, your own nation, but in relation to all humanity, then you have a cosmic emotion of the third or second order.   I say "third or second," because whether the emotion be second or third rate depends very much upon your conception of humanity as One.   But if you think of yourself in relation not to this world only but to the whole universe of hundreds of millions of stars and planets—in relation to the whole mystery of existence— then you have a cosmic emotion of the highest order.   Of course there are degrees even in this; the philosopher or the metaphysician will probably have a finer quality of cosmic emotion than the poet or the artist is able to have.   But lovers very often, according to their degree of intellectual culture, experience a kind of cosmic emotion; and Victor Hugo's little poem illustrates this.   Night and the stars and the abyss of the sky all seem to be thrilling with love and beauty to the lover's eyes, because he himself is in a state of loving happiness; and then he begins to think about his relation to the universal life, to the supreme mystery beyond all Form and Name.

A third or fourth class of such emotion may be illustrated by the beautiful sonnet of Keats, written not long before his death.   Only a very young man could have written this, because only a very young man loves in this way—but how delightful it is!   It has no title.

> Bright star! would I were steadfast as thou art—
>   Not in lone splendour hung aloft the night
> And watching, with eternal lids apart,
>   Like nature's patient, sleepless Eremite,
> The moving waters at their priest-like task
>   Of pure ablution round earth's human shores,
> Or gazing on new soft-fallen mask
>   Of snow upon the mountains and the moors—

> No—yet still steadfast, still unchangeable,
> Pillow'd upon my fair love's ripening breast,
> To feel forever its soft fall and swell,
> Awake forever in a sweet unrest,
> Still, still to hear her tender-taken breath,
> And so live ever—or else swoon to death.

Tennyson has charmingly represented a lover wishing that he were a necklace of his beloved, or her girdle, or her earring; but that is not a cosmic emotion at all.   Indeed, the idea of Tennyson's pretty song was taken from old French and English love songs of the peasants—popular ballads.   But in this beautiful sonnet of Keats, where the lover wishes to be endowed with the immortality and likeness of a star only to be forever with the beloved, there is something of the old Greek thought which inspired the beautiful lines written between two and three thousand years ago, and translated by J. A. Symonds:

> Gazing on stars, my Star!   Would that I were the welkin,
> Starry with myriad eyes, ever to gaze upon thee!

But there is more than the Greek beauty of thought in Keats's sonnet, for we find the poet speaking of the exterior universe in the largest relation, thinking of the stars watching forever the rising and the falling of the sea tides, thinking of the sea tides themselves as continually purifying the world, even as a priest purifies a temple.   The fancy of the boy expands to the fancy of philosophy; it is a blending of poetry, philosophy, and sincere emotion.

You will have seen by the examples which we have been reading together that English love poetry, like Japanese love poetry, may be divided into many branches and classified according to the range of subject from the very simplest utterance of feeling up to that highest class expressing cosmic emotion.   Very rich the subject is; the student is only puzzled where to choose.   I should again suggest to you to observe the value of the theme of illusion, especially as illustrated in our examples. There are indeed multitudes of Western love poems that would probably appear to you very strange, perhaps very foolish. But you will certainly acknowledge that there are some varieties of English love poetry which are neither strange nor foolish, and which are well worth studying, not only in themselves but in their relation to the higher forms of emotional expression in all literature. Out of love poetry belonging to the highest class, much can be drawn that would serve to enrich and to give a new colour to your own literature of emotion.

CHAPTER II

STUDIES IN TENNYSON

(A Fragment)

WITH perhaps one exception, the great poets of the Victorian period only carried on and developed the traditions of the preceding era. This is curious. The poets of the Lake School and of the other schools who were contemporary with it have their counterparts in the men of the Victorian age. Tennyson is Keats perfected and enriched. Wordsworth is represented also partly by Tennyson, but much more by Matthew Arnold, both as to his faults and as to his merits. Coleridge reblossoms in Rossetti. Shelley and Byron both reappear in Swinburne, but without any of the faults of the Satanic School as to form, Swinburne being the greatest master of form in all modern literature. But the Satanic spirit of Byron is there—larger, stronger, fiercer, and all the grace and passion and music of Shelley, magnified miraculously, with a new and strange quality of beauty borrowed from former times. Even Sir Walter Scott is reborn in the poetry of William Morris, who inherited the same extraordinary faculty for romance in verse, though he falls far below Scott as a lyrical poet. There is only one great figure of the Victorian era for whom we cannot find any prototype; that is Robert Browning. Browning alone belongs to no school, and makes a tradition of his own, the future of which is very doubtful. It might be said that Tennyson is not a fair representative of the philosophical tradition of Wordsworth, and that Matthew Arnold does not go much beyond Wordsworth in range of thought. This is true. I think that the man who most expanded the Wordsworthian tradition and brought it into perfect har-

mony with nineteenth century philosophy, is George Meredith, whose faults of style alone prevent him from taking
place in the very front rank. As a philosopher I hold him
to be the largest thinker of the century.

Alfred Tennyson is the first figure that rises up before
us—the first great star that showed itself in the poetical sky
after the sinking of those two constellations of which
Wordsworth and Shelley were respectively the principal
luminaries. The serious and self-controlled character expressed in his familiar portraits appears to have distinguished him even in childhood. Nevertheless, it is
curious that as a boy he absolutely worshipped Byron, and
afterwards thought that the death of Byron was the greatest
possible misfortune that could have happened to the human
race. Even as a child he composed somewhat, but none of
his very youthful poems was suffered to see the light. As
he grew older, Wordsworth began to influence him considerably, together with Scott and Coleridge. Then it appears
that he had an enthusiasm for Shelley. But by the time
that he had reached maturity, his great source of inspiration
became Keats; and it is the tradition of Keats that he
chiefly followed.

Considering the extraordinary perfection of his work as
we now have it, you might find it difficult to believe that
the first work which he published was bad—weak, sentimental, gushing—somewhat in the style of Mrs. Hemans
and the lady-poets before the Victorian period. There
were beauties in it; but it was deserving of severe criticism,
and it was criticised very severely indeed. Previously, in
1826, Tennyson had been in print; he and his brothers,
Charles and Frederick, had published a little volume entitled "Poems by Two Brothers." We do not know now
why it was so called, but we do know that three and not
two persons composed it. But this anonymous publication
cannot be said to have much connection with Alfred's career.
The first book that he published bearing his own name was

a volume simply entitled "Poems," printed in 1830. This was the book that deserved severe criticism, and received it. The criticism was very beneficial to Tennyson, probably because of his extremely strong character. Instead of being downcast by it, he set to work to correct his faults, quietly, slowly, patiently, and twelve years later he printed a second volume of poems, containing, besides much new matter, the best of the bad poems of 1830 entirely changed, trans- formed, and beautified. This time he was not severely criticised; men of letters saw that a very great poet was coming. Five years later appeared "The Princess." Then Tennyson's reputation suddenly blazed up and he became famous; no such poetry had ever been read in England before. Then in rapid succession followed "In Memo- riam," "Maud," and the first half of the "Idylls of the King"—these last appearing in 1859. Tennyson mean- time had become poet laureate after the death of Words- worth; and there can be no doubt that the honour greatly increased his popularity. When "Enoch Arden" was pub- lished, in 1864, seventeen thousand copies were sold on the morning of publication. Thenceforth the poet's fortune was in every way secure. He rose from honour to honour; he was made a peer; he became as rich as he could possibly have wished; and he continued the dominant figure in Eng- lish literature during the latter half of the century. Even to-day we must confess that, in a general way, the greatest literary figure of the nineteenth century is Tennyson. He died in 1892, and was buried in Westminster Abbey with extraordinary honours, his death being considered as a national calamity.

No other English poet, except perhaps Pope, has ever given so many familiar quotations to the English language; and nobody else, certainly not Pope, has influenced and enriched the English language so much as Tennyson. Probably his influence will be felt for hundreds of years to come. In spite of the predictions of Matthew Arnold and others, that influence is growing. And it is an influence not only artistic and philosophical, but also educational and moral in the highest degree. The whole English world from Great Britain to India, from Canada in the North down to South Africa and Australia in the other hemisphere, studies Tennyson, and will long continue to study him. Let us now try to understand the reason of this great influence and this extraordinary recognition of an excellence as exquisite as it is rare.

The first fact to bear in mind about the character of Tennyson's work as individual labour is this, that no other man in our literary history, not even Pope, ever polished his work so much. He was not simply satisfied with keeping work back for years rather than print it before feeling quite sure that he had done his best upon it; but he subsequently corrected it in almost every one of the many editions which it afterwards went through. For, as a man grows older, his capacity for literary judgment, his faculty of literary perception, and the range of his knowledge, are all constantly increasing in breadth and depth; and Tennyson, recognising this fact, has given to even the work of his early years the most highly developed powers of his old age. In critical editions of poets, it is necessary that all different versions of each poem be presented to the student; and it has been well said that if such an edition of Tennyson should ever be published it must be the most enormous production of its kind in existence.

As a result of this perpetual polishing, the work of Tennyson has an exquisiteness not to be surpassed in any literature. Of no other poet can it be said that the exquisiteness is so uniform. You cannot find in the whole immense body of this man's verse inequalities of construction. You may find inequalities of other kinds, but not of workmanship. And were there no other merit in Tennyson at all, this single merit would still give him the first place as a wordsmith.

But there are many other qualities in Tennyson, some of which are even greater than merits of workmanship. There is thought, singularly broad and liberal, with just a little of that English conservatism which we may not be able to sympathise with, but which we are obliged to confess healthy and dignified. Then there is the splendid sense of sound and colour. There is fine observation of nature, and fine observation of human character. And all these abilities were directed especially toward the painting of English subjects as a rule—English life, English landscape, English women, English ideals of heroism and of duty. Tennyson seldom ventures into classical or ancient themes, though when he does, as in "Lucretius," "Ulysses," "Tithonus," or the translations from Homer, he is still peerless within the limits which he has set himself. Even in the Idylls, and other studies of which the subject is mediæval, it is always English life and English character that are described under a thin disguise. The knights of Arthur's court are not really the men of the Middle Ages; they are ideals of English gentlemen, and have long been so recognised by the people. The Princess and her girl-students and her lady professor and all the figures of that wonderful medley are figures familiar to every English reader; they are nineteenth century people wearing the robes of other days; they are actors and actresses acting out a lesson both didactic and æsthetic. How should the English people not love work that painted them in such splendid colours?

This would alone explain popularity. Besides the pleasure found in the subject, and in the artistic treatment of the subject, there is yet another quality to ensure popularity—the quality of clearness. Great scholar though he was, Tennyson could be understood by any person with a moderate degree of education. It is true that some of his thoughts could be read at once only by a philosopher, but the proportion of these to the rest of the text is rather small; and we may generally say that even where Tennyson's sen-

tences seem at first sight most difficult, a little patient thinking and study can always straighten out the difficulty. I
am speaking of course of English readers. When we study
Tennyson in Japan we have to explain almost every line of
certain poems. But that is because those poems are full
of English idioms and English allusions which, though familiar to the English reader from local habit and experience, are necessarily very obscure for one who reads in a
language not his own.

And there is yet another curious quality in Tennyson's
compositions—a teaching quality. He has brought back
to the English language, out of the cemetery of dead words,
a great many expressions from Middle English and other
obsolete English, and given them new life; and he has done
this in such a way that the reader is taught the meaning of
these unfamiliar words without looking at the dictionary.
The context teaches the value of the words better than any
dictionary could teach it to you. I may say that I myself,
as a boy, learned more English from Tennyson than I learned
in any other way; and even now I cannot read him over
again without constantly learning something new. The
more you study him, the more you will find in him; and the
more you will be astonished at the perception of the labour
and the learning that such work must have cost. I consider Tennyson the greatest educational influence in English literature; and the etymologists, now engaged upon the
colossal dictionary of the English language, would probably be the first to recognise Tennyson's influence upon that
language. No small portion of the three millions of quotations that are to appear in that dictionary will be quotations from Tennyson.

Some of you may have read Taine's criticism upon
Tennyson; and I wish to say a word about that. Taine,
who was a very great critic, one of the greatest artists that
literature ever produced, made a very unfavourable comparison of Tennyson with Alfred de Musset. From Taine's

point of view, I venture to assure you, Taine is quite right. He explains his partiality perfectly well. He found Tennyson too correct, too genteel, too conservative, too cold, and altogether too English. Tennyson was not, in his judgment, a world-poet—that is, a poet who can touch equally well the hearts of the men in all languages, a poet who sings only of emotions common to all mankind. But de Musset is a poet of passion; and passion is universal. True, there is not much passion in Tennyson. True, also, Tennyson is not really a world-poet. But as an English poet, as a master of all the beauties and riches and powers of the English language, he is unique. And for the study of language, rather than for the study of emotion, there is no one like him. Upon this point, which Taine did not sufficiently recognise, it is necessary that you should think clearly.

CHAPTER III

STUDIES IN ROSSETTI

I

We must rank Dante Gabriel Rossetti as not inferior to Tennyson in workmanship—therefore as occupying the very first rank in nineteenth century poetry. He was not inferior to Tennyson either as a thinker, but his thinking was in totally different directions. He had no sympathy with the ideas of his own century; he lived and thought in the Middle Ages; and while one of our very greatest English poets, he takes a place apart, for he does not reflect the century at all. He had the dramatic gift, but it was a gift in his case much more limited than that of Browning. Altogether we can safely give him a place in the first rank as a maker of poetry, but in all other respects we cannot classify him in any way. He remains a unique figure in the Victorian age, a figure such as may not reappear for hundreds of years to come. It was as if a man of the thirteenth century had been reborn into the nineteenth century, and, in spite of modern culture, had continued to think and to feel very much as men felt and thought in the time of the great Italian poet Dante.

One reason for this extraordinary difference between himself and his contemporaries was that Rossetti was not an Englishman but an Italian by blood, religion, and feeling. In his verse we might expect to find something that we cannot find in any other English poet; and I think that we shall find it. The facts of his life—strange and pathetic— need not occupy us now. You need only remember for the present that he was a great painter before becoming a great poet, and that his painting, like his poetry, was the painting

37

of another century than his own.   Also it will be well to
bear in mind that he detested modern science and modern
philosophy—which fact makes it all the more remarkable
that he uttered some great thoughts quite in harmony with
the most profound philosophy of the Orient.

In studying the best of his poetry, it will be well for us
to consider it by groups, taking a few specimens from each
group as examples of the rest; since we shall not have time
to read even a quarter of all his production. Taking the
very simplest of his work to begin with, I shall make a selection from what I might call the symbolic group, for want
of a better name.   I mean those poems which are parables,
or symbolic illustrations of deep truths—poems which seem
childishly simple, but are nevertheless very deep indeed.
We may begin with a little piece called "The Mirror."

> She knew it not,—most perfect pain
>   To learn: this too she knew not. Strife
>   For me, calm hers, as from the first.
>   'Twas but another bubble burst
>   Upon the curdling draught of life,—
> My silent patience mine again.
>
> As who, of forms that crowd unknown
>   Within a distant mirror's shade,
>   Deems such a one himself, and makes
>   Some sign; but when the image shakes
>   No whit, he finds his thought betray'd,
> And must seek elsewhere for his own.

So far as the English goes, this verse is plain enough;
but unless you have met with the same idea in some other
English writer, you will find the meaning very obscure.
The poet is speaking of a universal, or almost universal, experience of misplaced love.   A man becomes passionately
attached to a woman, who treats him with cold indifference.
Finally the lover finds out his mistake; the woman that he
loved proves not to be what he imagined; she is not worthy

of his love. Then what was he in love with? With a shadow out of his brain, with an imagination or ideal very pure and noble, but only an imagination. Supposing that he was worshipping good qualities in a noble woman, he deceived himself; the woman had no such qualities; they existed only in his fancy. Thus he calls her his mirror, the human being that seemed to be a reflection of all that was good in his own heart. She never knows the truth as to why the man loved her and then ceased to love her; he could not tell her, because it would have been to her "most perfect pain to learn."

A less obscure but equally beautiful symbolism, in another metre, is "The Honeysuckle."

> I plucked a honeysuckle where
>   The hedge on high is quick with thorn,
>   And climbing for the prize, was torn,
> And fouled my feet in quag-water;
>   And by the thorns and by the wind
>   The blossom that I took was thinn'd,
> And yet I found it sweet and fair.
>
> Thence to a richer growth I came,
>   Where, nursed in mellow intercourse,
>   The honeysuckle sprang by scores,
> Not harried like my single stem,
>   All virgin lamps of scent and dew,
>   So from my hand that first I threw,
> Yet plucked not any more of them.

It often happens that a young man during his first struggle in life, when all the world seems to be against him, meets with some poor girl who loves him. She is not educated as he has been; she is ignorant of many things, and she has suffered herself a great deal of hardship, so that although beautiful naturally and good-hearted, both her beauty and her temper have been a little spoiled by the troubles of life. The young man whom she loves is obliged to mix with a very poor and vulgar class of people in order to become intimate with her.   There are plenty of rough common men who would like to get that girl; and the young man has a good deal of trouble in winning her away from them.   With all her small faults she seems for the time very beautiful to her lover, because he cannot get any finer woman while he remains poor.   But presently success comes to him, and he is able to enter a much higher class of society, where he finds scores of beautiful girls, much more accomplished than his poor sweetheart; and he becomes ashamed of her and cruelly abandons her.   But he does not marry any of the rich and beautiful women.   Perhaps he is tired of women; perhaps his heart has been spoiled.   The poet does not tell us why.   He simply tells a story of human ingratitude which is as old as the world.

One more simple poem before we take up the larger and more complicated pieces of the group.

THE WOODSPURGE

The wind flapped loose, the wind was still,
Shaken out dead from tree and hill:
I had walked on at the wind's will,—
I sat now, for the wind was still.

Between my knees my forehead was,—
My lips, drawn in, said not Alas!
My hair was over in the grass,
My naked ears heard the day pass.

My eyes, wide open, had the run
Of some ten weeds to fix upon;
Among those few, out of the sun,
The woodspurge flower'd, three cups in one.

From perfect grief there need not be
Wisdom or even memory:
One thing then learnt remains to me,—
The woodspurge has a cup of three!

The phenomenon here described by the poet is uncon-

sciously familiar to most of us. Any person who has suffered some very great pain, moral pain, is apt to observe
during that instant of suffering things which he never observed before, or to notice details never noticed before in
common things. One reason is that at such a time sense-
impressions are stimulated to a strange degree by the increase of circulation, while the eyes and ears remain auto-
matically active only. Whoever among you can remember
the pain of losing a parent or beloved friend, will probably
remember with extraordinary vividness all kinds of little
things seen or heard at the time, such as the cry of a bird
or a cricket, the sound of the dripping of water, the form
of a sunbeam upon a wall, the shapes of shadows in a garden. The personage of this poem often before saw the
woodspurge, without noticing anything particular about it;
but in a moment of great sorrow observing the plant, he
learns for the first time the peculiar form of its flower. In
a wonderful novel by Henry Kingsley, called "Ravenshoe,"
there is a very striking example of the same thing. A cav-
alry-soldier, waiting in the saddle for the order to charge
the enemy, observes on the back of the soldier before him
a grease-spot which looks exactly like the map of Sweden,
and begins to think that if the outline of Norway were beside it, the upper part of the map would go over the shoulder
of the man. This fancy comes to him in a moment when
he believes himself going to certain death.

Now we will take a longer poem, very celebrated, entitled "The Cloud Confines."

> The day is dark and the night
>   To him that would search their heart;
>   No lips of cloud that will part
> Nor morning song in the light:
>   Only, gazing alone,
>   To him wild shadows are shown,
>   Deep under deep unknown,
> And height above unknown height.

Still we say as we go,—
  "Strange to think by the way,
Whatever there is to know,
  That shall we know one day."

The Past is over and fled;
  Named new, we name it the old;
  Thereof some tale hath been told,
But no word comes from the dead;
  Whether at all they be,
  Or whether as bond or free,
  Or whether they too were we,
Or by what spell they have sped.
  Still we say as we go,—
    "Strange to think by the way,
  Whatever there is to know,
    That shall we know one day."

What of the heart of hate
  That beats in thy breast, O Time?—
  Red strife from the furthest prime,
And anguish of fierce debate;
  War that shatters her slain,
  And peace that grinds them as grain,
  And eyes fixed ever in vain
On the pitiless eyes of Fate.
  Still we say as we go,—
    "Strange to think by the way,
  Whatever there is to know,
    That shall we know one day."

What of the heart of love
  That bleeds in thy breast, O Man?—
  Thy kisses snatched 'neath the ban
Of fangs that mock them above;
  Thy bells prolonged unto knells,
  Thy hope that a breath dispels,
  Thy bitter forlorn farewells
And the empty echoes thereof?
  Still we say as we go,—
    "Strange to think by the way,
  Whatever there is to know,
    That shall we know one day."

The sky leans dumb on the sea,
    Aweary with all its wings;
    And oh! the song the sea sings
Is dark everlastingly.
    Our past is clean forgot,
    Our present is and is not,
    Our future's a sealed seedplot,
And what betwixt them are we?
    Still we say as we go,—
        "Strange to think by the way,
    Whatever there is to know,
        That shall we know one day."

This dark poetry is very different from the optimism of
Tennyson; and we uncomfortably feel it to be much more
true.   In spite of all its wonderful tenderness and caressing
hopefulness, we feel that Tennyson's poetry does not illuminate the sombre problems of life.   But Rossetti will not be
found to be a pessimist.   I shall presently show, by examples, the difference between poetical pessimism and Rossetti's thoughtful melancholy.   He is simply communing
with us about the mystery of the universe—sadly enough,
but always truthfully.   We may even suspect a slight
mockery in the burthen of his poem:

        Whatever there is to know,
        That shall we know one day.

Suppose there is nothing to know?   "Very well," the poet
would answer, "then we shall know nothing."   Although
by education and by ancestry a Roman Catholic, Rossetti
seems to have had just as little faith as any of his great
contemporaries; the artistic and emotional side of Catholi-
cism made strong appeal to his nature as an artist, but so far
as personal belief is concerned we may judge him by his
own lines:

        Would God I knew there were a God to thank
        When thanks arise in me!

Nevertheless we have here no preacher of negation, but a sincere doubter. We know nothing of the secret of the universe, the meaning of its joy and pain and impermanency; we do not know anything of the dead; we do not know the meaning of time or space or life. But just for that reason there may be marvellous things to know. The dead do not come back, but we do not know whether they could come back, nor even the real meaning of death. Do we even know, he asks, whether the dead were not ourselves? This thought, like the thought in the poem "Sudden Light," is peculiar to Rossetti. You will find nothing of this thought in any other Victorian poet of great rank—except, indeed, in some of the work of O'Shaughnessy, who is now coming into a place of eminence only second to that of the four great masters.

Besides this remarkable line, which I have asked you to put in italics, you should remember those two very splendid lines in the third stanza:

> War that shatters her slain,
> And peace that grinds them as grain.

These have become famous. The suggestion is that peace is more cruel than war. In battle a man is dashed to pieces, and his pain is immediately over. In the competition of civil life, the weak and the stupid, no matter how good or moral they may be, are practically crushed by the machinery of Western civilisation, as grain might be crushed in a mill.

In the last stanza of the composition you will doubtless have observed the pathetic reference to the meaning of the song of the sea, mysterious and awful beyond all other sounds of nature. Rossetti has not failed to consider this sound, philosophically and emotionally, in one of his most beautiful poems. And now I want to show you, by illustration, the difference between a really pessimistic treatment of a subject and Rossetti's treatment of it. Perhaps the very finest example of pessimism in Victorian poetry is a sonnet by Lee-Hamilton, on the subject of a sea-shell. You know that if you take a large sea-shell of a particular form, and hold it close to your ear, you will hear a sound like the sound of the surf, as if the ghost of the sea were in the shell. Nearly all English children have the experience of listening to the sound of the sea in a shell; it startles them at first; but nobody tells them what the sound really is, for that would spoil their surprise and delight. You must not tell a child that there are no ghosts or fairies. Well, Rossetti and Lee-Hamilton wrote about this sound of the sea in a shell—but how differently! Here is Lee-Hamilton's composition:

> The hollow sea-shell, which for years hath stood
> On dusty shelves, when held against the ear
> Proclaims its stormy parent; and we hear
> The faint far murmur of the breaking flood.
> We hear the sea. The sea? It is the blood
> In our own veins, impetuous and near,
> And pulses keeping pace with hope and fear,
> And with our feelings' ever-shifting mood.
>
> Lo! in my heart I hear, as in a shell,
> The murmur of a world beyond the grave,
> Distinct, distinct, though faint and far it be.
> Thou fool; this echo is a cheat as well,—
> The hum of earthly instincts; and we crave
> A world unreal as the shell-heard sea.

Of course this is a very fine poem, so far as the poetry is concerned. But it is pessimism absolute. Its author, a brilliant graduate of Oxford University, entered the English diplomatic service as a young man, and in the middle of a promising career was attacked by a disease of the spine which left him a hopeless invalid. We might say that he had some reason to look at the world in a dark light. But such poetry is not healthy. It is morbid. It means retrogression. It brings a sharp truth to the mind with a painful shock, and leaves an after-impression of gloom unspeak-

able.   As I said before, we must not spoil the happiness of
children by telling them that there are no ghosts or fairies.
So we must not tell the humanity which believes in happiness after death that there is no heaven.   All progress is
through faith and hope in something.   The measure of a
poet is in the largeness of the thought which he can apply
to any subject, however trifling.   Bearing this in mind, let
us now see how the same subject of the sea-shell appeals
to the thought of Rossetti.   You will then perceive the
difference between pessimism and philosophical humani-
tarianism.

THE SEA-LIMITS

Consider the sea's listless chime:
   Time's self it is, made audible,—
   The murmur of the earth's own shell.
Secret continuance sublime
   Is the sea's end: our sight may pass
   No furlong further.   Since time was,
This sound hath told the lapse of time.

No quiet, which is death's,—it hath
   The mournfulness of ancient life,
   Enduring always at dull strife.
As the world's heart of rest and wrath,
   Its painful pulse is in the sands.
   Last utterly, the whole sky stands,
Grey and not known, along its path.

Listen alone beside the sea,
   Listen alone among the woods;
   Those voices of twin solitudes
Shall have one sound alike to thee:
   Hark where the murmurs of thronged men
   Surge and sink back and surge again,—
Still the one voice of wave and tree.

Gather a shell from the strown beach
   And listen at its lips: they sigh
   The same desire and mystery,

> The echo of the whole sea's speech.
> And all mankind is thus at heart
> Not anything but what thou art:
> And Earth, Sea, Man, are all in each.

In the last beautiful stanza we have a comparison as sublime as any ever made by any poet—of the human heart, the human life, re-echoing the murmur of the infinite Sea of Life. As the same sound of the sea is heard in every shell, so in every human heart is the same ghostly murmur of Universal Being. The sound of the sea, the sound of the forest, the sound of men in cities, not only are the same to the ear, but they tell the same story of pain. The sound of the sea is a sound of perpetual strife, the sound of the woods in the wind is a sound of ceaseless struggle, the tumult of a great city is also a tumult of effort. In this sense all the three sounds are but one, and that one is the sound of life everywhere. Life is pain, and therefore sadness. The world itself is like a great shell full of this sound. But it is a shell on the verge of the Infinite. The millions of suns, the millions of planets and moons, are all of them but shells on the shore of the everlasting sea of death and birth, and each would, if we could hear it, convey to our ears and hearts the one same murmur of pain. This is, to my thinking, a much vaster conception than anything to be found in Tennyson; and such a poem as that of Lee-Hamilton dwindles into nothingness beside it, for we have here all that man can know of our relation to the universe, and the mystery of that universe brought before us by a simile of incomparable sublimity.

Before leaving this important class of poems, let me cite another instance of the comparative nearness of Rossetti at times to Oriental thought. It is the fifteenth of that wonderful set of sonnets entitled the "House of Life."

THE BIRTH-BOND

> Have you not noted, in some family
> Where two were born of a first marriage-bed,

How still they own their gracious bond, though fed
And nursed on the forgotten breast and knee?—
How to their father's children they shall be
    In act and thought of one goodwill; but each
    Shall for the other have, in silence speech,
And in a word complete community?

Even so, when I first saw you, seemed it, love,
    That among souls allied to mine was yet
One nearer kindred than life hinted of.
    O born with me somewhere that men forget,
    And though in years of sight and sound unmet,
Known for my soul's birth-partner well enough!

This beautiful little thought of love is almost exactly the
same as that suggested in a well-known Japanese proverb
about the relations of a previous existence. We have here,
in an English poet, who very probably never read anything
about Buddhism, the very idea of the Buddhist *en*. The
whole tendency of the poet's mind was toward larger things
than his early training had prepared him for.

Yet it would be a mistake to suppose Rossetti a pure
mystic; he was too much of an artist for that. No one felt
the sensuous charm of life more keenly, nor the attraction
of plastic beauty and grace. By way of an interlude, we
may turn for a time to his more sensuous poetry. It is by
this that he is best known; for you need not suppose that
the general English public understands such poems as those
which we have been examining. Keep in mind that there
is a good deal of difference between the adjectives "sensuous" and "sensual." The former has no evil meaning; it
refers only to sense-impression—to sensations visual, audi-
tory, tactile. The other adjective is more commonly used
in a bad sense. At one time an attempt was made to injure
Rossetti by applying it to his work; but all good critics have
severely condemned that attempt, and Rossetti must not be
regarded as in any sense an immoral poet.

II

To the cultivated the very highest quality of emotional poetry is that given by blending the artistically sensuous with the mystic. This very rare quality colours the greater part of Rossetti's work. Perhaps one may even say that it is never entirely absent. Only, the proportions of the blending vary, like those mixtures of red and blue, crimson and azure, which may give us either purple or violet of different shades according to the wish of the dyer. The quality of mysticism dominates in the symbolic poems; we might call those deep purple. The sensuous element dominates in most of the ballads and narrative poems; we might say that these have rather the tone of bright violet. But even in the ballads there is a very great difference in the proportions of the two qualities. The highest tone is in the "Blessed Damozel," and in the beautiful narrative poem of the "Staff and Scrip"; while the lowest tone is perhaps that of the ballad of "Eden Bower," which describes the two passions of lust and hate at their greatest intensity. But everything is beautifully finished as work, and unapproachably exquisite in feeling. I think the best example of what I have called the violet style is the ballad of "Troy Town."

> Heavenborn Helen, Sparta's Queen,
> (*O Troy Town!*)
> Had two breasts of heavenly sheen,
> The sun and moon of the heart's desire:
> All Love's lordship lay between.
> (*O Troy's down!*
> *Tall Troy's on fire!*)
>
> Helen knelt at Venus' shrine,
> (*O Troy Town!*)
> Saying, "A little gift is mine,
> A little gift for a heart's desire.

Hear me speak and make me a sign!
  (*O Troy's down!*
  Tall Troy's on fire!)

"Look! I bring thee a carven cup;
  (*O Troy Town!*)
See it here as I hold it up,—
Shaped it is to the heart's desire,
Fit to fill when the gods would sup.
  (*O Troy's down!*
  Tall Troy's on fire!)

"It was moulded like my breast;
  (*O Troy Town!*)
He that sees it may not rest,
Rest at all for his heart's desire.
O give ear to my heart's behest!
  (*O Troy's down!*
  Tall Troy's on fire!)

"See my breast, how like it is;
  (*O Troy Town!*)
See it bare for the air to kiss!
Is the cup to thy heart's desire?
O for the breast, O make it his!
  (*O Troy's down!*
  Tall Troy's on fire!)

"Yea, for my bosom here I sue;
  (*O Troy Town!*)
Thou must give it where 'tis due,
Give it there to the heart's desire.
Whom do I give my bosom to?
  (*O Troy's down!*
  Tall Troy's on fire!)

"Each twin breast is an apple sweet!
  (*O Troy Town!*)
Once an apple stirred the beat
Of thy heart with the heart's desire:—
Say, who brought it then to thy feet?
  (*O Troy's down!*
  Tall Troy's .on fire!).

"They that claimed it then were three:
  (*O Troy Town!*)
For thy sake two hearts did he
Make forlorn of the heart's desire.
Do for him as he did for thee!
  (*O Troy's down!*
  Tall Troy's on fire!)

"Mine are apples grown to the south,
  (*O Troy Town!*)
Grown to taste in the days of drouth,
Taste and waste to the heart's desire:
Mine are apples meet for his mouth!"
  (*O Troy's down!*
  Tall Troy's on fire!)

Venus looked on Helen's gift,
  (*O Troy Town!*)
Looked and smiled with subtle drift,
Saw the work of her heart's desire:—
"There thou kneel'st for Love to lift!"
  (*O Troy's down!*
  Tall Troy's on fire!)

Venus looked in Helen's face,
  (*O Troy Town!*)
Knew far off an hour and place,
And fire lit from the heart's desire;
Laughed and said, "Thy gift hath grace!"
  (*O Troy's down!*
  Tall Troy's on fire!)

Cupid looked on Helen's breast,
  (*O Troy Town!*)
Saw the heart within its nest,
Saw the flame of the heart's desire,—
Marked his arrow's burning crest.
  (*O Troy's down!*
  Tall Troy's on fire!)

Cupid took another dart,
  (*O Troy Town!*)
Fledged it for another heart,

Winged the shaft with the heart's desire,
Drew the string, and said "Depart!"
  (*O Troy's down!*
  Tall Troy's on fire!)

Paris turned upon his bed,
  (*O Troy Town!*)
Turned upon his bed, and said,
Dead at heart with the heart's desire,—
"O to clasp her golden head!"
  (*O Troy's down!*
  Tall Troy's on fire!)

This wonderful ballad, with its single and its double re-
frains, represents Rossetti's nearest approach to earth,
except the ballad of "Eden Bower." Usually he seldom
touches the ground, but moves at some distance above it,
just as one flies in dreams. But you will observe that the
mysticism here has almost vanished. There is just a little
ghostliness to remind you that the writer is no common
singer, but a poet able to give a thrill. The ghostliness is
chiefly in the fact of the supernatural elements involved;
Helen with her warm breast we feel to be a real woman,
but Venus and love are phantoms, who speak and act as
figures in sleep. This is true art under the circumstances.
We feel nothing more human until we come to the last
stanza; then we hear it in the cry of Paris. But why do
I say that this is high art to make the gods as they are made
here? The Greeks would have made Venus and Cupid
purely human. But Rossetti is not taking the Greek view
of the subject at all. He is taking the mediæval one. He
is writing of Greek gods and Greek legends as such subjects
were felt by Chaucer and by the French poets of the thirteenth and fourteenth centuries. It would not be easy to
explain the mediæval tone of the poem to you; that would
require a comparison with the work of very much older
poets. I only want now to call your attention to the fact
that even in a Greek subject of the sensuous kind Rossetti

always keeps the tone of the Middle Ages; and that tone was mystical.

Having given this beautiful example of the least mystical class of Rossetti's light poems, let us pass at once to the most mystical. These are in all respects, I am not afraid to say, far superior. The poem by which Rossetti became first widely known and admired was "The Blessed Damozel." This and a lovely narrative poem entitled "Staff and Scrip" form the most exquisite examples of the poet's treatment of mystical love. You should know both of them; but we shall first take "The Blessed Damozel."

This is the story of a woman in heaven, speaking of the man she loved on earth. She is waiting for him. She watches every new soul that comes to heaven, hoping that it may be the soul of her lover. While waiting thus, she talks to herself about what she will do to make her lover happy when he comes, how she will show him all the beautiful things in heaven, and will introduce him to the holy saints and angels. That is all. But it is very wonderful in its sweetness of simple pathos, and in a peculiar, indescribable quaintness which is not of the nineteenth century at all. It is of the Middle Ages, the Italian Middle Ages before the time of Raphael. The heaven painted here is not the heaven of modern Christianity—if modern Christianity can be said to have a heaven; it is the heaven of Dante, a heaven almost as sharply defined as if it were on earth.

THE BLESSED DAMOZEL

> The blessed damozel leaned out
>   From the gold bar of Heaven;
> Her eyes were deeper than the depth
>   Of waters stilled at even;
> She had three lilies in her hand,
>   And the stars in her hair were seven.

Damozel. This is only a quaint form of the same word which in modern French signifies a young lady—demoiselle.

The suggestion is not simply that it is a maiden that speaks, but a maiden of noble blood. The idea of the poet is exactly that of Dante in speaking of Beatrice. Seven is the mystical number of Christianity.

> Her robe, ungirt from clasp to hem,
>   No wrought flowers did adorn,
> But a white rose of Mary's gift,
>   For service meetly worn;
> Her hair that lay along her back
>   Was yellow like ripe corn.

Clasp. The ornamental fastening of the dress at the neck. "From clasp to hem" thus signifies simply "from neck to feet," for the hem of a garment means especially its lower edge. *Wrought flowers* here means embroidered flowers. The dress has no ornament and no girdle; it is a dress of the thirteenth century as to form; but it may interest you to know that usually in religious pictures of angels and heavenly souls (the French religious prints are incomparably the best) there is no girdle, and the robe falls straight from neck to feet. *Service.* The maiden in heaven becomes a servant of the Mother of God. But the mediæval idea was that the daughter of a very noble house, entering heaven, might be honoured by being taken into the service of Mary, just as in this world one might be honoured by being taken into the personal service of a queen or emperor. A white rose is worn as the badge or mark of this distinction, because white is the symbol of chastity, and Mary is especially the patron of chastity. In heaven also—the heaven of Dante—the white rose has many symbolic significations. *Yellow.* Compare "Elle est *blonde comme le blé.*" (De Musset.)

> Herseemed she scarce had been a day
>   One of God's choristers;
> The wonder was not yet quite gone
>   From that still look of hers;

> Albeit, to them she left, her day
> Had counted as ten years.

Herseemed. This word is very unusual, even obsolete. Formerly instead of saying "it seems to me," "it seems to him," English people used to say meseems, himseems, herseems. The word "meseems" is still used, but only in the present, with rare exceptions. It is becoming obsolete also. *Choristers.* Choir-singers. The daily duty of angels and souls in heaven was supposed to be to sing the praises of God, just as on earth hymns are sung in church. *Albeit.* An ancient form of "although."

> (To one, it is ten years of years,
>   . . . Yet now, and in this place,
> Surely she leaned o'er me—her hair
>   . Fell all about my face. . . .
> Nothing: the autumn-fall of leaves.
>   The whole year sets apace.)

Ten years of years. That is, years composed not of three hundred and sixty-five days, but of three hundred and sixty-five years. To the lover on earth, deprived of his beloved by death, the time passes slowly so that a day seems as long as a year. Sometimes he imagines that he feels the dead bending over him—that he feels her hair falling over his face. When he looks, he finds that it is only the leaves of the trees that have been falling upon him; and he knows that the autumn has come, and that the year is slowly dying.

> It was the rampart of God's house
>   That she was standing on;
> By God built over the sheer depth
>   The which is Space begun;
> So high, that looking downward thence
>   She scarce could see the sun.

Rampart, you know, means part of a fortification; all the nobility of the Middle Ages lived in castles or fortresses,

and their idea of heaven was necessarily the idea of a splendid castle. In the "Song of Roland" we find the angels
and the saints spoken of as knights and ladies, and the language they use is the language of chivalry. *Sheer depth*,
straight down, perpendicularly, absolute. God's castle
overlooks, not a landscape, but space; the sun and the stars
lie far below.

> It lies in Heaven, across the flood
>   Of ether, as a bridge.
> Beneath, the tides of day and night
>   With flame and darkness ridge
> The void, as low as where this earth
>   Spins like a fretful midge.
>
> Around her, lovers, newly met
>   'Mid deathless love's acclaims,
> Spoke ever more among themselves
>   Their heart-remembered names;
> And the souls mounting up to God
>   Went by her like thin flames.

Ether. This is not the modern word, the scientific ether,
but the Greek and also mediæval ether, the most spiritual
form of matter. The house of God, or heaven, rests upon
nothing, but stretches out like a bridge over the ether itself.
Far below something like enormous waves seem to be sound-
lessly passing, light and dark. Even in heaven, and
throughout the universe, it was supposed in the Middle Ages
that there were successions of day and night independent of
the sun. These are the "tides" described. *Ridge the void*
means, make ridges or wave-like lines in the ether of space.
Midge is used in English just as the word *kobai* is used in
Japanese. Fretful midge, a midge that moves very quickly
as if fretted or frightened.

> And still she bowed herself and stooped
>   Out of the circling charm;
> Until her bosom must have made
>   The bar she leaned on warm,

> And the lilies lay as if asleep
>   Along her bended arm.

Charm. The circling charm is not merely the gold railing upon which she leans, but the magical limits of heaven itself which holds the souls back. She cannot pass beyond them. Otherwise her wish would take her back to this world to watch by her living lover. But only the angels, who are the messengers of heaven, can go beyond the boundaries.

> From the fixed place of Heaven she saw
>   Time like a pulse shake fierce
> Through all the worlds. Her gaze still strove
>   Within the gulf to pierce
> Its path; and now she spoke as when
>   The stars sang in their spheres.

Shake. Here in the sense of to beat like a heart or pulse. Heaven about her is motionless, fixed; but looking down upon the universe she sees a luminous motion, regular like a heart-beat; that is Time. *Its path.* Her eyes tried to pierce a way or path for themselves through space; that is, she made a desperate effort to see farther than she could see. She is looking in vain for the coming of her lover. *Their spheres.* This is an allusion to a biblical verse, "when the morning stars sang together." It was said that when the world was created the stars sang for joy.

> The sun was gone now; the curled moon
>   Was like a little feather
> Fluttering far down the gulf; and now
>   She spoke through the still weather.
> Her voice was like the voice the stars
>   Had when they sang together.
>
> (Ah sweet! Even now, in that bird's song,
>   Strove not her accents there,
> Fain to be hearkened? When those bells
>   Possessed the mid-day air,

> Strove not her steps to reach my side
> Down all the echoing stair?)

Stair. We must suppose the lover to be in or near a church with a steeple, or lofty bell tower. Outside he hears a bird singing; and in the sweetness of its song he thinks that he hears the voice of the dead girl speaking to him. Then, as the church bells send down to him great sweet waves of sound from the tower, he imagines that he can hear, in the volume of the sound, something like a whispering of robes and faint steps as of a spirit trying to descend to his side.

> "I wish that he were come to me,
> For he will come," she said.
> "Have I not prayed in Heaven?—on earth,
> Lord, Lord, has he not prayed?
> Are not two prayers a perfect strength?
> And shall I feel afraid?

An allusion to a verse in the New Testament—"if two of you shall agree on earth as touching anything that they shall ask, it shall be done for them." She is a little afraid that her lover may not get to heaven after all, but she suddenly remembers this verse, and it gives her encouragement. *Perfect strength* means strength of prayer, the power of the prayer to obtain what is prayed for. As she and he have both been praying for reunion in heaven, and as Christ has promised that whatever two people pray for, shall be granted, she feels consoled.

> "When round his head the aureole clings,
> And he is clothed in white,
> I'll take his hand and go with him
> To the deep wells of light;
> As unto a stream we will step down,
> And bathe there in God's sight.

The *aureole* is the circle or disk of golden light round the head of a saint. Sometimes it is called a "glory." In some respects the aureole of Christian art much resembles that of Buddhist art, with this exception, that some of the Oriental forms are much richer and more elaborate. Three forms in Christian art are especially common—the plain circle; the disk, like a moon or sun, usually made in art by a solid plate of gilded material behind the head; the full "glory," enshrining the whole figure. There is only one curious fact to which I need further refer here; it is that the Holy Ghost in Christian art has a glory of a special kind—the triangle. *White.* This is a reference to the description of heaven in the paradise of St. John's vision, where all the saints are represented in white garments. *Deep wells of light.* Another reference to St. John's vision, Rev. xxii, 1—"And he showed me a pure river of water of life, clear as crystal, proceeding out of the throne of God." In the heaven of the Middle Ages, as in the Buddhist paradise, we find also lakes and fountains of light, or of liquid jewels.

> "We two will stand beside that shrine,
>   Occult, withheld, untrod,
> Whose lamps are stirred continually
>   With prayer sent up to God;
> And see our old prayers, granted, melt
>   Each like a little cloud.

Shrine. The Holy of Holies, or innermost sanctuary of heaven, imagined by mediæval faith as a sort of reserved chapel. But the origin of the fancy will be explained in the next note. *Lamps.* See again St. John's vision, Rev. iv, 5—"And there were seven lamps of fire burning before the throne, which are the seven Spirits of God." These mystical flames, representing special virtues and powers, would be agitated according to the special virtues corresponding to them in the ascending prayers of men. But now we come to another and stranger thought. *A little cloud.* See again Rev. v, 8, in which reference is made to "golden vials, full of incense, which are the prayers of the saints." Here we see the evidence of a curious belief that prayers in heaven actually become transformed into the substance of incense. By the Talmudists it was said that they were turned into beautiful flowers. Again, in Rev. viii, 3, we have an allusion to this incense, made of prayer, being burned in heaven—"And there was given unto him much incense, that he should offer it with the prayers of all saints." Now the poem can be better understood. The Blessed Damozel thinks that her old prayers, that is to say, the prayers that she made on earth, together with those of her lover, are in heaven in the shape of incense. As long as prayer is not granted, it remains incense; when granted it becomes perfume smoke and vanishes. Therefore she says, "We shall see our old prayers, granted, melt each like a little *cloud*"—that is, a cloud of smoke of incense.

> "We two will lie i' the shadow of
>   That living mystic tree
> Within whose secret growth the Dove
>   Is sometimes felt to be,
> While every leaf that His plumes touch
>   Saith His Name audibly.

The heavenly tree of life is described in Rev. xxvii, 2, as bearing twelve different kinds of fruit, one for each of the twelve months of the year, while its leaves heal all diseases or troubles of any kind. The Dove is the Holy Ghost, who is commonly represented in Christian art by this bird, when he is not represented by a tongue or flame of fire. Every time that a leaf touches the body of the Dove, we are told that the leaf repeats the name of the Holy Ghost. In what language? Probably in Latin, and the sound of the Latin name would be like the sound of the motion of leaves, stirred by a wind: *Sanctus Spiritus*.

> "And I myself will teach to him,
>   I myself, lying so,

The songs I sing here; which his voice
  Shall pause in, hushed and slow,
And find some knowledge at each pause,
  Or some new thing to know."

(Alas! we two, we two, thou say'st!
  Yea, one wast thou with me
That once of old. But shall God lift
  To endless unity
The soul whose likeness with thy soul
  Was but its love for thee?)

It is the lover who now speaks, commenting upon the
imagined words of the beloved in heaven. *Endless unity*
here has a double meaning, signifying at once the mystical
union of the soul with God, and the reunion forever of
lovers separated by death. The lover doubts whether he
can be found worthy to enter heaven, because his only likeness to the beloved was in his love for her; that is to say,
his merit was not so much in being good as in loving good
in another.

"We two," she said, "will seek the groves
  Where the lady Mary is,
With her fine handmaidens, whose names
  Are five sweet symphonies,
Cecily, Gertrude, Magdalen,
  Margaret, and Rosalys.

Notice the mediæval method of speaking of the mother
of God as "the lady Mary"; such would have been the form
of address for a princess or queen in those times. So King
Arthur's wife, in the old romance, is called the lady Guinevere. *Symphonies* here has only the simplest meaning of
a sweet sound, not of a combination of sounds; but the use
of the word nevertheless implies to a delicate ear that the
five names make harmony with each other. They are
names of saints, but also favourite names given to daughters
of great families as Christian names. The picture is simply

that of the lady of a great castle, surrounded by her waiting women, engaged in weaving and sewing.

> "Circlewise sit they, with bound locks
>   And foreheads garlanded;
> Into the fine cloth white like flame
>   Weaving the golden thread,
> To fashion the birth-robes for them
>   Who are just born, being dead.

With bound locks means only with the hair tied up, not
flowing loose, as was usual in figures of saints and angels.
They are weaving garments for new souls received into
heaven, just as mothers might weave cloth for a child soon
to be born. The description of the luminous white cloth
might be compared with descriptions in Revelation. *Being
dead.* Christianity, like the Oriental religions, calls death
a rebirth; but the doctrinal idea is entirely different. You
will remember that the Greeks represented the soul under
the form of a butterfly. Christianity approaches the Greek
fancy by considering the human body as a sort of caterpil-
lar, which enters the pupa-state at death; the soul is like
the butterfly leaving the chrysalis. So far everything is
easy to understand; but this rebirth of the soul is only half
a rebirth in the Christian sense. The body is also to be
born again at a later day. At present there are only souls
in heaven; but after the judgment day the same bodies
which they used to have during life are to be given back
to them. Therefore Rossetti is not referring here to rebirth
except in the sense of spiritual rebirth, as Christ used it, in
saying "Ye must be born again"—that is, obtain new
hearts, new feelings. What in Oriental poetry would represent a fact of belief, here represents only the symbol of a
belief, a belief of a totally different kind.

> "He shall fear, haply, and be dumb:
>   Then will I lay my cheek
> To his, and tell about our love,
>   Not once abashed or weak:

And the dear Mother will approve
 My pride, and let me speak.

"Herself shall bring us, hand in hand,
 To Him round whom all souls
Kneel, the clear-ranged unnumbered heads
 Bowed with their aureoles:
And angels meeting us shall sing
 To their citherns and citoles.

"There will I ask of Christ the Lord
 Thus much for him and me:—
Only to live as once on earth
 With Love, only to be,
As then awhile, forever now
 Together, I and he."

The Damozel's idea is that her lover will be ashamed
and afraid to speak to the mother of God when he is introduced to her; but she will not be afraid to say how much
she loves her lover, and she will cause the lady Mary to
bring them both into the presence of God himself, identified
here rather with the Son than with the Father. *Citherns
and citoles.* Both words are derived from the Latin
cithara, a harp, and both refer to long obsolete kinds of
stringed instruments used during the twelfth, thirteenth,
and fourteenth centuries.

She gazed and listened and then said,
 Less sad of speech than mild,—
"All this is when he comes." She ceased.
 The light thrilled toward her, filled
With angels in strong level flight.
 Her eyes prayed, and she smiled.

(I saw her smile.) But soon their path
 Was vague in distant spheres:
And then she cast her arms along
 The golden barriers,
And laid her face between her hands,
 And wept. (I heard her tears.)

In these beautiful lines we are reminded of the special duty of angels, from which they take their name, "messenger"—the duty of communicating between earth and heaven and bringing the souls of the dead to paradise. The Damozel, waiting and watching for her lover, imagines, whenever she sees the angels coming from the direction of the human world, that her lover may be coming with them. At last she sees a band of angels flying straight toward her through the luminous ether, which shivers and flashes before their coming. "Her eyes prayed," that is, expressed the prayerful desire that it might be her beloved; and she feels almost sure that it is. Then comes her disappointment, for the angels pass out of sight in another direction, and she cries—even in heaven. At least her lover imagines that he saw and heard her weeping.

The use of the word Damozel needs a little more explanation, that you may understand the great art with which the poem was arranged. The Old French *damoisel* (later *damoiseau*) signified a young lad of noble birth or knightly parentage, employed in a noble house as page or squire. Originally there was no feminine form; but afterwards the form *damoselle* came into use, signifying a young lady in the corresponding capacity. Thus Rossetti in choosing the old English form *damozel* selected perhaps the only possible word which could exactly express the position of the Damozel in heaven, as well as the mediæval conception of that heaven. Our English word "damsel," so common in the Bible, is a much later form than damozel. There was, however, a Middle English form spelled almost like the form used by Rossetti, except that there was an "s" instead of a "z."

Now you will better see the meaning of Rossetti's mysticism. When you make religion love, without ceasing to be religious, and make love religion, without ceasing to be human and sensuous, in the good sense of the word, then you have made a form of mysticism. The blending in

Rossetti is very remarkable, and has made this particular poem the most famous thing which he wrote. We have here a picture of heaven, with all its mysteries and splendours, suspended over an ocean of ether, through which souls are passing like an upward showering of fire; and all this is spiritual enough. But the Damozel, with her yellow hair, and her bosom making warm what she leans upon, is very human; and her thoughts are not of the immaterial kind. The suggestions about bathing together, about embracing, cheek against cheek, and about being able to love in heaven as on earth, have all the delightful innocence of the Middle Ages, when the soul was thought of only as another body of finer substance. Now it is altogether the human warmth of the poem that makes its intense attraction. Rarely to-day can any Western poet write satisfactorily about heavenly things, because we have lost the artless feeling of the Middle Ages, and we cannot think of the old heaven as a reality. In order to write such things, we should have to get back the heart of our fathers; and Rossetti happened to be born with just such a heart. He had probably little or no real faith in religion; but he was able to understand exactly how religious people felt hundreds of years ago.

Let us now turn to a more earthly phase of the same tone of love which appears in "The Blessed Damozel." Now it is the lover himself on earth who is speaking, while contemplating the portrait of the dead woman whom he loved. We shall only make extracts, on account of the extremely elaborate and difficult structure of the poem.

THE PORTRAIT

This is her picture as she was:
  It seems a thing to wonder on,
As though mine image in the glass
  Should tarry when myself am gone.
I gaze until she seems to stir,—
Until mine eyes almost aver

That now, even now, the sweet lips part
　　To breathe the words of the sweet heart:—
And yet the earth is over her.

　．　　．　　．　　．　　．　　．　　．　　．

Even so, where Heaven holds breath and hears
　　The beating heart of Love's own breast,—
Where round the secret of all spheres
　　All angels lay their wings to rest,—
How shall my soul stand rapt and awed,
When, by the new birth borne abroad
Throughout the music of the suns,
　　It enters in her soul at once
And knows the silence there for God!

Here is the very highest form of mystical love; for love
is identified with God, and the reunion in heaven is a blending, not with a mere fellow soul, but with the Supreme
Being.　By "silence" here you must understand rest, heavenly peace.　The closing stanza of the poem contains one
of the most beautiful images of comparison ever made in
any language.

Here with her face doth memory sit
　　Meanwhile, and wait the day's decline,
Till other eyes shall look from it,
　　Eyes of the spirit's Palestine,
Even than the old gaze tenderer:
While hopes and aims long lost with her
Stand round her image side by side,
　　Like tombs of pilgrims that have died
About the Holy Sepulchre.

What the poet means is this:　"Now I sit, remembering
the past, and look at her face in the picture, as long as the
light of day remains.　Presently, with twilight the stars
will shine out like eyes in heaven—heaven which is my
Holy Land, because she is there.　Those stars will then
seem to me even as her eyes, but more beautiful, more loving than the living eyes.　The hopes and the projects which
I used to entertain for her sake, and which died when she

died—they come back to mind, but like the graves ranged around the grave of Christ at Jerusalem." The reference is of course to the great pilgrimages of the Middle Ages made to Jerusalem.

More than the artist speaks here; and if there be not strong faith, there is at least beautiful hope. A more tender feeling could not be combined with a greater pathos; but Rossetti often reaches the very same supreme quality of sentiment, even in poems of a character closely allied to romance. We can take "The Staff and Scrip" as an example of mediæval story of the highest emotional quality.

"Who rules these lands?" the Pilgrim said.
　"Stranger, Queen Blanchelys."
"And who has thus harried them?" he said.
　"It was Duke Luke did this;
　　God's ban be his!"

The Pilgrim said, "Where is your house?
　I'll rest there, with your will."
"You've but to climb these blackened boughs
　And you'll see it over the hill,
　　For it burns still."

"Which road, to seek your Queen?" said he.
　"Nay, nay, but with some wound
You'll fly back hither, it may be,
　And by your blood i' the ground
　　My place be found."

"Friend, stay in peace. God keep your head,
　And mine, where I will go;
For He is here and there," he said.
　He passed the hillside, slow,
　　And stood below.

So far the poem is so simple that no one could expect anything very beautiful in the sequence. We only have a conversation between a pilgrim from the Holy Land, returned to his native country (probably mediæval France),

and a peasant or yeoman belonging to the estate of a certain
Queen.   We may suspect, however, from the conversation,
that the pilgrim is a knight or noble, and probably has been
a crusader.   He sees that the country has been ravaged by
some merciless enemy; and the peasant tells him that it was
Duke Luke.   The peasant's house is burning; he himself
is hiding in terror of his life.   But the pilgrim is not afraid,
and goes to see the Queen in spite of all warning.   One can
imagine very well that the purpose of the Duke in thus
making war upon a woman was to force a marriage as well
as to acquire territory.   Now it was the duty of a true
knight to help any woman unjustly oppressed or attacked;
therefore the pilgrim's wish to see the Queen is prompted
by this sense of duty.   Hereafter the poem has an entirely
different tone.

> The Queen sat idle by her loom:
>   She heard the arras stir,
> And looked up sadly: through the room
>   The sweetness sickened her
>   Of musk and myrrh.
>
> Her women, standing two and two,
>   In silence combed the fleece.
> The Pilgrim said, "Peace be with you,
>   Lady"; and bent his knees.
>   She answered, "Peace."
>
> Her eyes were like the wave within;
>   Like water-reeds the poise
> Of her soft body, dainty-thin;
>   And like the water's noise
>   Her plaintive voice.

The naked walls of rooms during the Middle Ages were
covered with drapery or tapestry, on which figures were
embroidered or woven.   *Arras* was the name given to a
kind of tapestry made at the town of Arras in France.

For him, the stream had never well'd
  In desert tracts malign
So sweet; nor had he ever felt
  So faint in the sunshine
    Of Palestine.

Right so, he knew that he saw weep
  Each night through every dream
The Queen's own face, confused in sleep
  With visages supreme
    Not known to him.

At this point the poem suddenly becomes mystical. It is not chance nor will that has brought these two together, but some divine destiny. As he sees the Queen's face for the first time with his eyes, he remembers having seen the same face many times before in his dreams. And when he saw it in dreams, it was also the face of a woman weeping; and there were also other faces in the dream, not human but "supreme"—probably angels or other heavenly beings.

"Lady," he said, "your lands lie burnt
  And waste: to meet your foe
All fear: this I have seen and learnt.
  Say that it shall be so,
    And I will go."

She gazed at him. "Your cause is just,
  For I have heard the same:"
He said: "God's strength shall be my trust.
  Fall it to good or grame,
    'Tis in His name."

"Sir, you are thanked. My cause is dead.
  Why should you toil to break
A grave, and fall therein?" she said.
  He did not pause but spake:
    "For my vow's sake."

"Can such vows be, Sir—to God's ear,
  Not to God's will?" "My vow

Remains : God heard me there as here,"
He said, with reverent brow,
"Both then and now."

They gazed together, he and she,
The minute while he spoke;
And when he ceased, she suddenly
Looked round upon her folk
As though she woke.

"Fight, Sir," she said; "my prayers in pain
Shall be your fellowship."
He whispered one among her train,—
"To-morrow bid her keep
This staff and scrip."

The scrip was a kind of wallet or bag carried by pilgrims. Now we have a few sensuous touches, of the kind
in which Rossetti excels all other poets, because they always
are kept within the extreme limits of artistic taste.

She sent him a sharp sword, whose belt
About his body there
As sweet as her own arms he felt.
He kissed its blade, all bare,
Instead of her.

She sent him a green banner wrought
With one white lily stem,
To bind his lance with when he fought.
He writ upon the same
And kissed her name.

"Wrought" here signifies embroidered with the design
of the white lily. Remember that the Queen's name is
white lily (Blanchelys), and the flower is her crest. It was
the custom for every knight to have fastened to his lance a
small flag or pennon—also called sometimes "pennant."

She sent him a white shield, whereon
She bade that he should trace

His will. He blent fair hues that shone,
And in a golden space
He kissed her face.

Being appointed by the Queen her knight, it would have
been more customary that she should tell him what design
he should put upon his shield—heraldic privileges coming
from the sovereign only. But she tells him generously
that he may choose any design that he pleases. He returns
the courtesy very beautifully by painting the Queen's face
on the shield upon a background of gold, and kissing the
image. By "space" here must be understood a quarter, or
compartment, of the shield, according to the rules of her-
aldry.

Born of the day that died, that eve
Now dying sank to rest;
As he, in likewise taking leave,
Once with a heaving breast
Looked to the west.

And there the sunset skies unseal'd,
Like lands he never knew,
Beyond to-morrow's battle-field
Lay open out of view
To ride into.

Here we have the suggestion of emotions known to us
all, when looking into a beautiful sunset sky in which there
appeared to be landscapes of gold and purple and other
wonderful colours, like some glimpse of a heavenly world.
Notice the double suggestion of this verse. The knight,
having bidden the Queen good-bye, is riding home, looking,
as he rides, into the sunset and over the same plain where
he must fight to-morrow. Looking, he sees such landscapes
—strangely beautiful, more beautiful than anything in the
real world. Then he thinks that heaven might be like
that. At the same time he has a premonition that he is

going to be killed the next day, and this thought comes to him: "Perhaps I shall ride into that heaven to-morrow."

> Next day till dark the women pray'd;
>   Nor any might know there
> How the fight went; the Queen has bade
>   That there do come to her
>   No messenger.

> The Queen is pale, her maidens ail;
>   And to the organ-tones
> They sing but faintly, who sang well
>   The matin-orisons,
>   The lauds and nones.

Orison means a prayer; *matin* has the same meaning as the French word, spelled in the same way, for morning. Matin-orisons are morning prayers, but special prayers belonging to the ancient church services are intended; these prayers are still called matins. *Lauds* is also the name of special prayers of the Roman morning service; the word properly means "praises." *Nones* is the name of a third special kind of prayers, intended to be repeated or sung at the ninth hour of the morning—hence nones.

> Lo, Father, is thine ear inclin'd,
>   And hath thine angel pass'd?
> For these thy watchers now are blind
>   With vigil, and at last
>   Dizzy with fast.

> Weak now to them the voice o' the priest
>   As any trance affords;
> And when each anthem failed and ceas'd,
>   It seemed that the last chords
>   Still sang the words.

By *Father* is here meant God—probably in the person of Christ. To incline the ear means to listen. When this expression is used of God it always means listening to

prayer. In the second line angel has the double signification of spirit and messenger, but especially the latter.
Why is the expression "at last" used here? It was the
custom when making special prayer both to remain without
sleep, which was called "keeping vigil" or watch, and to
remain without food, or "to fast." The evening has come
and the women have not eaten anything all day. At first
they were too anxious to feel hungry, but *at last* as the night
advances, they become too weak.

> "Oh, what is the light that shines so red?
>   'Tis long since the sun set";
> Quoth the youngest to the eldest maid:
>   " 'Twas dim but now, and yet
>   The light is great."
>
> Quoth the other: " 'Tis our sight is dazed
>   That we see flame i' the air."
> But the Queen held her brows and gazed,
>   And said, "It is the glare
>   Of torches there."

Held her brows—that is, put her hand above her eyes
so as to see better by keeping off the light in the room.
There is a very nice suggestion here; the Queen hears and
sees better than the young girls, not simply because she has
finer senses, or because she has more to fear by the loss of
her kingdom. It is the intensification of the senses caused
by love that makes her see and hear so well.

> "Oh what are the sounds that rise and spread?
>   All day it was so still";
> Quoth the youngest to the eldest maid:
>   "Unto the furthest hill
>   The air they fill."
>
> Quoth the other: " 'Tis our sense is blurr'd
>   With all the chants gone by."
> But the Queen held her breath and heard,
>   And said, "It is the cry
>   Of Victory."

> The first of all the rout was sound,
>   The next were dust and flame,
> And then the horses shook the ground;
>   And in the thick of them
>   A still band came.

I think that no poet in the world ever performed a greater feat than this stanza, in which, and in three lines only, the whole effect of the spectacle and sound of an army returning at night has been given. We must suppose that the women have gone out to wait for the army. It comes; but the night is dark, and they hear at first only the sound of the coming, the tramp of black masses of men passing. Probably these would be the light troops, archers and footmen. The lights are still behind, with the cavalry. Then the first appearance is made in the light of torches—foot soldiers still, covered with dust and carrying lights with them. Then they feel the ground shake under the weight of the feudal cavalry—the knights come. But where is the chief? No chief is visible; but, surrounded by the mounted knights, there is a silent company of men on foot carrying something. The Queen wants to know what it is. It is covered with leaves and branches so that she cannot see it.

> "Oh what do ye bring out of the fight,
>   Thus hid beneath these boughs?"
> "Thy conquering guest returns to-night,
>   And yet shall not carouse,
>   Queen, in thy house."

After a victory there was always in those days a great feast of wine-drinking, or carousal. *To carouse* means to take part in such noisy festivity. When the Queen puts her question, she is kindly but grimly answered, so that she knows the dead body of her knight must be under the branches. But being a true woman and lover, her love conquers her fear and pain; she must see him again, no matter how horribly his body may have been wounded.

"Uncover ye his face," she said.
"O changed in little space!"
She cried, "O pale that was so red!
O God, O God of grace!
Cover his face!"

His sword was broken in his hand
Where he had kissed the blade.
"O soft steel that could not withstand!
O my hard heart unstayed,
That prayed and prayed!"

Why does she call her heart hard? Because she naturally reproaches herself with his death. *Unstayed* means uncomforted, unsupported. There is a suggestion that she prayed and prayed in vain because her heart had suffered her to send that man to battle.

His bloodied banner crossed his mouth
Where he had kissed her name.
"O east, and west, and north, and south,
Fair flew my web, for shame,
To guide Death's aim!"

The tints were shredded from his shield
Where he had kissed her face.
"Oh, of all gifts that I could yield,
Death only keeps its place,
My gift and grace!"

The expression "*my* web" implies that the Queen had herself woven the material of the flag. The word "web" is not now often used in modern prose in this sense—we say texture, stuff, material instead. *A shred* especially means a small *torn* piece. "To shred from" would therefore mean to remove in small torn pieces—or, more simply expressed, to scratch off, or rend away. Of course the rich thick painting upon the shield is referred to. Repeated blows upon the surface would remove the painting in small shreds. This is very pathetic when rightly studied. She sees that all the presents she made to him, banner, sword, shield, have been destroyed in the battle; and with bitter irony, the irony of grief, she exclaims, "The only present I made him that could not be taken back or broken was death. Death was my grace, my one kindness!"

> Then stepped a damsel to her side,
>   And spoke, and needs must weep;
> "For his sake, lady, if he died,
>   He prayed of thee to keep
>   This staff and scrip."

> That night they hung above her bed,
>   Till morning wet with tears.
> Year after year above her head
>   Her bed his token wears,
>   Five years, ten years.

> That night the passion of her grief
>   Shook them as there they hung
> Each year the wind that shed the leaf
>   Shook them and in its tongue
>   A message flung.

We must suppose the Queen's bed to have been one of the great beds used in the Middle Ages and long afterwards, with four great pillars supporting a kind of little roof or ceiling above it, and also supporting curtains, which would be drawn around the bed at night. The staff and scrip and the token would have been hung to the ceiling, or as the French call it *ciel*, of the bed; and therefore they might be shaken by a passion of grief—because a woman sobbing in the bed would shake the bed, and therefore anything hung to the awning above it.

> And once she woke with a clear mind
>   That letters writ to calm
> Her soul lay in the scrip; to find
>   Only a torpid balm
>   And dust of palm.

Sometimes when we are very unhappy, we dream that what we really wish for has happened, and that the sorrow is taken away. And in such dreams we are very sure that what we were dreaming is true. Then we wake up to find the misery come back again. The Queen has been greatly sorrowing for this man, and wishing she could have some news from his spirit, some message from him. One night she dreams that somebody tells her, "If you will open that scrip, you will find in it the message which you want." Then she wakes up and finds only some palm-dust, and some balm so old that it no longer has any perfume—but no letter.

> They shook far off with palace sport
>   When joust and dance were rife;
> And the hunt shook them from the court;
>   For hers, in peace or strife,
>   Was a Queen's life.
>
> A Queen's death now: as now they shake
>   To gusts in chapel dim,—
> Hung where she sleeps, not seen to wake
>   (Carved lovely white and slim),
>   With them by him.

It would be for her, as for any one in great sorrow, a consolation to be alone with her grief. But this she cannot be, nor can she show her grief to any one, because she is a Queen. Only when in her chamber, at certain moments, can she think of the dead knight, and see the staff and scrip shaking in their place, as the castle itself shakes to the sound of the tournaments, dances, and the gathering of the great hunting parties in the court below.

In that age it was the custom when a knight died to carve an image of him, lying asleep in his armour, and this image was laid upon his long tomb. When his wife died, or the lady to whom he had been pledged, she was represented as lying beside him, with her hands joined, as if in prayer.

You will see plenty of these figures upon old tombs in England.   Usually a nobleman was not buried in the main
body of a large church, but in a chapel—which is a kind
of little side-church, opening into the great church.   Such
is the case in many cathedrals; and some cathedrals, like
Westminster, have many chapels used as places of burial
and places of worship.   On the altar in these little chapels
special services are performed for the souls of the dead
buried in the chapel.   It is not uncommon to see, in such
a chapel, some relics of the dead suspended to the wall, such
as a shield or a flag.   In this poem, by the Queen's own
wish, the staff and scrip of the dead knight are hung on
the wall above her tomb, where they are sometimes shaken
by the wind.

> Stand up to-day, still armed, with her,
>   Good knight, before His brow
> Who then as now was here and there,
>   Who had in mind thy vow
>   Then even as now.
>
> The lists are set in Heaven to-day,
>   The bright pavilions shine;
> Fair hangs thy shield, and none gainsay;
>   The trumpets sound in sign
>   That she is thine.
>
> Not tithed with days' and years' decease
>   He pays thy wage He owed,
> But with imperishable peace
>   Here in His own abode,
>   Thy jealous God.

Still armed refers to the representation of the dead knight
in full armour.   Mediæval faith imagined the warrior
armed in the spiritual world as he was in this life; and the
ghosts of dead knights used to appear in armour.   The general meaning of these stanzas is, "God now gives you the
reward which he owed to you; and unlike rewards given

to men in this world, your heavenly reward is not diminished by the certainty that you cannot enjoy it except for a certain number of days or years. God does not keep anything back out of his servants' wages—no tithe or tenth. You will be with her forever." The adjective "jealous" applied to God is a Hebrew use of the term; but it has here a slightly different meaning. The idea is this, that Heaven is jealous of human love when human love alone is a motive of duty. Therefore the reward of duty need not be expected in this world but only in Heaven.

Outside of the sonnets, which we must consider separately, I do not know any more beautiful example of the mystical feeling of love in Rossetti than this. It will not be necessary to search any further for examples in this special direction; I think you will now perfectly understand one of the peculiar qualities distinguishing Rossetti from all the other Victorian poets—the mingling of religious with amatory emotion in the highest form of which the language is capable.

III

While we are discussing the ballads and shorter narrative poems, let us now consider Rossetti simply as a story-teller, and see how wonderful he is in some of those lighter productions in which he brought the art of the refrain to a perfection which nobody else, except perhaps Swinburne, has equalled. Among the ballads there is but one, "Stratton Water," conceived altogether after the old English fashion; and this has no refrain. I do not know that any higher praise can be given to it than the simple statement that it is a perfect imitation of the old ballad—at least so far as perfect imitation is possible in the nineteenth century. Should there be any criticism allowable, it could be only this, that the tenderness and pathos are somewhat deeper, and somewhat less rough in utterance, than we ex-

pect in a ballad of the fourteenth or fifteenth century.
Yet there is no stanza in it for which some parallel might
not be found in ballads of the old time.   It is nothing more
than the story of a country girl seduced by a nobleman,
who nevertheless has no intention of being cruel or un-
faithful.   Just as she is about to drown herself, or rather
to let herself be drowned, he rescues her from the danger,
marries her in haste to save appearances, and makes her his
wife.   There is nothing more of narrative, and no narrative could be more simple.   But as the great pains and
great joys of life are really in simple things, the simplest is
capable of almost infinite expansion when handled by a true
artist.   Certainly in English poetry there is no ballad more
beautiful than this; nor can we imagine it possible to do
anything more with so slight a theme.   It contains nothing, however, calling for elaborate explanation or comment;
I need only recommend you to read it and to feel it.

It is otherwise in the case of such ballads as "Sister
Helen" and "The White Ship."   "The White Ship" is a
little too long for full reproduction in the lecture; but we
can point out its special beauties.   "Sister Helen," although rather long also, we must study the whole of, partly
because it has become so very famous, and partly because
it deals with emotions and facts of the Middle Ages requiring careful interpretation.   Perhaps it is the best example of story telling in the shorter pieces of Rossetti—not
because its pictures are more objectively vivid than the
themes of the "White Ship," but because it is more subjectively vivid, dealing with the extremes of human passion,
hate, love, revenge, and religious despair.   All these are
passions peculiarly coloured by the age in which the story
is supposed to happen, the age of belief in magic, in ghosts,
and in hell-fire.

I think that in nearly all civilised countries, East and
West, from very old times there has been some belief in the
kind of magic which this poem describes.   I have seen refer-

ences to similar magic in translations of Chinese books, and
I imagine that it may have been known in Japan. In
India it is still practised. At one time or other it was
practised in every country of Europe. Indeed, it was only
the development of exact science that rendered such beliefs
impossible. During the Middle Ages they caused the misery of many thousands of lives, and the fear born of them
weighed upon men's minds like a nightmare.

This superstition in its simplest form was that if you
wished to kill a hated person, it was only necessary to make
a small statue or image of that person in wax, or some other
soft material, and to place the image before a fire, after
having repeated certain formulas. As the wax began to
melt before the fire, the person represented by the image
would become sick and grow weaker and weaker, until with
the complete melting of the image, he would die. Sometimes when the image was made of material other than wax,
it was differently treated. Also it was a custom to stick
needles into such images, for the purpose of injuring rather
than of killing. By putting the needles into the place of
the eyes, for example, the person would be made blind; or
by putting them into the place of the ears, he might be
rendered deaf. A needle stuck into the place of the heart
would cause death, slow or quick according to the slowness
with which the needle was forced in.

But there were many penalties attaching to the exercise
of such magic. People convicted of having practised it
were burned alive by law. However, burning alive was
not the worst consequence of the practice, according to general belief; for the church taught that such a crime was
unpardonable, and that all guilty of it must go to hell for
all eternity. You might destroy your enemy by magic, but
only at the cost of your own soul. A soul for a life. And
you must know that the persons who did such things believed the magic was real, believed they were killing, and
believed they were condemned to lose their souls in conse-

quence.   Can we conceive of hatred strong enough to satisfy itself at this price?   Certainly, there have been many examples in the history of those courts in which trials for witchcraft were formerly held.

Now we have the general idea behind this awful ballad. The speakers in the story are only two, a young woman and her brother, a little boy.   We may suppose the girl to be twenty and the boy about five years old or even younger. The girl is apparently of good family, for she appears to be living in a castle of her own—at least a fortified dwelling of some sort.   We must also suppose her to be an orphan, for she avenges herself—as one having no male relative to fight for her.   She has been seduced under promise of marriage; but before the marriage day, her faithless lover marries another woman.   Then she determines to destroy his life by magic.   While her man of wax is melting before the fire, the parents, relatives, and newly-wedded bride of her victim come on horseback to beg that she will forgive. But forgive she will not, and he dies, and at the last his ghost actually enters the room.   This is the story.

You will observe that the whole conversation is only between the girl and this baby-brother.   She talks to the child in child language, but with a terrible meaning behind each simple word.   She herself will not answer the prayers of the relatives of the dying man; she makes the little brother act as messenger.   So all that is said in the poem is said between the girl and the little boy.   Even in the opening of the ballad there is a terrible pathos in the presence of this little baby brother.   What does he know of horrible beliefs, hatred, lust, evil passion of any sort?   He only sees that his sister has made a kind of wax-doll, and he thinks that it is a pretty doll, and would like to play with it.   But his sister, instead of giving him the doll, begins to melt it before the fire, and he cannot understand why.

One more preliminary observation.   What is the meaning of the refrain?   This refrain, in italics, always represents the secret thought of the girl, what she cannot say to the little brother, but what she thinks and suffers. The references to Mary refer to the Virgin Mary of course, but with the special mediæval sense. God would not forgive certain sins; but, during the Middle Ages at least, the Virgin Mary, the mother of God, was a refuge even for the despairing magician or witch. We could not expect one practising witchcraft to call upon the name of Christ. But the same person, in moments of intense pain, might very naturally ejaculate the name of Mary. And now we can begin the poem.

SISTER HELEN

"Why did you melt your waxen man,
  Sister Helen?
To-day is the third since you began."
"The time was long, yet the time ran,
  Little brother."
  (*O Mother, Mary Mother,*
Three days to-day, between Hell and Heaven!)

"But if you have done your work aright,
  Sister Helen,
You'll let me play, for you said I might."
"Be very still in your play to-night,
  Little brother."
  (*O Mother, Mary Mother,*
Third night, to-night, between Hell and Heaven!)

"You said it must melt ere vesper-bell,
  Sister Helen;
If now it be molten, all is well."
"Even so,—nay, peace! you cannot tell,
  Little brother!"
  (*O Mother, Mary Mother!*
O what is this, between Hell and Heaven?)

"Oh, the waxen knave was plump to-day,
  Sister Helen;
How like dead folk he has dropped away!"

"Nay now, of the dead what can you say,
  Little brother?"
  (*O Mother, Mary Mother!*
What of the dead, between Hell and Heaven?)

"See, see, the sunken pile of wood,
  Sister Helen,
Shines through the thinned wax red as blood!"
"Nay now, when looked you yet on blood,
  Little brother?"
  (*O Mother, Mary Mother!*
How pale she is, between Hell and Heaven!)

"Now close your eyes, for they're sick and sore
  Sister Helen,
And I'll play without the gallery door."
"Aye, let me rest,—I'll lie on the floor,
  Little brother."
  (*O Mother, Mary Mother!*
What rest to-night, between Hell and Heaven?)

"Here high up in the balcony,
  Sister Helen,
The moon flies face to face with me."
"Aye, look and say whatever you see,
  Little brother,"
  (*O Mother, Mary Mother!*
What sight to-night, between Hell and Heaven?)

"Outside, it's merry in the wind's wake,
  Sister Helen;
In the shaken trees the chill stars shake."
"Hush, heard you a horse-tread as you spake,
  Little brother?"
  (*O Mother, Mary Mother!*
What sound to-night, between Hell and Heaven?)

"I hear a horse-tread, and I see,
  Sister Helen,
Three horsemen that ride terribly."
"Little brother, whence come the three,
  Little brother?"

(O Mother, Mary Mother!
Whence should they come, between Hell and Heaven?)

In this last stanza the repetition of the words "little brother" indicates intense eagerness.   The girl has been expecting that the result of her enchantments would force the relatives of her victim to come and beg for mercy.   The child's words therefore bring to her a shock of excitement.

> "They come by the hill-verge from Boyne Bar,
>   Sister Helen,
> And one draws nigh, but two are afar."
> "Look, look, do you know them who they are,
>   Little brother?"
>   *(O Mother, Mary Mother,*
> *Who should they be, between Hell and Heaven?)*
>
> "Oh, it's Keith of Eastholm rides so fast,
>   Sister Helen,
> For I know the white mane on the blast."
> "The hour has come, has come at last,
>   Little brother!"
>   *(O Mother, Mary Mother,*
> *Her hour at last, between Hell and Heaven!)*

Those who come are knights, and the child can know them only by the crest or by the horses; as they are very far he can distinguish only the horses, but he knows the horse of Keith of Eastholm, because of its white mane, floating in the wind.   From this point the poem becomes very terrible, because it shows us a play of terrible passion—passion all the more terrible because it is that of a woman.

> "He has made a sign and called Halloo!
>   Sister Helen,
> And he says that he would speak with you."
> "Oh tell him I fear the frozen dew
>   Little brother."
>   *(O Mother, Mary Mother,*
> *Why laughs she thus, between Hell and Heaven?)*

"The wind is loud, but I hear him cry,
    Sister Helen,
That Keith of Ewern's like to die."
"And he and thou, and thou and I,
    Little brother."
    (*O Mother, Mary Mother,*
And they and we, between Hell and Heaven.)

"Three days ago, on his marriage-morn,
    Sister Helen,
He sickened, and lies since then forlorn."
"For bridegroom's side is the bride a thorn,
    Little brother?"
    (*O Mother, Mary Mother,*
Cold bridal cheer, between Hell and Heaven!)

We now can surmise the story from the girl's own lips.
There are wrongs that a woman cannot forgive, unless she
is of very weak character indeed. But this woman is no
weakling; she can kill, and laugh while killing, because she
is a daughter of warriors, and has been cruelly injured.
Notice the bitter mockery of every word she utters, especially the exulting reference to the unhappy bride. We
imagine that she might be sorry for killing a man whom
she once loved; but we may be perfectly sure that she will
feel no pity for the woman that he married.

"Three days and nights he has lain abed,
    Sister Helen,
And he prays in torment to be dead."
"The thing may chance, if he have prayed,
    Little brother!"
    (*O Mother, Mary Mother,*
If he have prayed, between Hell and Heaven!)

"But he has not ceased to cry to-day,
    Sister Helen,
That you should take your curse away."
"*My* prayer was heard,—he need but pray,
    Little brother?"
    (*O Mother, Mary Mother,*
Shall God not hear, between Hell and Heaven?)

"But he says till you take back your ban,
    Sister Helen,
His soul would pass, yet never can."
"Nay then, shall I slay a living man,
    Little brother?"
    (*O Mother, Mary Mother,
A living soul, between Hell and Heaven!)

"But he calls for ever on your name,
    Sister Helen,
And says that he melts before a flame."
"My heart for his pleasure fared the same,
    Little brother."
    (*O Mother, Mary Mother!
Fire at the heart, between Hell and Heaven!)

"Here's Keith of Westholm riding fast,
    Sister Helen,
For I know the white plume on the blast."
"The hour, the sweet hour I forecast,
    Little brother!"
    (*O Mother, Mary Mother,
Is the hour sweet, between Hell and Heaven?)

"He stops to speak, and he stills his horse,
    Sister Helen,
But his words are drowned in the wind's course."
"Nay hear, nay hear, you must hear, perforce,
    Little brother!"
    (*O Mother, Mary Mother!
What word now heard, between Hell and Heaven?)

"Oh, he says that Keith of Ewern's cry,
    Sister Helen,
Is ever to see you ere he die."
"In all that his soul sees, there am I,
    Little brother!"
    (*O Mother, Mary Mother,
The soul's one sight, between Hell and Heaven!)

"He sends a ring and a broken coin,
    Sister Helen,
And bids you mind the banks of Boyne."

"What else he broke will he ever join,"
          Little brother?"
          (*O Mother, Mary Mother,*
No, never joined, between Hell and Heaven!)

It was a custom, and in some parts of England still is
a custom, for lovers not only to give each other rings, but
also to divide something between them—such as a coin or
a ring, for pledge and remembrance. Sometimes a ring
would be cut in two, and each person would keep one-half.
Sometimes a thin coin, gold or silver money, was broken
into halves and each of the lovers would wear one-half
round the neck fastened to a string. Such pledges would
be always recognised, and were only to be sent back in time
of terrible danger—in a matter of life and death. There
are many references to this custom in the old ballads.

"He yields you these, and craves full fain,
          Sister Helen,
You pardon him in his mortal pain."
"What else he took will he give again,
          Little brother?"
          (*O Mother, Mary Mother,*
Not twice to give, between Hell and Heaven!)

"He calls your name in an agony,
          Sister Helen,
That even dead Love must weep to see."
"Hate, born of Love, is blind as he,
          Little brother!"
          (*O Mother, Mary Mother,*
Love turned to hate, between Hell and Heaven!)

"Oh it's Keith of Keith now that rides fast,
          Sister Helen,
For I know the white hair on the blast."
"The short, short hour will soon be past,
          Little brother!"
          (*O Mother, Mary Mother,*
Will soon be past, between Hell and Heaven!)

"He looks at me and he tries to speak,
    Sister Helen,
But oh! his voice is sad and weak!"
"What here should the mighty Baron seek,
    Little brother?"
  (*O Mother, Mary Mother,*
Is this the end, between Hell and Heaven?)

"Oh his son still cries, if you forgive,
    Sister Helen,
The body dies, but the soul shall live."
"Fire shall forgive me as I forgive,
    Little brother!"
  (*O Mother, Mary Mother,*
As she forgives, between Hell and Heaven!)

This needs some explanation in reference to religious belief. The witch, you will observe, has the power to destroy the soul as well as the body, but on the condition of suffering the same loss herself. Yet how can this be? It could happen thus: if the dying man could make a confession before he dies, and sincerely repent of his sin before a priest, his soul might be saved; but while he remains in the agony of suffering caused by the enchantment, he cannot repent. Not to repent means to go to Hell for ever and ever. If the woman would forgive him, withdrawing the curse and pain for one instant, all might be well. But she answers, "Fire shall forgive me as I forgive"—she means, "The fire of Hell shall sooner forgive me when I go to Hell, than I shall forgive him in this world." There will be other references to this horrible belief later on. It was very common in the Middle Ages.

"Oh he prays you, as his heart would rive,
    Sister Helen,
To save his dear son's soul alive."
"Fire cannot slay it, it shall thrive,
    Little brother!"
  (*O Mother, Mary Mother,*
Alas, alas, between Hell and Heaven!)

Rive is seldom used now in prose, though we have "riven" very often. To rive is to tear. The last line of this stanza is savage, for it refers to the belief that the black fire of Hell preserves the body of the damned person instead of consuming it.

> "He cries to you, kneeling in the road,
> Sister Helen,
> To go with him for the love of God!"
> "The way is long to his son's abode,
> Little brother!"
> (*O Mother, Mary Mother,*
> *The way is long, between Hell and Heaven!*)
>
> "A lady's here, by a dark steed brought,
> Sister Helen,
> So darkly clad, I saw her not."
> "See her now or never see aught,
> Little brother!"
> (*O Mother, Mary Mother,*
> *What more to see, between Hell and Heaven?*)

As the horse was black and the lady was all dressed in black, the child could not at first notice either in the shadows of the road. On announcing that he had seen her at last, the excitement of the sister reaches its highest and wickedest; she says to him, "Nay, you will never be able to see anything in this world, unless you can see that woman's face and tell me all about it." For it is the other woman, who has made forgiveness impossible; it is the other woman, the object of her deepest hate.

> "Her hood falls back, and the moon shines fair,
> Sister Helen,
> On the Lady of Ewern's golden hair."
> "Blest hour of my power and her despair,
> Little brother!"
> (*O Mother, Mary Mother,*
> *Hour blessed and bann'd, between Hell and Heaven!*)

"Pale, pale her cheeks, that in pride did glow,
        Sister Helen,
'Neath the bridal-wreath three days ago."
"One morn for pride, and three days for woe,
        Little brother!"
    (*O Mother, Mary Mother,*
Three days, three nights, between Hell and Heaven!)

"Her clasped hands stretch from her bending head,
        Sister Helen;
With the loud wind's wail her sobs are wed."
"What wedding-strains hath her bridal bed,
        Little brother?"
    (*O Mother, Mary Mother,*
What strain but death's, between Hell and Heaven?)

You must remember that the word "strains" is nearly always used in the sense of musical tones, and that "wedding-strains" means the joyful music played at a wedding. Thus the ferocity of Helen's mockery becomes apparent, for it was upon the bridal night that the bridegroom was first bewitched; and from the moment of his marriage, therefore, he has been screaming in agony.

The climax of hatred is in the next stanza. After that the tone begins to reverse, and gradually passes away in the melancholy of eternal despair.

"She may not speak, she sinks in a swoon,
        Sister Helen,—
She lifts her lips and gasps on the moon."
"Oh! might I but hear her soul's blithe tune,
        Little brother!"
    (*O Mother, Mary Mother,*
Her woe's dumb cry, between Hell and Heaven!)

To "gasp" means to open the mouth in the effort to get breath, as one does in a fit of hysterics, or in time of great agony. "Gasps on the moon" means that she gasps with her face turned up toward the moon. In the last line we have the words "blithe tune" used in the same tone of terrible irony as that with which the words "wedding strain" was used in the preceding stanza. "Blithe" means "merry." Helen is angry because the other woman has fainted; having fainted, she has become for the moment physically incapable of suffering. But Helen thinks that her soul must be conscious and suffering as much as ever; therefore she wishes that she could hear the suffering of the soul, since she cannot longer hear the outcries of the body.

> "They've caught her to Westholm's saddle-bow,
>   Sister Helen,
> And her moonlit hair gleams white in its flow."
> "Let it turn whiter than winter-snow,
>   Little brother!"
>   (*O Mother, Mary Mother,*
> *Woe-withered gold, between Hell and Heaven.*)

The allusion is to the physiological fact that intense moral pain, or terrible fear, sometimes turns the hair of a young person suddenly white.

> "O Sister Helen, you heard the bell,
>   Sister Helen!
> More loud than the vesper-chime it fell."
> "No vesper-chime, but a dying knell,
>   Little brother!"
>   (*O Mother, Mary Mother,*
> *His dying knell, between Hell and Heaven!*)

> "Alas, but I fear the heavy sound,
>   Sister Helen;
> Is it in the sky or in the ground?"
> "Say, have they turned their horses round,
>   Little brother?"
>   (*O Mother, Mary Mother,*
> *What would she more, between Hell and Heaven?*)

> "They have raised the old man from his knee,
>   Sister Helen,
> And they ride in silence hastily."

"More fast the naked soul doth flee,
    Little brother !"
    (*O Mother, Mary Mother,*
The naked soul, between Hell and Heaven!)

"Flank to flank are the three steeds gone,
    Sister Helen,
But the lady's dark steed goes alone."
"And lonely her bridegroom's soul hath flown,
    Little brother !"
    (*O Mother, Mary Mother,*
The lonely ghost, between Hell and Heaven!)

"Oh the wind is sad in the iron chill,
    Sister Helen,
And weary sad they look by the hill."
"But he and I are sadder still,
    Little brother !"
    (*O Mother, Mary Mother,*
Most sad of all, between Hell and Heaven!)

"See, see, the wax has dropped from its place,
    Sister Helen,
And the flames are winning up apace !"
"Yet here they burn but for a space,
    Little brother !"
    (*O Mother, Mary Mother,*
Here for a space, between Hell and Heaven!)

"Ah ! what white thing at the door has cross'd,
    Sister Helen ?
Ah ! what is this that sighs in the frost ?"
"A soul that's lost as mine is lost,
    Little brother !"
    (*O Mother, Mary Mother,*
Lost, lost, all lost, between Hell and Heaven!)

Notice how the action naturally dies off into despair.
From the beginning until very nearly the close, we had an
uninterrupted crescendo, as we should say in music—that
is, a gradual intensification of the passion expressed.   With

the stroke of the death-bell the passion subsides.   The revenge is satisfied, the irreparable wrong is done to avenge a wrong, and with the entrance of the ghost the whole consequence of the act begins to appear within the soul of the actor.   I know of nothing more terrible in literature than this poem, as expressing certain phases of human feeling, and nothing more intensely true.   The probability or improbability of the incidents is of no more consequence than is the unreality of the witch-belief.   It is enough that such beliefs once existed to make us know that the rest is not only possible but certain.   For a time we are really subjected to the spell of a mediæval nightmare.

As we have seen, the above poem is mainly a subjective study.   As an objective study, "The White Ship" shows us an equal degree of power, appealing to the visual faculty. We cannot read it all, nor is this necessary.   A few examples will be sufficient.   This ballad is in distichs, and has a striking refrain.   The story is founded upon historical fact.   The son and heir of the English king Henry I, together with his sister and many knights and ladies, was drowned on a voyage from France to England, and it is said that the king was never again seen to smile after he had heard the news.   Rossetti imagines the story told by a survivor—a butcher employed on the ship, the lowest menial on board.   Such a man would naturally feel very differently toward the prince from others of the train, and would criticise him honestly from the standpoint of simple morality.

> Eighteen years till then he had seen,
> And the devil's dues in him were eighteen.

The peasant thus estimates the ruler who breaks the common laws of God and man.   Nevertheless he is just in his own way, and can appreciate unselfishness even in a man whom he hates.

He was a Prince of lust and pride;
He showed no grace till the hour he died.

. . . .

God only knows where his soul did wake,
But I saw him die for his sister's sake.

It is a simple mind of this sort that can best tell a tragical story; and the butcher's story is about the most perfect thing imaginable of its kind. Here also we have one admirable bit of subjective work, the narration of the butcher's experience in the moment of drowning. I suppose you all know that when one is just about to die, or in danger of sudden death, the memory becomes extraordinarily vivid, and things long forgotten flash into the mind as if painted by lightning, together with voices of the past.

I Berold was down in the sea;
Passing strange though the thing may be,
Of dreams then known I remember me.

Not dreams in the sense of visions of sleep, but images of memory.

Blithe is the shout on Harfleur's strand
When morning lights the sails to land:

And blithe is Honfleur's echoing gloam
When mothers call the children home:

And high do the bells of Rouen beat
When the Body of Christ goes down the street.

These things and the like were heard and shown
In a moment's trance 'neath the sea alone;

And when I rose, 'twas the sea did seem,
And not these things, to be all a dream.

In the moment after the sinking of the ship, under the water, the man remembers what he most loved at home—

mornings in a fishing village, seeing the ships return; evenings in a like village, and the sound of his own mother's voice calling him home, as when he was a little child at play; then the old Norman city that he knew well, and the church processions of Corpus Christi (Body of Christ), the great event of the year for the poorer classes. Why he remembered such things at such a time he cannot say; it seemed to him a very ghostly experience, but not more ghostly than the sight of the sea and the moon when he rose again.

> The ship was gone and the crowd was gone,
> And the deep shuddered and the moon shone;
>
> And in a strait grasp my arms did span
> The mainyard rent from the mast where it ran;
> And on it with me was another man.
>
> Where lands were none 'neath the dim sea-sky,
> We told our names, that man and I.
>
> "O I am Godefroy de l'Aigle hight,
> And son I am to a belted knight."
>
> "And I am Berold the butcher's son,
> Who slays the beasts in Rouen town."

The touch here, fine as it is, is perfectly natural. The common butcher finds himself not only for the moment in company with a nobleman, but able to talk to him as a friend. There is no rank or wealth between sky and sea— or, as a Japanese proverb says, "There is no king on the road of death." The refrain of the ballad utters the same truth:

> *Lands are swayed by a king on a throne,*
> *The sea hath no King but God alone.*

Both in its realism and in its emotion this ballad is a great masterpiece. It is much superior to "The King's

Tragedy," also founded upon history. "The King's Tragedy" seems to us a little strained; perhaps the poet attempted too much. I shall not quote from it, but will only recommend a reading of it to students of English literature because of its relation to a very beautiful story—the story of the courtship of James I of Scotland, and of how he came to write his poem called "The King's Quhair."

Another ballad demands some attention and explanation, though it is not suitable for reading in the classroom. It is an expression of passion—but not passion merely human; rather superhuman and evil. For she who speaks in this poem is not a woman like "Sister Helen"; she is a demon.

> Not a drop of her blood was human,
> But she was made like a soft sweet woman.

Perhaps the poet desired to show us here the extremest imaginative force of hate and cruelty—not in a mortal being, because that would repel us, but in an immortal being, in whom such emotion can only inspire fear. Emotionally, the poet's conception is of the Middle Ages, but the tradition is incomparably older; we can trace it back to ancient Assyrian beliefs. Coming to us through Hebrew literature, this strange story has inspired numberless European poets and painters, besides the author of "Eden Bower." You should know the story, because you will find a great many references to it in the different literatures of Europe.

Briefly, Lilith is the name of an evil spirit believed by the ancient Jews and by other Oriental nations to cause nightmare. But she did other things much more evil, and there were curious legends about her. The Jews said that before the first woman, Eve, was created, Adam had a demon wife by whom he became the father of many evil spirits. When Eve was created and given to him in marriage, Lilith was necessarily jealous, and resolved to avenge herself upon the whole human race. It is even to-day the custom among Jews to make a charm against Lilith on their marriage night; for Lilith is especially the enemy of brides.

But the particular story about Lilith that mostly figures in poetry and painting is this: If any young man sees Lilith, he must at once fall in love with her, because she is much more beautiful than any human being; and if he falls in love with her, he dies. After his death, if his body is opened by the doctors, it will be found that a long golden hair, one strand of woman's hair, is fastened round his heart. The particular evil in which Lilith delights is the destruction of youth.

In Rossetti's poem Lilith is represented only as declaring to her demon lover, the Serpent, how she will avenge herself upon Adam and upon Eve. The ideas are in one way extremely interesting; they represent the most tragical and terrible form of jealousy—that jealousy written of in the Bible as being like the very fires of Hell. We might say that in Victorian verse this is the unique poem of jealousy, in a female personification. For the male personification we must go to Robert Browning.

But there is a masterly phase of jealousy described in one of Rossetti's modern poems, "A Last Confession." Here, however, the jealousy is of the kind with which we can humanly sympathise; there is nothing monstrous or distorted about it. The man has reason to suspect unchastity, and he kills the woman on the instant. I should, therefore, consider this poem rather as a simple and natural tragedy than as a study of jealousy. It is to be remarked here that Rossetti did not confine himself to mediæval or supernatural subjects. Three of his very best poems are purely modern, belonging to the nineteenth century. This "Last Confession," appropriately placed in Italy, is not the most remarkable of the three, but it is very fine. I do not know anything in even French literature to be compared with the pathos of the murder scene, unless it be the terrible closing chapter of Prosper Merimée's "Carmen." The story of "Carmen" is also a confession; but there is a great difference

in the history of the tragedies. Carmen's lover does not
kill in a moment of passion. He kills only after having
done everything that a man could do in order to avoid killing. He argues, prays, goes on his knees in supplication—
all in vain. And then we know that he must kill, that any
man in the same terrible situation must kill. He stabs her;
then the two continue to look at each other—she keeping
her large black eyes fixed on the face of her murderer, till
suddenly they close, and she falls. No simpler fact could
occur in the history of an assassination; yet how marvellous
the power of that simple fact as the artist tells it. We
always see those eyes. In the case of Rossetti's murderer,
the incidents of the tragedy differ somewhat, because he
is blind with passion at the moment that he strikes, and
does not see. When his vision clears again, he sees the
girl fall, and

> —her stiff bodice scooped the sand
> Into her bosom.

As long as he lived, he always saw that—the low stiff front
of the girl's dress with the sand and blood. In its way this
description is quite as terrible as the last chapter of "Carmen"; and it would be difficult to say which victim of passion most excites our sympathies. The other two poems of
modern life to which I have referred are "The Card-Dealer"
and "Jenny." "The Card-Dealer" represents a singular
faculty on the poet's part of seeing ordinary facts in their
largest relations. In many European gambling houses of
celebrity, the cards used are dealt—that is, given to the
players—by a beautiful woman, usually a woman not of
the virtuous kind. The poet, entering such a place, watches
the game for a time in silence, and utters his artistic admiration of the beauty of the card-dealer, merely as he would
admire a costly picture or a statue of gold. Then suddenly
comes to him the thought that this woman, and the silent
players, and the game, are but symbols of eternal fact.

The game is no longer to his eyes a mere game of cards; it is the terrible game of Life, the struggle for wealth and vain pleasures. The woman is no longer a woman, but Fate; she plays the game of Death against Life, and those who play with her must lose. However, the allusions in this poem would require for easy understanding considerable familiarity with the terms of card-play and the names of the cards. If you know these, I think you will find this poem a very solemn and beautiful composition.

Much more modern is "Jenny," a poem which greatly startled the public when it was first published. People were inclined for the moment to be shocked; then they studied and admired; finally they praised unlimitedly, and the poem deserved all praise. But the subject was a very daring one to put before a public so prudish as the English. For Jenny is a prostitute. Nevertheless the prudish public gladly accepted this wonderful psychological study, which no other poet of the nineteenth century, except perhaps Browning, could have attempted.

The plan of the poem is as follows: A young man, perhaps the poet himself, finds at some public place of pleasure a woman of the town who pleases him, and he accompanies her to her residence. Although the young man is perhaps imprudent in seeking the company of such a person, he is only doing what tens of thousands of young men are apt to do without thinking. He represents, we might say, youth in general. But there is a difference between him and the average youth in one respect—he thinks. On reaching the girl's room, he is already in a thoughtful mood; and when she falls asleep upon his knees, tired with the dancing and banqueting of the evening, he does not think of awakening her. He begins to meditate. He looks about the room and notices the various objects in it, simple enough in themselves, but strangely significant by their relation to such a time and place—a vase of flowers, a little clock ticking, a bird in a cage. The flowers make him think

of the symbolism of flowers—lilies they are, but faded.
Lilies, the symbol of purity, in Jenny's room! But once
she herself was a lily—now also morally faded. Then the
clock, ticking out its minutes, hours—what strange hours it
has ticked out! He looks at the sleeping girl again, but
with infinite pity. She dreams; what is she dreaming of?
To wake her would be cruel, for in the interval of sleep
she forgets all the sorrows of the world. He thinks:

> For sometimes, were the truth confess'd,
> You're thankful for a little rest,—
> Glad from the crush to rest within,
> From the heart-sickness and the din
> Where envy's voice at virtue's pitch
> Mocks you because your gown is rich;
> And from the pale girl's dumb rebuke,
> Whose ill-clad grace and toil-worn look
> Proclaims the strength that keeps her weak.
>
> .   .   .   .
>
> Is rest not sometimes sweet to you?—
> But most from the hatefulness of man,
> Who spares not to end what he began,
> Whose acts are ill and his speech ill,
> Who, having used you at his will,
> Thrusts you aside, as when I dine
> I serve the dishes and the wine.

Then he begins to think of the terrible life of the prostitute,
what it means, the hideous and cruel part of it, and the end
of it. Here let me say that the condition of such a woman
in England is infinitely worse than it is in many other countries; in no place is she treated with such merciless cruelty
by society. He asks himself why this should be so—how
can men find pleasure in cruelty to so beautiful and simple-
hearted a creature? Then, suddenly looking at her asleep,
he is struck by a terrible resemblance which she bears to the
sweetest woman that he knows, the girl perhaps that he
would marry. Seen asleep, the two girls look exactly the

same.   Each is young, graceful, and beautiful; yet one is
a girl adored by society for all that makes a woman lovable,
and the other is—what?   These lines best explain the
thought:

> Just as another woman sleeps!
> Enough to throw one's thoughts in heaps
> Of doubt and horror,—what to say
> Or think,—this awful secret sway,
> The potter's power over the clay!
> Of the same lump (it has been said)
> For honour and dishonour made,
> Two sister vessels.   Here is one.
>
> My cousin Nell is fond of fun,
> And fond of dress, and change, and praise,
> So mere a woman in her ways:
> And if her sweet eyes rich in youth
> Are like her lips that tell the truth,
> My cousin Nell is fond of love.
> And she's the girl I'm proudest of.
> Who does not prize her, guard her well?
> The love of change, in cousin Nell,
> Shall find the best and hold it dear:
> The unconquered mirth turn quieter
> Not through her own, through others' woe:
> The conscious pride of beauty glow
> Beside another's pride in her.
>
> .   .   .   .
>
> Of the same lump (as it is said),
> For honour and dishonour made,
> Two sister vessels.   Here is one.
> It makes a goblin of the sun!

For, judging by the two faces, the two characters were
originally the same.   Yet how terrible the difference now.
This woman likes what all women like; his cousin, the girl
he most loves in the world, has the very same love of nice
dresses, pleasures, plays.   There is nothing wrong in liking
these things.   But in the case of the prostitute all pleasure

must turn for her to ashes and bitterness. The pure girl
will have in this world all the pretty dresses, and pleasures,
and love that she can wish for; and will never have reason
to feel unhappy except when she hears of the unhappiness
of somebody else. And it seems a monstrous thing under
heaven that such a different destiny should be portioned out
to beings at first so much alike as those two women. Even
to think of his cousin looking like her, gives him a shudder
of pain—not because he cruelly despises the sleeping girl,
but because he thinks of what might have happened to his
own dearest, under other chances of life.

Yet again, who knows what may be in the future, any
more than what has been in the past? All this world is
change. The fortunate of to-day may be unfortunate in
their descendants; the fortunate of long ago were perhaps
the ancestors of the miserable of to-day. And everything
may in the eternal order of change have to rise and sink
alternately. Cousin Nell is to-day a fortunate woman; he,
the dreamer at the bed-side of the nameless girl, is a fortunate man. But what might happen to their children? He
thinks again of the strange resemblance of the two women,
and murmurs:

> So pure,—so fall'n! How dare to think
> Of the first common kindred link?
> Yet, Jenny, till the world shall burn
> It seems that all things take their turn;
> And who shall say but this fair tree
> May need, in changes that may be,
> Your children's children's charity?
> Scorned then, no doubt, as you are scorn'd!
> Shall no man hold his pride forewarn'd
> Till in the end, the Day of Days,
> At Judgment, one of his own race,
> As frail and lost as you, shall rise.—
> His daughter, with his mother's eyes?

Then he begins to think more deeply on the great wrongs
of this world, the great misery caused by vice, the cruelty

of lust in itself.   The ruined life of this girl represents but one fact of innumerable facts of a like kind.   Millions of beautiful and affectionate women have been, and are being, and will be through all time to come, sacrificed in this way to lust—selfish and foolish and cruel lust, that destroys mind and body together.   The mystery of the dark side of life comes to him in a new way.   He cannot explain it— who can explain the original meaning of pain in this world? But he begins to get at least a new gleam of truth—this great truth, that every one who seeks pleasure in the way that he at first intended to seek it that night, adds a little to the great sum of human misery.   For vice exists only at the cost of misery.   The question is not, "Is it right for me or wrong for me to take what is forbidden if I pay for it."   The real question is, "Is it right for me or wrong for me to help in any way to support that condition of society which sacrifices lives, body, and soul, to cruelty and selfishness."   We all of us in youth think chiefly about right and wrong in their immediate relations to ourselves and our friends.   Only later in life, after we have seen a great deal of the red of human pain, do we begin to think of the consequences of an act in relation to the happiness or unhappiness of humanity.

Suddenly the morning comes as he is thinking thus.   At once he ceases to be the philosopher, and becomes again the gentleman of the world.   The girl's head is still upon his knees; he looks at the sleeping face, and wonders whether any painter could have painted a face more beautiful.   But the beauty does not appeal to his senses in any passional way; it only fills him with unspeakable compassion.   He does not awake her, but lifts her into a more comfortable position for sleeping, and leaves beside her pillow a present of gold coins, and then steals away without bidding her good-bye.   The night has not given him pleasure, but pain only—yet a pain that has made his heart more kindly and his thoughts more wise than they had been before.

IV

Our last lecture dealt with the shorter narrative poems of Rossetti, including the ballads. There remain to be considered two other narrative poems of a much more extended kind. They are quite unique in English literature; and both of them deal with mediæval subjects. One, again, is chiefly objective in its treatment; and the other chiefly subjective—that is to say, psychological. One is a fragment, but the most wonderful fragment of its kind in existence; more wonderful, I think, than even the fragments of Coleridge, both as to volume and finish. The other is complete, a story of magic and passion entitled "Rose Mary." We may first deal with "Rose Mary," giving the general plan of the poem, rather than extracts of any length; for this narration cannot very well be illustrated by examples. We shall make some quotations only in illustration of the finish and the beauty of the work.

The subject of "Rose Mary" was peculiarly adapted to Rossetti's genius. In the Middle Ages there was a great belief in the virtue of jewels and crystals of a precious kind. Belief in the magical power of rubies, diamonds, emeralds, and opals was not confined either to Europe or to modern civilisation; it had existed from great antiquity in the Orient, and had been accepted by the Greeks and Romans. This belief was perhaps forgotten after the destruction of the Roman Empire, for a time at least, in Europe; but the Crusades revived it. Talismanic stones were brought back from Palestine by many pilgrim-knights; and as some of these were marked with Arabic characters, then supposed by the ignorant to be characters of magic, supernatural legends were invented to account for the history of not a few. Also there was a certain magical use to which precious stones were put during the Middle Ages, and to which they are still sometimes put in Oriental countries. This is called crystallomancy. Crystallomancy is the art of seeing the future in crystals, or glass, or transparent substances of jewels. The same art can be practised even with ink—a drop of ink, held in the hand, offering to the eye the same reflecting surface that a black jewel would do. In Egypt, Arabia, Persia, and India divination is still practised with ink. This is the same thing as crystallomancy. Usually in those countries a young boy or a young girl is used by the diviner. He mesmerises the boy or the girl, and bids him or her look into the crystal or the ink-drop, as the case may be, and say what he or she sees there. In this way, the future is supposed to be told. Modern investigation has taught us how the whole thing is done, though science has not been able yet to explain all that goes on in the mind of the "subject." But in the Middle Ages, when the whole process was absolutely mysterious, it was thought to be the work of spirits inside the stone, or crystal, or ink-drop. And this is the superstition to which Rossetti refers in his poem "Rose Mary."

Now there is one more fact which must be explained in connection with crystallomancy. It has always been thought that the "subject"—that is, the boy or girl who looks into the stone, crystal, or ink-drop—must be absolutely innocent. The "subject" must be virtuous. In the Catholic Middle Ages the same idea took form especially in relation to the chastity of the "subject." Chastity was, in those centuries, considered a magical virtue. A maiden, it was thought, could play with lions or tigers, and not be hurt by them. A maiden—and the word was then used for both sexes, as it is sometimes used by Tennyson in his Idylls—could see ghosts or spirits, and could be made use of for purposes of crystallomancy even by a very wicked person. But should the subject have been secretly guilty of any fault, then the power to see would be impaired. The tragedy of Rossetti's poem turns upon this fact.

In the poem a precious stone, of the description called

beryl, is the instrument of divination. This beryl is round, like a terrestrial globe, and is supposed to be of the shape of the world. It is half transparent, but there are cloudings inside of it. Hidden among these cloudings are a number of evil spirits, who were enclosed in the jewel by magic. These spirits make the future appear visible to any virtuous person who looks into the stone; but they have power to deceive and to injure any one coming to consult them who is not perfectly chaste. The stone came from the East, and it was obtained only at the sacrifice of the soul of the person who obtained it. Having been brought to England, it became the property of a knightly family. This family consists only of a widow and her daughter Rose Mary. The daughter is in a state of great anxiety. She was to be married to a certain knight, who has not kept his affectionate promises. The daughter and the mother both fear that the knight may have been killed by some of his enemies. So they resolve to consult the beryl-stone. The mother does not know that her daughter has been too intimate with the absent knight. Believing that Rose Mary is all purity, the mother makes her the subject of an experiment in crystallomancy; and she looks into the beryl.

First she sees an old man with a broom, sweeping away dust and cobwebs; that is always the first thing seen. Then the inside of the beryl becomes perfectly clear, and the girl can see the open country, and the road along which her lover is expected to travel. And she sees him too. But there are perhaps enemies waiting for him. The mother tells her to look for those enemies. She looks; she sees the points of lances, in a hiding place by a roadside, and there is the evidence of what the lover has to fear in that direction. "Now look in the other direction," says the mother. The girl does so, and sees the whole road clearly, except in one place, in a valley. There she says that there is a mist; and she cannot see under the mist. This surprises the mother, and she takes away the beryl. The presence of the mist indicates that Rose Mary has committed some sin.

As a consequence the daughter confesses to the mother all that has occurred. She is not severely blamed; she is only gently rebuked, and forgiven with great love and tenderness. But it is probable that the sin must be expiated. Both are afraid. Then the expiation comes. The lover is killed by his enemies, and killed exactly on that part of the road where the mist was in the image seen in the beryl-stone. The mother goes to the dead knight's home, and examines the body. Evidently the man had died fighting bravely. The woman at first is all pity for him, as well as for her daughter. Suddenly she notices something in the dead man's breast. She takes it out, and finds that it is a package containing a love-letter, and a lock of hair. The hair is bright gold—while the hair of Rose Mary is black. This makes the mother suspicious, and she reads the letter. Then she no longer pities but abhors the dead man; for the letter proves him to have had another sweetheart, and that he had intended to betray Rose Mary.

When the daughter learns of her lover's death, she suffers terribly; but she makes sincere repentance for her fault, and then in her mother's absence she determines to destroy the beryl-stone, as a devilish thing. This is another way of committing suicide, because whoever breaks the stone is certain to be killed by the enraged spirits cast out of it. By one blow of a sword the stone is broken, and Rose Mary atones for all her faults by death. This is the whole of the story.

The extraordinary charm of the story is in its vividness— a vividness perhaps without equal even in the best work of Tennyson (certainly much finer than similar work in Coleridge), and in the attractive characterisation of mother and daughter. There is this great difference between the mediæval poems of Coleridge or Scott, and those of Rossetti, that when you are reading "The Lay of the Last Minstrel" or the wonderful "Christabel," you feel that you are reading a fairy-tale, but when you read Rossetti you are looking at life and feeling human passion. It is a great puzzle to critics how any man could make the Middle Ages live as Rossetti did. One reason, I think, is that Rossetti was a great painter as well as a great poet, and he studied the life of the past in documents and in museums until it became to him as real as the present. But we must also suppose that he inherited a great deal of his peculiar power. This power never wearies. Although the romance of Rose Mary is not very short, you do not get tired of wondering at its beauty until you reach the end. It is divided into three parts, which is a good thing for the student, as he can see the structure of the composition at once. It is written in stanzas of five lines, thus arranged—*a, a, b, b, b*. You would think this measure monotonous, but it is not. I give two examples. The first is the description of the magic jewel.

> The lady unbound her jewelled zone
> And drew from her robe the Beryl-stone.
> Shaped it was to a shadowy sphere,—
> World of our world, the sun's compeer,
> That bears and buries the toiling year.
>
> With shuddering light 'twas stirred and strewn
> Like the cloud-nest of the wading moon:
> Freaked it was as the bubble's ball,
> Rainbow-hued through a misty pall,
> Like the middle light of the waterfall.
>
> Shadows dwelt in its teeming girth
> Of the known and unknown things of earth;
> The cloud above and the wave around,—
> The central fire at the sphere's heart bound,
> Like doomsday prisoned underground.

I feel quite sure that even Tennyson could not have done this. Only a great painter, as well as a great observer, could have done it; and the choice of words is astonishing in its exquisiteness. Most of them have more than one meaning, and both meanings are equally implied by their use. Take, for example, the word "shadowy"; it means cloudy and it also means ghostly. Thus it is peculiarly appropriate to picture the magic stone as full of moving shadows, themselves of ghostly character. Or take the word "shuddering"; it means trembling with cold or fear, and it means also a quick trembling, never a slow motion. Just such a word might be used to describe the strange vibration of air-bubbles enclosed in a volcanic crystal. But we have also the suggestion here of a ghostly motion, a motion that gives a shiver of fear to the person who sees it. Or take the word "freaked." "Freak" is commonly used to signify a mischievous bit of play, a wild fancy. "Fancifully marked" would be the exact meaning of "freaked" in the ordinary sense; but here it is likewise appropriate as a description of the streams and streaks of colour playing over the surface of a bubble without any apparent law, as if they were made by some whimsical spirit. Now every verse of the whole long poem is equally worthy of study for its astonishing finish. I shall give a few more verses merely to show the application of the same power to a description of pain. The girl has just been told of her lover's murder; and the whole immediate consequence is told in five lines.

> Once she sprang as the heifer springs
> With the wolf's teeth at its red heart-strings:
> First 'twas fire in her breast and brain,
> And then scarce hers but the whole world's pain,
> As she gave one shriek and sank again.

The first two lines might give you an undignified image unless you understood the position of the girl when she received the news. She was kneeling at her mother's feet, with her mother's arms around her. On being told the terrible thing, she tries to spring up, because of the shock of the pain—just as a young heifer would leap when the wolf had seized it from underneath. A wolf snaps at the belly of the animal, close to the heart. Therefore the comparison is admirable. As for the rest of the verse, any physician can confirm its accuracy. The up-rush of blood at the instant of a great shock of pain feels like a great sudden heat, burning up toward the head. And in such a time one realises that certain forms of pain, moral pain, are larger than oneself—too great to be borne. Psychologically, great moral pain depends upon nervous development; and this nervous susceptibility to pain is greater than would seem fitted to the compass of one life. Moral pain can kill. It is said that in such times we feel not only our own pain, but the pain of all those among our ancestors who suffered in like manner. Thus, by inheritance, individual pain is more than individual. At all events the fourth line of the stanza I have quoted will appear astonishingly true to anybody who knows the greater forms of mental suffering.

Leaving this poem, which could not be too highly praised, we may turn to "The Bride's Prelude," the greatest of the longer compositions, therefore the greatest thing that Rossetti did. Unfortunately, perhaps, it is unfinished. It is only a fragment; death overtook the writer before he was able to complete it. Like "Rose Mary," it leads us back to the Middle Ages. But here there is no magic, nothing ghostly, nothing impossible; there is only truth, atrocious, terrible truth—a tale of cruelty, treachery, and pain related by the victim. The victim is a bride. She is just going to be married. But before her marriage, she has a story to tell her sister—a story so sad and so frightful that it requires strong nerves to read the thing without pain.

We may suppose that the incident occurred in old France, or—though I doubt it—in Norman England. The scenery and the names remind us rather of Southern France. All the facts belong to the life of the feudal aristocracy. We are among princes and princesses; great lords of territory and great lords of battle are introduced to us, with their secret sorrows and shames. Great ladies, too, open their hearts to us, and prove so intensely human that it is very hard to believe the whole story is a dream. It rather seems as if we had known all these people, and that our lives had at some time been mingled with theirs. The eldest daughter of one great house, very beautiful, and very innocent, is taken advantage of by a retainer in the castle. She is foolish and unable to imagine that any gentleman could intend to do her a wrong. The retainer, on the other hand, is a very cunning villain. His real purpose is to bring shame upon the daughter of the house. Why? Because, as he is only a poor knight, he could not hope to marry into a princely family. But if he can seduce one of the girls, then perhaps the family will be only too glad to have him marry his victim, because that will hide their shame. Evidently he has plotted for this. But his plans, and everybody's plans, are affected by unexpected results of civil war. His masters, being defeated in a great battle, have to retreat to the mountains for a time; and then he deserts them in the basest manner. Meantime the unhappy girl is found to be with child. Death was the rule in those days for such a case—burning alive. Her brothers wish to kill her. But her father interferes and saves her. It is decided only that the child shall be taken from her—to be killed, probably. Everybody is forbidden to speak of the matter. Some retainers who did speak of it are hanged for an example. Presently, by another battle, the family return into their old possessions, and enormously increase their ancient power. When this happens the scoundrel that seduced the daughter of the house and then deserted the family returns. Why does he return? Now is the time to fulfil his purpose. He has become a great soldier and a nobleman in his own right. Now he can ask for that young lady in marriage, and they dare not refuse. If they refuse, he can revenge himself by telling the story of her disgrace. If they accept him as a son-in-law, they will also be obliged to make him very powerful; and he will know how to take every advantage. The girl is not consulted at all. Her business is to obey. She thinks that it would be better to die than to marry the wicked man that had wronged her; but she must obey and she is ordered to marry him. He cares nothing about her; she is only the tool by which he wishes to win his way into power. But, cunning as he is, the brothers of the girl are even more cunning. They wish for the marriage only for the purpose of getting the man into their hands, just for one moment. He shall marry her, but immediately afterwards he shall disappear forever from the sight of men. The bride does not know the purpose of her terrible brothers; she thinks they are cruel to her when she tells her story, but they only wish to avenge her, and they are much too prudent to tell her what they are going to do. The poem does not go any further than the moment before the marriage. The first part is quite finished; but the second part was never written.

The whole of this great composition is in verses of five lines, curiously arranged. Rossetti adopts a different form of verse for almost every one of his narrations. This is quite as unique a measure in its way—that is, in nineteenth century poetry—as was the measure of Tennyson's "In Memoriam" in elegiac poetry. Now we shall try to illustrate the style of the poem.

> Against the haloed lattice-panes
>   The bridesmaid sunned her breast;
> Then to the glass turned tall and free,
> And braced and shifted daintily
> Her loin-belt through her côte-hardie.
>
> The belt was silver, and the clasp
>   Of lozenged arm-bearings;
> A world of mirrored tints minute
> The rippling sunshine wrought into 't,
> That flushed her hand and warmed her foot.

> At least an hour had Aloÿse,—
>   Her jewels in her hair,—
> Her white gown, as became a bride,
> Quartered in silver at each side,—
> Sat thus aloof, as if to hide.
>
> Over her bosom, that lay still,
>   The vest was rich in grain,
> With close pearls wholly overset:
> Around her throat the fastenings met
> Of chevesayle and mantelet.

Absolutely real as this seems, we know that the details must have been carefully studied in museums. Elsewhere, except perhaps in very old pictures, these things no longer exist. There are no more loin-belts of silver, no côte-hardies, no chevesayle or mantelet. I cannot explain to you what they are without pictures—further than to say that they were parts of the attire of a lady of rank about the thirteenth and fourteenth centuries. Brides do not now have their white robes "quartered in silver"—that is, figured with the family crest or arms. Why silver instead of gold? Simply because of the rule that brides should be all in white; therefore even the crest was worked in white metal instead of gold. By the word vest, you must also understand an ancient garment for women; the modern word signifies a garment worn only by men. "Grain" is an old term for texture. The description of the light playing on the belt-clasp of the bridesmaid, in the second stanza, is a marvellous bit of work, the effect being given especially by three words—"lozenged," "rippling," for the sunshine, and "minute," for the separate flushes or sparklings thrown off from the surface. But all is wonderful; this is painting with words exactly as a painter paints with colours. Sounds are treated with the same wonderful vividness:

> Although the lattice had dropped loose,
>   There was no wind; the heat

Being so at rest that Amelotte
Heard far beneath the plunge and float
Of a hound swimming in the moat.

Some minutes since, two rooks had toiled
  Home to the nests that crowned
Ancestral ash-trees. Through the glare
Beating again, they seemed to tear
With that thick caw the woof o' the air.

One must have been in the tower of a castle to feel the
full force of the first stanza. The two girls are in a room
perhaps one hundred and fifty or two hundred feet above
the water of the moat, so that except in a time of extraordinary stillness they would not hear ordinary sounds from so
far below. And notice that the poet does not tell us that
this was because the air did not move; he says that the heat
was at rest. Very expressive—in great summer heat, without wind, the air itself seems to our senses not air but fluid
heat. And the same impression of summer is given by the
description of the two crows flying to their nest and back
again, and screaming as they fly. The poet does not say
that they flew; he says they toiled home—because flying in
that thick warm air is difficult for them. When they return he uses another word, still more impressive; he says
they beat again through the glare. This makes you hear
the heavy motion of the wings. And he describes the crow
as seeming to tear the air, because that air is so heavy that
it seems like a thing woven.

Here is a strangely powerful stanza describing the difficulty of speaking about a painful subject that for many
years one has tried to forget:

Her thought, long stagnant, stirred by speech,
  Gave her a sick recoil;
As, dip thy fingers through the green
That masks a pool,—where they have been
The naked depth is black between.

Any of you who as boys have played about a castle moat, and stirred the green water weeds covering the still water, must have remarked that the water looks black as ink underneath. Of course it is not black in itself; but the weeds keep out the sun, so that it seems black because of the shadow. The poet's comparison has a terrible exactness here. The mind is compared to stagnant water covered with water-weeds. Weeds grow upon water in this way only when there has been no wind for a long time, and no current. The condition of a mind that does not think, that dares not think, is like stagnant water in this way. Memory becomes covered up with other things, matters not relating to the past.

Now we can take four stanzas from the scene of the secret family meeting, after the shame has been confessed and is known. They are very powerful.

> "Time crept. Upon a day at length
>   My kinsfolk sat with me:
> That which they asked was bare and plain:
> I answered: the whole bitter strain
> Was again said, and heard again.
>
> "Fierce Raoul snatched his sword, and turned
>   The point against my breast.
> I bared it, smiling: 'To the heart
> Strike home,' I said; 'another dart
> Wreaks hourly there a deadlier smart.'
>
> " 'Twas then my sire struck down the sword,
>   And said, with shaken lips:
> 'She from whom all of you receive
> Your life, so smiled; and I forgive.'
> Thus for my mother's sake, I live.
>
> "But I, a mother even as she,
>   Turned shuddering to the wall:
> For I said: 'Great God! and what would I do,
> When to the sword, with the thing I knew,
> I offered not one life, but two!' "

This is now the most terrible part of the story; and it has a humanity about it that almost makes us doubt. Fancy the situation. The daughter of a prince unchaste with a common retainer. Now in princely families chastity was of as much importance as physical strength and will; it meant everything—honour, purity of race, the possibility of alliance. And a great house is thus disgraced. We can sympathise with the horrible mental suffering of the girl, but it is impossible not to sympathise also even with the terrible brother that wishes to kill her. He is right, she deserves death; but he is young, and cruel because young. The father sorrows, and seeing the girl smiling, thinks of the dead mother, and forgives. This is the only point at which we feel inclined to lay down the book and ask questions. Would a father in such a position have done this in those cruel ages? Would he have allowed himself to pity? —or rather, could he have allowed himself to pity? Tender-hearted men did not rule in those days. We have records of husbands burning their wives, of fathers killing their sons. All we can say is that an exception might have existed, just as Rossetti imagines. Human nature was of course not different then from what it is now, but it is quite certain that the gentle side of human nature seldom displayed itself in the families of the feudal princes; a man who was gentle could not rule. In Italy sons who did not show the ruling character were apt to be killed or poisoned. One must understand that feudal life was not much more moral than other life.

I think we can here turn to another department of Rossetti's verse. I only hope that the examples given from the "Bride's Prelude" will interest you sufficiently to make you at a later day turn to this wonderful poem for a careful study of its beauty and power.

V

When we come to the study of the lives of the Victorian poets, we shall find that Rossetti's whole existence was governed by his passion for one woman, whom he loved in a strange mystical way, with a love that was half art (art in the good sense) and half idolatry. To him she was much more than a woman; she was a divinity, an angel, a model for all things beautiful. You know that he was a great painter, and in a multitude of beautiful pictures he painted the face of this woman. He composed his poems also in order to please her. He lost her within a little more than a year after winning her, and this nearly killed him. I may say that throughout all his poems, speaking in a general way, there are references to this great love of his life; but there is one portion of his work that we must consider as especially illustrating it, and that is the "House of Life," a collection of more than one hundred sonnets upon the subject of love and its kindred emotions. But the love of which Rossetti sings is not the love of a young man for a girl—not the love of youth and maid. It is married love carried to the utmost degree of worship. You will think this a strange subject; and I confess that it is. Very few men could be praised for touching such a subject. Coventry Patmore, you know, was an exception. He made the subject of his own courtship, wedding, and married life the subject of his poetry, and he did it so nicely and so tenderly that his book had a great success. But Rossetti did his work in an entirely different way, which I must try to explain.

Unlike Patmore, Rossetti did not openly declare that he took any personal experience for the subject of his study; we only perceive, through knowledge of his life, and through suggestions obtained from other parts of his work, that personal love and personal loss were his great inspira-

tion. As a matter of fact, any man who sings about love
must draw upon his own personal experience of the passion.
Every lover thinks of love in his own way. But the value
of a love poem is not the personal part of it; the value of
a love poem is according to the degree in which it represents
universal experience, or experience of a very large kind.
It must represent to some degree a general philosophy of
life. Even the commonest little love-song, such as a peasant might sing in the streets of Tokyo, as he comes in from
the country walking beside his horse, will represent something of the philosophy of life if it is a good and true composition, no matter how vulgar may be the idiom of it.
When we come to think about it, we shall find that all great
poetry is in this sense also philosophical poetry.

Rossetti, as I have already shown you, was a true philosopher in certain directions; and he applied his philosophical
powers, as well as his artistic powers, to his own experiences, so as to adapt them to the uses of great poetry. He
is never narrowly impersonal. And his sonnets are really
very wonderful compositions—not reflecting universal experience so as to be universally understood, but reflecting
universal experience so as to be understood by cultivated
minds only. These productions are altogether above the
range of the common mind; they are extremely subtle and
elaborate, both as to thought and as to form. But their
subject is not at all special. Rossetti had the idea that
every phase of happiness and sorrow belonging to married
life, from the hour of the wedding night to the hour of
death, was worthy of poetical treatment, because married
life is related to the deepest human emotions. And in the
space of one hundred sonnets he treats every phase. This
series of sonnets is divided into two groups. The first contains poems relating to the early conditions of love in marriage; the second group treats especially of the more
sorrowful aspects of a married life—the trials of death, the
pains of memory, and the hopes and fears of reuniting after

death.   The second part does not, however, contain all the sad pieces; there are very sad ones in the first group of fifty-nine.   We have already studied one of the first group, the piece called "The Birth-Bond."   There is another piece in this group, the first of four sonnets, which is exquisite as a bit of fancy.   It is entitled "Willowwood."

I sat with Love upon a woodside well,
    Leaning across the water, I and he;
    Nor ever did he speak nor looked at me,
But touched his lute wherein was audible
The certain secret thing he had to tell:
    Only our mirrored eyes met silently
    In the low wave; and that sound came to be
The passionate voice I knew; and my tears fell.

And at their fall, his eyes beneath grew hers;
And with his foot and with his wing-feathers
    He swept the spring that watered my heart's drouth.
Then the dark ripples spread to waving hair,
And as I stooped, her own lips rising there
    Bubbled with brimming kisses at my mouth.

This is a dream of the dead woman loved.   The lover finds himself seated with the god of love, the little naked boy with wings, as the ancients represented him, at the edge of a spring near the forest.   He does not look at the god of love, neither does the god look at him; they were friends long ago, but now—what is the use?   She is dead.   By the reflection in the water only he knows that Love is looking down, and he does not wish to speak to him.   But Love will not leave him alone.   He hears the tone of a musical instrument, and that music makes him suddenly very sad, for it seems like the voice of the dead for whom he mourns. It makes his tears fall into the water; and immediately, magically, the reflection of the eyes of Love in the water become like the eyes of the woman he loved.   Then while he looks in wonder, the little god stirs the surface of the water with wings and feet, and the ripples become like the hair of the dead woman, and as the lover bends down, her lips rise up through the water to kiss him. You may ask, what does all this mean? Well, it means as much as any dream means; it is all impossible, no doubt, but the impossible in dreams often makes us very sad indeed—especially if the dead appear to come back in them.

Another example of regret, very beautiful, is the sonnet numbered ninety-one in this collection. It is called "Lost on Both Sides."

> As when two men have loved a woman well,
>   Each hating each, through Love's and Death's deceit;
>   Since not for either this stark marriage-sheet
> And the long pauses of this wedding-bell;
> Yet o'er her grave the night and day dispel
>   At last their feud forlorn, with cold and heat;
>   Nor other than dear friends to death may fleet
> The two lives left that most of her can tell :—
>
> So separate hopes, which in a soul had wooed
>   The one same Peace, strove with each other long,
>   And Peace before their faces perished since:
> So through that soul, in restless brotherhood,
>   They roam together now, and wind among
>   Its bye-streets, knocking at the dusty inns.

The comparison is of the hopes and aims of the artist to a couple of men in love with the same woman—bitter enemies while she lives, because of their natural rivalry, but loving each other after her death, simply because each can understand better than anybody else in the world the pain of the other. Afterward the men, once rivals, passed all their time together, wandering about at night in search of some quiet place, where they can sit down and drink and talk together. In Rossetti's time such quiet places were not to be found in the main streets, but in the little side streets called bye-streets. After this explanation, the comparison should not be obscure. The artist who loves does all his work with the thought of the woman that he loves before him; his hope to win fame is that he may make her proud of him; his aims are in all cases to please her.   After he has lost her, these hopes and aims, which might have been antagonists to each other in former days, are now reconciled within him; her memory alone is now the inspiration and the theme.   I hope you will notice the curious and exquisite value of certain words here.   "Stark," meaning stiff, nearly always refers to the rigidness of death; it is especially used of the appearance and attitude of corpses, and its application in this poem to the cover of the marriage bed is quite enough to convey the sense of death without any more definite observation.   Again the expression "long pauses," referring to the sound of the church bells, makes us understand that the bells are really ringing a funeral knell; for the ringing of wedding bells ought to be quick and joyous.   It might seem a strange contradiction, this simile, but the poet has in his mind an old expression about the death of a maiden: "She became the bride of Death." Thus the effect is greatly intensified by the sombre irony of the simile itself.

We might extract a great many beauties from this wonderful collection of sonnets; but time is precious, and we shall have room for only another quotation or two.   The following is one to which I should like especially to invite your attention—not only because of its strange charm, but also because of the curious legend which it recalls—a legend which we have already studied:

BODY'S BEAUTY

Of Adam's first wife, Lilith, it is told
  (The witch he loved before the gift of Eve,)
  That, ere the snake's, her sweet tongue could deceive,
And her enchanted hair was the first gold.
And still she sits, young while the earth is old,
  And subtly of herself contemplative,
  Draws men to watch the bright web she can weave,
Till heart and body and life are in its hold.

The rose and poppy are her flowers ; for where
  Is he not found, O Lilith, whom shed scent
And soft-shed kisses and soft sleep shall snare ?
  Lo ! as that youth's eyes burned at thine, so went
  Thy spell through him, and left his straight neck bent,
And round his heart one strangling golden hair.

The reference to the rose and the poppy may need some
explanation. The rose has been for many centuries in
Western countries a symbol of love; and the poppy has
been a symbol of death and sleep from the time of the
Greeks. It is from the seeds of the poppy that opium is
extracted. The Greeks did not know the use of opium;
but they knew that the seeds of the flower produced sleep,
and might, in certain quantities, produce death. We have
the expression "poppied sleep" to express the sleep of death.

A final word must be said about Rossetti's genius as a
translator. He has given us, in one large volume, the most
precious anthology of the Italian poets of the Middle Ages
that ever has been made—the poets of the time of Dante,
under the title of "Dante and his Circle." This magnificent work would alone be sufficient to establish his supreme
excellence as a translator of poetry; but the material is
mostly of a sort that can appeal to scholars only. Rossetti
is better known as a translator through a very few short
pieces translated from French poets, chiefly. Such is the
wonderful rendering of Villon's "Ballad of Dead Ladies,"
beginning

Tell me now in what hidden way is
  Lady Flora, the lovely Roman ?
Where's Hipparchia, and where is Thais,
  Neither of them the fairer woman ?
Where is Echo, beheld of no man,
  Only heard on river and mere,—
She whose beauty was more than human ?—
  But where are the snows of yester-year ?

Even Swinburne, when making his splendid translations

from Villon, refrained from attempting to translate this ballad, saying that no man could surpass, even if he could equal, Rossetti's version. The burthen is said to be especially successful as a rendering of the difficult French refrain:

Mais ou sont les neiges d'antan?

You will find this matchless translation almost anywhere, so we need not occupy the time further with it; but I doubt whether you have noticed as yet other wonderful translations made by this master from the French. Such is the song from Victor Hugo's drama "Les Burgraves"; you will not forget Rossetti's translation after having once read it.

> Through the long winter the rough wind tears;
> With their white garments the hills look wan.
>   Love on: who cares?
>   Who cares? Love on!
> My mother is dead; God's patience wears;
> It seems my chaplain will not have done!
>   Love on: who cares?
>   Who cares? Love on!
> The Devil, hobbling up the stairs,
> Comes for me with his ugly throng.
>   Love on: who cares?
>   Who cares? Love on.

Another remarkable translation from the same drama is that of the song beginning:

> In the time of the civil broils
> Our swords are stubborn things.
> A fig for all the cities!
> A fig for all the kings!

and ending:

> Right well we hold our own
> With the brand and the iron rod.
> A fig for Satan, Burgraves;
> Burgraves, a fig for God!

But even more wonderful Rossetti seems when we go back to the old French, as in the translation which has been called "My Father's Close."

> Inside my father's close
> (*Fly away O my heart away!*)
> Sweet apple-blossom blows
> *So sweet.*
>
> Three kings' daughters fair,
> (*Fly away O my heart away!*)
> They lie below it there
> *So sweet!*

Now the Old French of the first stanza will show you the astonishing faithfulness of the rendering:

> Au jardin de mon père,
> (*Vole, mon coeur, vole!*)
> Il y a un pommier doux,
> *Tout doux.*

Besides the small exquisite things, there are long translations from mediæval writers, French and Italian, of wonderful beauty. Compare, for example, the celebrated episode of Francesca da Rimini in Dante (which Carlyle so beautifully called "a lily in the mouth of Hell"), as translated by Byron, and as translated by Rossetti, and observe the immeasurable superiority of the latter. It would be very pleasant, if we had time, to examine Rossetti's translations more in detail; but the year advances and we must turn to an even greater master of verse—Swinburne.

CHAPTER IV

STUDIES IN SWINBURNE

A GOOD modern critic has said that the resemblance between Shelley and Algernon Charles Swinburne is of so astonishing a kind that it tempts one to believe that Swinburne is Shelley in a new body, that the soul of the drowned poet really came back to life again, and returned to finish at Oxford University the studies interrupted by his expulsion at the beginning of the century. The fancy is pretty; and it is supported by a number of queer analogies. Swinburne, like Shelley, is well born; like Shelley, he has been from his early days at Eton a furious radical; like Shelley, he has always been an enemy of Christianity; and like Shelley, he has also been an enemy of conventions and prejudices of every description. At the beginning of the century Swinburne would certainly have been treated just as Byron and Shelley were treated, but times are changed to-day; the public has become more generous and more sensible, and critics generally recognise Swinburne as the greatest verse writer English literature produced. He will certainly have justice done him after his death, if not during his life.

If Swinburne were Shelley reborn, we should have to recognise that he gained a good deal of wisdom from the experiences of his former life. He is altogether an incomparably stronger character than Shelley. He kept his radicalism for his poetry, and never in any manner outraged the conventions of society in such matters as might relate to his private life. He is also a far greater poet than Shelley —greater than Tennyson, greater than Rossetti, greater than Browning, greater than any other Englishman, not excepting Milton, in the mastery of verse. He is also probably one of the greatest of scholars among the poets of any

country, writing poetry in English or French, in Greek and
Latin. For learning, there are certainly few among the
poets of England who would not have been obliged to bow
before him. He is also the greatest living English dramatist—I might as well say the greatest English dramatist of
the nineteenth century. Except the "Cenci" of Shelley,
there is no other great drama since 1800 to be placed beside
the dramas of Swinburne; and the "Prometheus Unbound"
by Shelley is far surpassed by Swinburne's Greek tragedy
of "Atalanta in Calydon." Another feature of Swinburne's
genius is his critical capacity. He is a great critic; so great
that he has been able to make his enemies afraid of him,
as well as to help to distinction struggling young men of
talent whose work he admires. You will perceive what
force there must be in the man. Born in 1837, he has never
ceased to produce poetry from the time of his University
days, and he still writes, with the result that the bulk of
his work probably exceeds the work of any other great poet
of the century. If he be indeed the reborn Shelley, it is
certain that Shelley has become a giant.

I may have surprised you by saying that Swinburne is
the greatest of all our poets. But understand that I am
speaking of poetry as distinguished from prose, of poetry as
rhythm and rhyme, as melody and measure. By greatest
of poets I mean the greatest master of verse. If you were
to ask me whether Swinburne has as great a quality as
Tennyson or as Rossetti or as Browning, either in the moral
or philosophical sense, I should say no. Greatest of all in
the knowledge and use of words, he is perhaps less than any
of the three in the higher emotional, moral, sympathetic,
and philosophical qualities that give poetry its charm for
even those who know nothing about the art of words. And
of all the Victorian poets, Swinburne will be the least useful to students of these literary classes. The extraordinary
powers that distinguish him are powers requiring not only
a perfect knowledge of English, but a perfect knowledge

of those higher forms of literary expression which are especially the outcome of classical study. Swinburne's scholarship is one of the great obstacles to his being understood by any who are not scholars themselves in the very same direction; in this sense he would be, I think, quite as useless to you as Milton in the matter of form. In value to you he would be far below Milton in the matter of thought and sentiment.

There are several ways of studying poetry. The greater number of people who buy the books of poets, and who find pleasure in them, do not know anything about the rules of verse. Out of one hundred thousand Englishmen who read Tennyson, I doubt very much if one thousand know the worth of his art. English University students, who have taken a literary course, probably do understand very well; but a poet's reputation and fortune are not made by scholars, but by the great mass of half-educated people. They read for sentiment, for emotion, for imagination; and they are quite satisfied with the pleasure given them by the poet in this way. They are improving and educating themselves when they read him, and for this it is not necessary that they should know the methods of his work, but only that they should know its results. The educators of the great mass of any people in Europe are, in this sense, the poets.

The other way of studying a poet is the scholarly way, the critical method (I do not mean the philosophical method; that is beside our subject); we read a poet closely, carefully, observing every new and unfamiliar word, every beautiful phrase and unaccustomed term, every device of rhythm or rhyme, sound or colour that he has to give us. Our capacity to study any poet in this way depends a good deal upon literary habit and upon educational opportunity. By the first method I doubt whether you could find much in Swinburne. He is like Shelley, often without substance of any kind. By the second method we can do a great deal with a choice of texts from his best work. I think it better to state this clearly beforehand, so that you may not be disappointed, failing to find in him the beautiful haunting thoughts that you can find in Rossetti or in Tennyson or in Browning.

Here I must digress a little. I must speak of the worst side of Swinburne as well as of the best. The worst is nearly all in one book, not a very large book, which made the greatest excitement in England that had been made since the appearance of Byron's "Don Juan." It is the greatest lyrical gift ever given to English literature, this book; but it is also, in some respects, the most immoral book yet written by an English poet. The work of Byron, at its worst, is pure and innocent by comparison with the work of Swinburne in this book. It is astonishing that the English public could have allowed the book to exist. Probably it was forgiven on account of its beauty. Some years ago, I remember, an excellent English review said, in speaking of a certain French poem, that it was the most beautiful poem of its kind in the French language, but that, unfortunately, the subject could not be mentioned in print. Of course when there is a great beauty and great voluptuousness at the same time, it is the former, not the latter, that makes the greatness of the work. There must be something very good to excuse the existence of the bad. Much of the work of Swinburne is like that French poem, valuable for the beauty and condemnable for the badness in it—and touching upon subjects which cannot be named at all. Why he did this work we must try to understand without prejudice.

First, as to the man himself. We must not suppose that a person is necessarily immoral in his life because he happens to write something which is immoral, any more than we should suppose a person whose writings are extremely moral to be incapable of doing anything of a vicious or foolish kind. Shelley, for example, is a very chaste poet— there is not one improper line in the whole of his poetry;

but his life was decidedly unfortunate. Exactly the reverse happens in the case of Swinburne, who has written thousands of immoral lines. The fact is that many persons are apt to mistake artistic feeling for vicious feeling, and a spirit of revolt against conventions for a general hatred of moral law. I must ask you to try to put yourselves for a moment in the place of a young student, such as Swinburne was at the time of these writings, and try to imagine how he felt about things. In every Western boy—indeed, I may say in every civilised boy—there are several distinct periods, corresponding to the various periods in the history of human progress. Both psychologically and physiologically the history of the race is repeated in the history of the individual. The child is a savage, without religion, without tenderness, with a good deal of cruelty and cunning in his little soul. He is this because the first faculties that are developed within him are the faculties for self-preservation, the faculties of primitive man. Then ideas of right and wrong and religious feelings are quickened within him by home-training, and he becomes somewhat like the man of the Middle Ages—he enters into his mediæval period. Then in the course of his college studies he is gradually introduced to a knowledge of the wonderful old Greek civilisation, civilisation socially and, in some respects, even morally superior to anything in the existing world; and he enters into the period of his Renaissance. If he be very sensitive to beauty, if he have the æsthetic faculty largely developed, there will almost certainly come upon him an enthusiastic love and reverence for the old paganism, and a corresponding dislike of his modern surroundings. This feeling may last only for a short time, or it may change his whole life. One fact to observe is this, that it is just about the time when a young man's passions are strongest that the story of Greek life is suddenly expounded to him in the course of his studies; and you must remember that the æsthetic faculty is primarily based upon the sensuous life. Now in

Swinburne's case we have an abnormal æsthetic and scholarly faculty brought into contact with these influences at a
very early age; and the result must have been to that young
mind like the shock of an earth-quake. We must also
imagine the natural consequence of this enthusiasm in a
violent reaction against all literary, religious, or social conventions that endeavour to keep the spirit of the old paganism hidden and suppressed within narrow limits, as a
dangerous thing. Finally we must suppose the natural effect of opposition upon this mind, the effect of threats,
sneers, or prohibitions, like oil upon fire. For young Swinburne was, and still is, a man of exceeding courage, incapable of fear of any sort. A great idea suddenly came to
him, and he resolved to put it into execution. This idea
was nothing less than to attempt to obtain for English
poetry the same liberty enjoyed by French poetry in recent
times, to attempt to obtain the right of absolute liberty of
expression in all directions, and to provoke the contest with
such a bold stroke as never had been dared before. The
result was the book that has been so much condemned.

We cannot say that Swinburne was successful in this attempt at reform. He attempted a little too much, and attempted it too soon. Even in his own time the great French
poet Charles Baudelaire was publicly condemned in a French
court for having written verse less daring than Swinburne's.
The great French novelist Flaubert also had to answer in
court for the production of a novel that is now thought to
be very innocent. It was only at a considerably later time
that the French poets obtained such liberty of expression
as allowed of the excesses of writers like Zola or of poets
like Richepin. Altogether Swinburne's fight was prema-
ture. He must now see that it was. But I should not like
to say that he was entirely wrong. The result of absolute
liberty in French literature gives us a good idea of what
would be the result of absolute liberty in English literature.
Extravagances of immorality were followed by extrava-

gances of vulgarity as well, and after the novelty of the thing was over a reaction set in, provoked by disgust and national shame. Exactly the same thing would happen in England after a brief period of vicious carnival; the English tide of opinion would set in the contrary direction with immense force, and would bring about such a tyrannical conservatism in letters as would signify, for the time being, a serious check upon progress. As a matter of fact, we cannot do in English literature what can be done in French literature. Swinburne might, but there is only one Swinburne. The English language is not perfect enough, not graceful and flexible enough, to admit of elegant immorality; and the English character is not refined enough. A Frenchman can say very daring things, very immoral things, gracefully; an Englishman cannot. Only one Englishman has approached the possibility; and that Englishman is Swinburne himself.

I think you will now understand what Swinburne's purpose was, and be able to judge of it. His mistakes were due not only to his youth but also to his astonishing genius; for he could not then know how much superior in ability he actually was to any other English poet. He imagined that there were many who might do what he could do. The truth is that hundreds of years may pass before another Englishman is born capable of doing what Swinburne could do. Men of letters have long ago forgiven him, because of this astonishing power. They say, "We know the poems are improper, but we have nothing else like them, and English literature cannot afford to lose them." The scholars have forgiven him, because his worst faults are always scholarly; and a common person cannot understand his worst allusions. Indeed, one must be much of a classical scholar to comprehend what is most condemnable in the first series of the "Poems and Ballads." Their extreme laxity will not be perceived without elaborate explanation, and no one can venture to explain—I do not mean in a university class

room only, I mean even in printed criticism. When this
was attempted by the poet's enemies, he was able to point
out, with great effect, that the explanations were much more
immoral than the poems.

Now in considering Swinburne's poetry in a short course
of lectures, I think it will be well to begin by explaining his
philosophical position; for every poet has a philosophy of
his own. As I have already said, there is less of this visible
in Swinburne than in the other Victorian poets, but the little
there is has a particular and beautiful interest, which we
shall be able to illustrate in a series of quotations. I am
presuming a little in speaking about his philosophy because
there has been nothing of importance written about his philosophy, nor has he himself ever made a plain statement of it. In such a case I can only surmise, and you
need not consider my opinion as definitive. Swinburne is,
like George Meredith, an evolutionist, and he has something of the spiritual element in him which we notice in
Meredith as a philosopher—but always with this difference,
that Meredith makes evolution preach a moral law, and
Swinburne does not. But here we notice that Swinburne's
evolution is something totally different from Meredith's
in its origin. I have said to you that Meredith expresses
evolutional philosophy according to Herbert Spencer; I
consider him the greatest of our philosophical poets for
that very reason. Swinburne does not appear to have felt
the influence of Herbert Spencer; he seems rather to reflect the opinions of Comte—especially of Comte as inter-
preted by Lewes, and perhaps by Frederic Harrison. He
speaks of the Religion of Humanity, of the Divinity of
Man, and of other things which indicate the influence of
Comte. Furthermore, I must say, being myself a disciple
of Spencer, that Swinburne's sociological and radical opinions are quite incompatible with evolutional philosophy as
expounded by Spencer. Indeed, Swinburne's views about
government, about fraternity and equality, about liberty

in all matters of thought and action, are heresies for the strictly scientific mind. The great thinkers of our century have exposed and overthrown the old fallacies of the French revolutionary school as to the equality of men and the meaning of liberty and fraternity. Swinburne still champions, or appears to champion, some of the erroneous ideas of Rousseau. Otherwise there is little fault to be found with his thoughts concerning the ultimate nature of things, except in the deep melancholy that always accompanies them. Meredith is a grand optimist. Swinburne is something very like a pessimist. There is no joy and no hope in his tone of speaking about the mystery of death; rather we find ourselves listening to the tone of the ancient Roman Epicureans, in the time when faith was dying, and when philosophy attempted, without success, to establish a religion of duty founded upon pure ethics.

An important test of any writer's metaphysical position is what he believes about the soul. Swinburne's idea is very well expressed in the prelude to his "Songs before Sunrise." A single stanza would be enough in this case; but we shall give two, in order to show the pantheistic side of the poet's faith.

> Because man's soul is man's God still,
> What wind soever waft his will
>   Across the waves of day and night
>   To port or shipwreck, left or right,
> By shores and shoals of good and ill;
>   And still its flame at mainmast height
> Through the rent air that foam-flakes fill
>   Sustains the indomitable light
> Whence only man hath strength to steer
> Or helm to handle without fear.
>
> Save his own soul's light overhead,
> None leads him, and none ever led,
>   Across birth's hidden harbour-bar,
>   Past youth where shoreward shallows are,

Through age that drives on toward the red
Vast void of sunset hailed from far,
To the equal waters of the dead;
  Save his own soul he hath no star,
And sinks, except his own soul guide,
Helmless in middle turn of tide.

This is a very plain statement not only that man has no
god, and that he makes his own gods, but that he never had
a creator or a god of any kind. He has no divine help,
no one to pray to, no one to trust except himself. So far
this is in tolerable accord with the teaching of the Buddha,
"Be ye lights unto yourselves; seek no refuge but in yourselves." But the question comes, What is man's soul? Is
it divine? Is it part of the universal soul, a supreme and
infinite intelligence? There is another meaning in the first
line of the first stanza which I quoted to you about man's
soul being man's god. Some verses from the wonderful
poem called "On the Downs" will make the meaning
plainer.

"No light to lighten and no rod
To chasten men? Is there no God?"
  So girt with anguish, iron-zoned,
Went my soul weeping as she trod
  Between the men enthroned
  And men that groaned.

O fool, that for brute cries of wrong
Heard not the grey glad mother's song
  Ring response from the hills and waves,
But heard harsh noises all day long,
  Of spirits that were slaves
  And dwelt in graves.

        .   .   .   .   .   .

With all her tongues of life and death,
With all her bloom and blood and breath,
  From all years dead and all things done,
In the ear of man the mother saith,
  "There is no God, O son,
  If thou be none."

This is the declaration of a belief in the divinity of man, a doctrine well known to students of Comte. It is not altogether in disaccord with Oriental philosophy; you must not suppose Swinburne to be speaking of individual divinity, but of a universal divinity expressing itself in human thought and feeling. His view of life is that the essential thing is to live as excellently as possible, but we must not suppose that excellence is used in the moral sense. Swinburne's idea of excellence is the idea of completeness. His notions of right and wrong are not the religious or the social notions of right and wrong. In this respect he sometimes seems to think very much like the German philosopher Nietzsche. Nevertheless he does tell us that the real spirit of the universe is a spirit of love, a doctrine at which Huxley would certainly have laughed. But it is beautiful doctrine in its way, even if not true, and admirably suits the purposes of poetry.

I think that I need not say much more here about Swinburne's philosophy; you will understand that he is at once a pantheist and an evolutionist, and that is sufficient for our purposes. But it is necessary to remember this in order to understand many things in his verse, and especially in order to understand some of his extraordinary attitudes in condemning what most men respect, and in praising what most men condemn. Remember also that his judgments, like those of Nature, are never moral; they are not always the reverse, but they are founded entirely upon æsthetic perception. Those who praise him especially are men in revolt like himself. Therefore he praised Walt Whitman, at a time when Walt Whitman was being condemned everywhere for certain faults in his compositions; therefore he sang the praises of Baudelaire, as none other had done before him (and here he is certainly right); therefore he praised Théophile Gautier's "Mademoiselle de Maupin," calling it "the golden book of spirit and sense"; therefore also he wrote a sonnet praising Burton's translation of the

Arabian Nights, which made a great scandal in England because it translated all the obscene passages which nobody else had ventured to put into English or French. The æsthetic judgment in all these cases is correct, but I will not venture to pronounce upon the moral judgment any further than to say this, that Swinburne delights in courage, and that literary courage in his eyes covers a multitude of sins.

Not a few, however, of these daring songs of praise are among the most wonderful triumphs of modern lyric verse. I should like, for example, to quote to you the whole of his ode to Villon, but I fear that because of its length, and the unfamiliarity of the subject, we cannot afford the time. I will quote the closing stanza as a specimen of the rest, and I am sure that you will see its beauty.

> Prince of sweet songs made out of tears and fire,
> A harlot was thy nurse, a God thy sire;
>   Shame soiled thy song, and song assoiled thy shame.
> But from thy feet now death has washed the mire,
> Love reads out first at head of all our quire,
>   Villon, our sad bad glad mad brother's name.

Each stanza ends with this strange refrain of "sad bad glad mad," adjectives, which excellently express the changeful and extraordinary character of that poor student of Paris with whose name modern French literature properly begins. He lived a terrible and reckless life, very nearly ending with the gallows; he was an associate at one time of princes and bishops, at another time of thieves and prostitutes; he would be one day a spendthrift, the next day a beggar or a prisoner; and he sang of all these experiences as no man ever sang before or since. Really Swinburne's praise in this case is not only just—it represents the best possible estimate of the singer's faults and virtues combined.

To speak in detail of the great range of subjects chosen by Swinburne is not possible within the limits of this lecture.   I am going to make selections from every part of his production, except the dramatic, as well as I can, and the selections will be made with a view especially to show you the music of his verse and the brilliance of his language. Most of his poems are above the ordinary lyrical length rather than below it, and I hope that you will not be disappointed if I do not often give the whole of a poem, for the selections will contain, I am sure, the best part of the poem.

Being a descendant of great seamen, Swinburne had every reason to sing of the sea; and he has sung of it better than any one else.   A great number of his poems are sea-poems, or poems containing descriptions of the sea in all its moods, splendours, or terrors.   Sun, sea, and wind are favourite subjects with him, and I know of nothing in the whole of his work finer than his description of the wind as the lover of the sea.   The verses I am going to quote are from a great composition entitled "By the North Sea."   The personal pronoun "he" in the first line means the wind. personified.

> The delight that he takes but in living
>   Is more than of all things that live:
> For the world that has all things for giving
>   Has nothing so goodly to give:
> But more than delight his desire is,
>   For the goal where his pinions would be
> Is immortal as air or as fire is,
>   Immense as the sea.
>
> Though hence come the moan that he borrows
>   From darkness and depth of the night,
> Though hence be the spring of his sorrows,
>   Hence too is the joy of his might;
> The delight that his doom is forever
>   To seek, and desire, and rejoice,
> And the sense that eternity never
>   Shall silence his voice.

That satiety never may stifle
  Nor weariness ever estrange
Nor time be so strong as to rifle
  Nor change be so great as to change
His gift that renews in the giving,
  The joy that exalts him to be
Alone of all elements living
  The lord of the sea.

What is fire, that its flame should consume her?
  More fierce than all fires are her waves:
What is earth, that its gulfs should entomb her?
  More deep are her own than their graves.
Life shrinks from his pinions that cover
  The darkness by thunders bedinned;
But she knows him, her lord and her lover,
  The godhead of wind.

This titanic personification of sea and wind is sublime, but Swinburne has many other ways of personifying wind and sea, and sometimes the element of tenderness and love is not wanting. Sometimes the sea is addressed as a goddess, but more often she is addressed as a mother, and some of the most exquisite forms of such address are found in poems which have, properly speaking, nothing to do with the sea at all. A good example is in the poem called "The Triumph of Time." The words are supposed to be spoken by a person who is going to drown himself.

O fair green-girdled mother of mine,
  Sea, that art clothed with the sun and the rain,
Thy sweet hard kisses are strong like wine,
  Thy large embraces are keen like pain.
Save me and hide me with all thy waves,
Find me one grave of thy thousand graves,
Those pure cold populous graves of thine,
  Wrought without hand in a world without stain.

We shall also find great wonder and beauty in Swinburne's hymns to the sun, which is also for him, as for the poets of old, a living god, and which certainly is, in a scientific sense, the lord of all life within this world. The best expression of this feeling is in a poem called "Off Shore," describing sunrise over the sea, and the glory of light.

> Light, perfect and visible
>   Godhead of God!
> God indivisible,
>   Lifts but his rod,
> And the shadows are scattered in sunder, and darkness
>   is light at his nod.

> At the touch of his wand,
>   At the nod of his head
> From the spaces beyond
>   Where the dawn hath her bed,
> Earth, water, and air are transfigured, and rise as one
>   risen from the dead.

> He puts forth his hand,
>   And the mountains are thrilled
> To the heart as they stand
>   In his presence, fulfilled
> With his glory that utters his grace upon earth, and
>   her sorrows are stilled.

> . . . .

> As a kiss on my brow
>   Be the light of thy grace,
> Be thy glance on me now
>   From the pride of thy place:
> As the sign of a sire to a son be the light on my face
>   of thy face.

> . . . .

> Fair father of all
>   In thy ways that have trod,
> That have risen at thy call,
>   That have thrilled at thy nod,
> Arise, shine, lighten upon me, O Sun that we see to
>   be God.

> . . . .

> Be praised and adored of us
>   All in accord,

Father and lord of us
Always adored,
The slayer, and the stayer, and the harper, the light
of us all and our lord.

Swinburne has no equal in enthusiastic celebration of the
beauties of sky and sea and wood, of light and clouds and
waters, of sound and perfume and blossoming. Indeed,
one of his particular characteristics, a characteristic very
seldom found in English masterpieces, though common in
the best French work, is his art for describing odours—
the smell of morning and evening, scents of the seasons,
scents also of life.   We shall have many opportunities to
notice this characteristic of Swinburne, even in his descriptions of human beauty.   What the French call the *parfum
de jeunesse* or odour of youth, the pleasant smell of young
bodies, the perfume that we notice, for example, in the hair
of a healthy child, is something which English writers very
seldom venture to treat of; but Swinburne has treated it
quite as delicately at times as a French poet could do,
though sometimes a little extravagantly.   You must think
of him as one whom no quality of beauty escapes, whether
of colour, odour, or motion; and as one who believes, I think
rightly, that whatever is in itself beautiful and natural is
worthy of song.   You will be able to imagine, from what
I have already quoted, how he feels in the presence of wild
nature.   How he considers human beauty is a more difficult matter to illustrate by quotation, at least by quotation
before a class.   But I shall try to offer some illustrations
from the "Masque of Queen Bersabe."   You all know what
a masque is.   The masque in question is a perfect imitation,
for the most part, of a mediæval masque, both as to form
and language.   But there is one portion of it which is
mediæval only in tone, not in language, since there never
lived in the Middle Ages any man capable of writing such
verse.   It is from this part that I want to quote.   But
I must first explain to you that the name Bersabe is only

a mediæval form of the Biblical name Bathsheba, the wife of Uriah, whom King David caused to be murdered. It is an ugly story.   The King committed adultery with Bathsheba; then he ordered her husband to be put into the front rank during a battle, in such a place that he must be killed.   Afterwards the King married Bathsheba; but the prophet Nathan heard of the wickedness, and threatened the King with the punishment of God.   This was the subject of several mediæval religious plays, and Swinburne adopted it for an imitation of such play.   The first part of his conception is that at the command of the prophet the ghosts of all the beautiful and wicked queens who ever lived come before Bathsheba, to reproach her with her sin, and to tell her how they had been punished in other time for sins of the same kind.   Each one speaks in turn; and though I cannot quote all of what they said, I can quote enough to illustrate the magnificence of the work. Each verse is a portrait in words, uttered by the subject.

CLEOPATRA

I am the queen of Ethiope.
Love bade my kissing eyelids ope
    That men beholding might praise love.
My hair was wonderful and curled;
My lips held fast the mouth of the world
    To spoil the strength and speech thereof.
The latter triumph in my breath
Bowed down the beaten brows of death,
    Ashamed they had not wrath enough.

.   .   .   .   .   .

AHOLAH

I am the queen of Amalek.
There was no tender touch or fleck
    To spoil my body or bared feet.
My words were soft like dulcimers,
And the first sweet of grape-flowers
    Made each side of my bosom sweet.
My raiment was as tender fruit

Whose rind smells sweet of spice-tree root,
Bruised balm-blossom and budded wheat.

· · · · · ·

SEMIRAMIS

I am the queen Semiramis.
The whole world and the sea that is
In fashion like a chrysopras,
The noise, of all men labouring,
The priest's mouth tired through thanksgiving,
The sound of love in the blood's pause,
The strength of love in the blood's beat,
All these were cast beneath my feet
And all found lesser than I was.

· · · · · ·

PASITHEA

I am the queen of Cypriotes.
Mine oarsmen, labouring with brown throats,
Sang of me many a tender thing.
My maidens, girdled loose and braced
With gold from bosom to white waist,
Praised me between their wool-combing.
All that praise Venus all night long
With lips like speech and lids like song
Praised me till song lost heart to sing.

ALACIEL

I am the queen Alaciel.
My mouth was like that moist gold cell
Whereout the thickest honey drips.
Mine eyes were as a grey-green sea;
The amorous blood that smote on me
Smote to my feet and finger-tips.
My throat was whiter than the dove,
Mine eyelids as the seals of love,
And as the doors of love my lips.

ERIGONE

I am the queen Erigone.
The wild wine shed as blood on me
Made my face brighter than a bride's.
My large lips had the old thirst of earth,

Mine arms the might of the old sea's girth
    Bound round the whole world's iron sides.
Within mine eyes and in mine ears
Were music and the wine of tears,
    And light, and thunder of the tides.

So pass the strange phantoms of dead pride and lust and power, together with many more of whom the descriptions are not less beautiful and strange, though much less suitable for quotation. I have made the citations somewhat long, but I have done so because they offer the best possible illustration of two things peculiar to Swinburne, the music and colour of his verse, and the peculiar mediæval tone which he sometimes assumes in dealing with antique subjects. These descriptions are quite unlike anything done by Tennyson, or indeed by any other poet except Rossetti. They represent, in a certain way, what has been called Pre-Raphaelitism in poetry. Swinburne was, with Rossetti, one of the great forces of the new movement in literature. Observe that the illustrations are chiefly made by comparisons—that the descriptions are made by suggestion; there is no attempt to draw a clear sharp line, nothing is described completely, but by some comparison or symbolism in praise of a part, the whole figure is vaguely brought before the imagination in a blaze of colour with strange accompaniment of melody. For example, you will have noticed that no face is fully pictured; you find only some praise of the eyes or the mouth, the throat or the skin, but that is quite enough to bring to your fancy the entire person. But there is another queer fact which you must be careful to notice—namely, that no comparison is modern. The language and the symbolism are Biblical or mediæval in every case. The European scholar who had made a special study of the literature of the Middle Ages would notice even more than this; he would notice that the whole tone is not of the later but of the earlier Middle Ages, that the old miracle plays, the old French romances, and the early Italian poets, have all contributed something to this splendour of expression. It is modern art in one sense, of course, but there is nothing modern about it except the craftsmanship; the material is all quaint and strange, and gives us the sensation of old tapestry or of the paintings that were painted in Italy before the time of Raphael.

Here I must say a word about the Pre-Raphaelite movement in nineteenth century literature. To explain everything satisfactorily, I ought to have pictures to show you; and that is unfortunately impossible. But I think I can make a very easy explanation of the subject. First of all you must be quite well aware that the literature of all countries seeks for a majority of its subjects in the past. The everyday, the familiar, does not attract us in the same way as that which is not familiar and not of the present. Distance, whether of space or time, lends to things a certain tone of beauty, just as mountains look more beautifully blue the further away they happen to be. This seeking for beauty in the past rather than in the present represents much of what is called romanticism in any literature.

Necessarily, even in this age of precise historical knowledge, the past is for us less real than the present; time has spread mists of many colours between it and us, so that we cannot be sure of details, distances, depths, and heights. But in other generations the mists were heavier, and the past was more of a fairy-land than now; it was more pleasant also to think about, because the mysterious is attractive to all of us, and men of letters delighted to write about it, because they could give free play to the imagination. Such stories of the past as we find even in what have been called historical novels, were called also, and rightly called, romances—works of imagination rather than of fact.

But still you may ask, why such words as romance and romantic? The answer is that works of imagination, dealing with past events, were first written in languages derived from the Latin, the romance languages; and at a very

early time it became the custom to distinguish work written in these modern tongues upon fanciful or heroic subjects, by this name and quality.   The romantic in the Middle Ages signified especially the new literature of fancy as
opposed to the old classical literature.   Remember, therefore, that this meaning is not yet entirely lost, though it has
undergone many modifications.   "Romantic" in literature
still means "not classical," and it also suggests imagination
rather than fact, and the past rather than the present.

When we say "mediæval" in speaking of nineteenth century poetry, we mean of course nineteenth century literature having a romantic tone, as well as reflecting, so far
as imagination can, the spirit of the Middle Ages.   But
what is the difference between the Pre-Raphaelite and
Mediæval?   The time before Raphael, the Pre-Raphaelite
period, would necessarily have been mediæval.   As a matter of fact, the term Pre-Raphaelite does not have the wide
general meaning usually given to it.   It is something of a
technical term, belonging to art rather than to literature,
and first introduced into literature by a company of painters.
The Pre-Raphaelite painters, in the technical sense, were a
special group of modern painters, distinguished by particular characteristics.

So much being clear, I may say that there was a school
of painting before Raphael of a very realistic and remarkable kind.   This school came to existence a little after the
true religious spirit of the Middle Ages had begun to weaken.
It sought the emotion of beauty as well as the emotion of
religion, but it did not yet feel the influence of the Renaissance in a strong way; it was not Greek nor pagan.   It
sought beauty in truth, studying ordinary men and women,
flowers and birds, scenery of nature or scenery of streets;
and it used reality for its model.   It was much less romantic
than the school that came after it; but it was very great
and very noble.   With Raphael the Greek feeling, the old
pagan feeling for sensuous beauty, found full expression,

and this Renaissance tone changed the whole direction and character of art. After Raphael the painters sought beauty before all things; previously they had sought for truth and sentiment even before beauty. Raphael set a fashion which influenced all arts after him down to our own time; for centuries the older painters were neglected and almost forgotten. Therefore Ruskin boldly declared that since Raphael's death Western art had been upon the decline and that the school of painters immediately before Raphael were greater than any who came after him. Gradually within our own time a new taste came into art-circles, a new love for the old forgotten masters of the fourteenth and fifteenth centuries. It was discovered that they were, after all, nearer to truth in many respects than the later painters; and then was established, by Rossetti and others, a new school of painting called the Pre-Raphaelite school. It sought truth to life as well as beauty, and it endeavoured to mingle both with mystical emotion.

At first this was a new movement in art only, or rather in painting and drawing only, as distinguished from literary art. But literature and painting and architecture and music are really all very closely related, and a new literary movement also took place in harmony with the new departure in painting. This was chiefly the work of Rossetti, Swinburne, and William Morris. They tried to make poems and to write stories according to the same æsthetic motives which seem to have inspired the school of painters before Raphael. This is the signification of the strange method and beauty of those quotations which I have been giving to you from Swinburne's masque. They represent very powerfully the Pre-Raphaelite feelings in English poetry. I know that this digression is somewhat long, but I believe that it is of great importance; without knowing these facts, it would be impossible for the student to understand many curious things in Swinburne's manner. Throughout even his lighter poems we find this curious habit of describing things in ways totally remote from nineteenth century feeling, and nevertheless astonishingly effective. Fancy such comparisons as these for a woman's beauty in the correct age of Wordsworth:

> I said "she must be swift and white,
> And subtly warm, and half perverse,
> And sweet like sharp soft fruit to bite,
> And like a snake's love lithe and fierce."
> Men have guessed worse.

Or take the following extraordinary description of a woman's name, perhaps I had better say of the sensation given by the name Félise, probably an abbreviation of Felicita, but by its spelling reminding one very much of the Latin word *felis*, which means a cat:

> Like colours in the sea, like flowers,
> Like a cat's splendid circled eyes
> That wax and wane with love for hours,
> Green as green flame, blue-grey like skies,
> And soft like sighs.

The third line refers to the curious phenomenon of the enlarging and diminishing of the pupil in a cat's eye according to the decrease or increase of light. It is said that you can tell the time of day by looking at a cat's eyes. Now all these comparisons are in the highest degree offences against classical feeling. The classical poet, even the half-classical poet of the beginning of our own century, would have told you that a woman must not be compared to a snake or a cat; that you must not talk about her sweetness being like the sweetness of fruit, or the charm of her presence being like the smell of perfume. All such comparisons seemed monstrous, unnatural. If such a critic were asked why one must not compare a woman to a snake or a cat, the critic would probably answer, "Because a snake is a hateful reptile and a cat is a hateful animal." What would Ruskin or Swinburne then say to the critic? He would say simply, "Did you ever look at a snake? Did you ever study a cat?" The classicist would soon be convicted of utter ignorance about snakes and cats. He thought them hateful simply because it was not fashionable to admire them a hundred years ago. But the old poets of the early Middle Ages were not such fools. They had seen snakes and admired them, because for any man who is not prejudiced, a snake is a very beautiful creature, and its motions are as beautiful as geometry. If you do not think this is true, I beg of you to watch a snake, where its body can catch the light of the sun. Then there is no more graceful or friendly or more attractively intelligent animal than a cat. The common feeling about snakes and cats is not an artistic one, nor even a true one; it is of ethical origin, and unjust. These animals are not moral according to our notions; they seem cruel and treacherous, and forgetting that they cannot be judged by our code of morals, we have learned to speak of them contemptuously even from the physical point of view. Well, this was not the way in the early Middle Ages. People were less sensitive on the subject of cruelty than they are to-day, and they could praise the beauty of snakes and tigers and all fierce or cunning creatures of prey, because they could admire the physical qualities without thinking of the moral ones. In Pre-Raphaelite poetry there is an attempt to do the very same thing. Swinburne does it more than any one else, perhaps even too much; but there is a great and true principle of art behind this revolution.

Now we can study Swinburne in some other moods. I want to show you the splendour of his long verse, verse of fourteen and sixteen syllables, of a form resurrected by him after centuries of neglect; and also verse written in imitation of Greek and Roman measures with more success than has attended similar efforts on the part of any other living poet. But in the first example that I shall offer, you will find matter of more interest than verse as verse. The poem is one

of Swinburne's greatest, and the subject is entirely novel.
The poet attempts to express the feeling of a Roman pagan,
perhaps one of the last Epicurean philosophers, living at the
time when Christianity was first declared the religion of the
Empire, and despairing because of the destruction of the
older religion and the vanishing of the gods whom he loved.
By law Christianity has been made the state-religion, and
it is forbidden to worship the other gods; the old man
haughtily refuses to become a Christian, even after an im-
partial study of Christian doctrine; on the contrary, he is
so unhappy at the fate of the religion of his fathers that he
does not care to live any longer without his gods.   And he
prays to the goddess of death to take him out of this world,
from which all the beauty and art, all the old loved customs and beliefs are departing.   We cannot read the whole
"Hymn to Proserpine"; but we shall read enough to illustrate the style and feeling of the whole.   At the head of the
poem are the words *Vicisti, Galilæe!*—"Thou hast conquered, O Galilean"—words uttered by the great Roman
Emperor Julian at the moment of his death in battle.
Julian was the last Emperor who tried to revive and purify
the decaying Roman religion, and to oppose the growth of
Christianity.   He was, therefore, the great enemy of Christianity.   His dying words were said to have been addressed
to Christ, when he felt himself dying, but it is not certain
whether he really ever uttered these words at all.

I have lived long enough, having seen one thing, that love hath
    an end;
Goddess and maiden and queen, be near me now, and befriend.
Thou art more than the day or the morrow, the seasons that laugh
    or that weep;
For these give joy and sorrow; but thou, Proserpina, sleep.
Sweet is the treading of wine, and sweet the feet of the dove:
But a goodlier gift is thine than foam of the grapes or love.

After speaking to the goddess of death, he speaks thus to
Christ:

Wilt thou yet take all, Galilean? but these thou shalt not take,
The laurel, the palms and the pæan, the breasts of the nymphs in
    the brake;
Breasts more soft than a dove's, that tremble with tenderer breath;
And all the wings of the Loves, and all the joy before death;
All the feet of the hours that sound as a single lyre,
Dropped and deep in the flowers, with strings that flicker like fire.
More than these wilt thou give, things fairer than all these things?
Nay, for a little we live, and life hath mutable wings.
A little while and we die; shall life not thrive as it may?
For no man under the sky lives twice, outliving his day.
And grief is a grievous thing, and a man hath enough of his tears:
Why should he labour, and bring fresh grief to blacken his years?
Thou hast conquered, O pale Galilean; the world has grown grey
    from thy breath;
We have drunken of things Lethean, and fed on the fulness of death.

Or, in other words, the pagan says: "O Christ, you
would wish to take everything from us, yet some things
there are which you cannot take: not the inspiration of the
poet, nor the spirit of art, nor the glory of heroism, nor the
dreams of youth and love, nor the great and gracious gifts
of time—the beauty of the seasons, the splendour of night
and day. All these you cannot deprive us of, though you
wish to; and what is better than these? Can you give us
anything more precious? Assuredly you cannot. For these
things are fitted to human life; and what do we know about
any other life? Life passes quickly; why should we make
it miserable with the evil dreams of a religion of sorrow?
Short enough is the time in which we have pleasure, and the
world is already full enough of pain; wherefore should we
try to make ourselves still more unhappy than we already
are? Yet you have conquered; you have destroyed the
beauty of life; you have made the world seem grey and old,
that was so beautiful and eternally young. You have made
us drink the waters of forgetfulness and eat the food of
death. For your religion is a religion of death, not of life;
you yourself and the Christian gods are figures of death,
not figures of life."

And how does he think of this new divinity, Christ? As a Roman citizen necessarily, and to a Roman citizen Christ was nothing more than a vulgar, common criminal executed by Roman law in company with thieves and murderers. Therefore he addresses such a divinity with scorn, even in the hour of his triumph:

O lips that the live blood faints in, the leavings of racks and rods!
O ghastly glories of saints, dead limbs of gibbeted Gods!
Though all men abase them before you in spirit, and all knees bend,
I kneel not, neither adore you, but standing, look to the end!

To understand the terrible bitterness of this scorn, it is necessary for the student to remember that a Roman citizen could not be tortured or flogged or gibbeted. Such punishments and penalties were reserved for slaves and for barbarians. Therefore to a Roman the mere fact of Christ's death and punishment—for he was tortured before being crucified—was a subject for contempt; accordingly he speaks of such a divinity as the "leavings of racks and rods"—that is, so much of a man's body as might be left after the torturers and executioners had finished with it. Should a Roman citizen kneel down and humble himself before that? A little while, some thousands of years, perhaps, Christianity may be a triumphant religion, but all religions must die and pass away, one after another, and this new and detestable religion, with its ugly gods, must also pass away. For although the old Roman has studied too much philosophy to believe in all that his fathers believed, he believes in a power that is greater than man and gods and the universe itself, in the unknown power which gives life and death, and makes perpetual change, and sweeps away everything that man foolishly believes to be permanent. He gives to this law of impermanency the name of the goddess of death, but the name makes little difference; he has recognised the eternal law. Time will sweep away Christianity itself, and his description of this mighty wave of time is one of the finest passages in all his poetry:

All delicate days and pleasant, all spirits and sorrows are cast
Far out with the foam of the present that sweeps to the surf of
the past:

.   .   .   .

Where, mighty with deepening sides, clad about with the seas as
with wings,
And impelled of invisible tides, and fulfilled of unspeakable things,
White-eyed and poisonous-finned, shark-toothed and serpentine-
curled,
Rolls, under the whitening wind of the future, the wave of the world.
The depths stand naked in sunder behind it, the storms flee away;
In the hollow before it the thunder is taken and snared as a prey;
In its sides is the north-wind bound; and its salt is of all men's tears;
With light of ruins and sound of changes, and pulse of years:
With travail of day after day, and with trouble of hour upon hour;
And bitter as blood is the spray; and the crests are as fangs that
devour:
And its vapour and storm of its steam as the sighing of spirits to be;
And its noise as the noise in a dream; and its depth as the roots of
the sea:
And the height of its heads as the height of the utmost stars of the
air:
And the ends of the earth at the might thereof tremble, and time
is made bare.

When the poet calls this the wave of the world, you must not understand world to mean our planet only, but the universe, the cosmos; and the wave is the great wave of impermanency, including all forces of time and death and life and pain.   But why these terrible similes of white eyes and poisonous things and shark's teeth, of blood and bitterness and terror?   Because the old philosopher dimly recognises the cruelty of nature, the mercilessness of that awful law of change which, having swept away his old gods, will just as certainly sweep away the new gods that have appeared.   Who can resist that mighty power, higher than

the stars, deeper than the depths, in whose motion even
gods are but as bubbles and foam?   Assuredly not Christ
and his new religion.   Speaking to the new gods the Roman
cries:

All ye as a wind shall go by, as a fire shall ye pass and be past;
Ye are Gods, and behold, ye shall die, and the waves be upon you
    at last,
.   .   .   .
Thy kingdom shall pass, Galilean, thy dead shall go down to thee
    dead.

Here follows a beautiful picture of the contrast between the
beauty of the old gods and the uninviting aspect of the
new.   It is a comparison between the Virgin Mary, mother
of Christ, and Venus or Aphrodite, the ancient goddess of
love, born from the sea.   For to the Roman mind the Christian gods and saints wanted even the common charm of
beauty and tenderness.   All the divinities of the old Greek
world were beautiful to look upon, and warmly human;
but these strange new gods from Asia seemed to be not even
artistically endurable.   Addressing Christ, he continues:

Of the maiden thy mother men sing as a goddess with grace clad
    around;
Thou art throned where another was king; where another was queen
    she is crowned.
Yea, once we had sight of another: but now she is queen, say these.
Not as thine, not as thine was our mother, a blossom of flowering seas,
Clothed around with the world's desire as with raiment and fair as
    the foam,.
And fleeter than kindled fire, and a goddess and mother of Rome.
For thine came pale and a maiden, and sister to sorrow; but ours,
Her deep hair heavily laden with odour and colour of flowers,
White rose of the rose-white water, a silver splendour, a flame,
Bent down unto us that besought her, and earth grew sweet with
    her name.
For thine came weeping, a slave among slaves, and rejected; but she
Came flushed from the full-flushed wave, and imperial, her foot on
    the sea.
And the wonderful waters knew her, the winds and the viewless ways,

And the roses grew rosier, and bluer the sea-blue stream of the bays.
Ye are fallen, our lords, by what token? we wist that ye should
   not fall.
Ye were all so fair that are broken; and one more fair than ye all.

Why, by what power, for what reason, should the old gods
have passed away?   Even if one could not believe in them
all, they were too beautiful to pass away and be broken,
as their statues were broken by the early Christians in the
rage of their ignorant and brutal zeal.   The triumph of
Christianity meant much more than the introduction of a
new religion; it meant the destruction of priceless art and
priceless literature, it signified the victory of barbarism over
culture and refinement.   Doubtless the change, like all
great changes, was for the better in some ways; but no lover
of art and the refinements of civilisation can read without
regret the history of the iconoclasm in which the Christian
fanatics indulged when they got the government and the
law upon their side.   It is this feeling of regret and horror
that the poet well expresses through the mouth of the
Roman who cares no more to live, because the gods and
everything beautiful must pass away.   But there is one
goddess still left for him, one whom the Christians cannot
break but who will at last break them and their religion,
and scatter them as dust—the goddess of death.   To her
he turns with a last prayer:

I turn to her still, having seen she shall surely abide in the end;
Goddess and maiden and queen, be near me now and befriend.
O daughter of earth, of my mother, her crown and blossom of birth,
I am also, I also, thy brother; I go as I came unto earth.

.   .   .   .

Thou art more than the Gods who number the days of our temporal
   breath;
For these give labour and slumber, but thou, Proserpina, death.
Therefore now at thy feet I abide for a season in silence.   I know
I shall die as my fathers died, and sleep as they sleep; even so.
For the glass of the years is brittle wherein we gaze for a span;
A little soul for a little bears up this corpse which is man.

So long I endure, no longer; and laugh not again, neither weep.
For there is no God found stronger than death; and death is a sleep.

The third line from the end, "a little soul for a little," is a translation from the philosopher Epictetus. It is the Epicurean philosophy especially which speaks in this poetry. The address to the goddess of death as the daughter of earth, cannot be understood without some reference to Greek mythology. Proserpina was the daughter of the goddess Ceres, whom the ancients termed the Holy Mother —queen of the earth, but especially the goddess of fruitfulness and of harvests. While playing in the fields as a young girl, Proserpina was seized and carried away by the god of the dead, Hades or Pluto, to become his wife. Everywhere her mother sought after her to no purpose; and because of the grief of the goddess, the earth dried up, the harvests failed, and all nature became desolate. Afterwards, finding that her daughter had become the queen of the kingdom of the dead, Ceres agreed that Proserpina should spend a part of every year with her husband, and part of the year with her mother. To this arrangement the Greeks partly attributed the origin of the seasons.

Incidentally in the poem there is a very beautiful passage describing the world of death, where no sun is, where the silence is more than music, where the flowers are white and full of strange sleepy smell, and where the sound of the speech of the dead is like the sound of water heard far away, or a humming of bees—whither the old man prays to go, to rest with his ancestors away from the light of the sun, and to forget all the sorrow of this world and its changes. But I think that you will do well to study this poem in detail by yourselves, when opportunity allows. It happens to be one of the very few poems in the first series of Swinburne's "Poems and Ballads" to which no reasonable exception can be made; and it is without doubt one of the very finest things that he has ever written. I could recommend this for translation; there are many pieces in the same book which I could not so recommend, notwith-standing their beauty. For instance, the poem entitled "Hesperia," with its splendid beginning:

Out of the golden remote wild west where the sea without shore is,
Full of the sunset, and sad, if at all, with the fulness of joy.

There is nothing more perfect in modern literature than the beginning of this poem, which gives us an exact imitation in English words of the sound of the Greek hexameter and pentameter. But much of this work is too passionate and violent for even the most indulgent ears; and though I think that you ought to study the beginning, I should never recommend it for translation.

The comparison of the wave in the hymn to Proserpina must have given you an idea of Swinburne's power to deal with colossal images. I know of few descriptions in any literature to be compared with that picture of the wave; but Swinburne himself in another poem has given us descriptions nearly as surprising, if not as beautiful. There is a poem called "Thalassius," a kind of philosophical moral fable in Greek form, that contains a surprise of this kind. The subject is a young man's first experience with love. Walking in the meadows he sees a pretty boy, or rather child, just able to walk—a delicious child, tender as a flower, and apparently needing kindly care. So he takes the child by the hand, wondering at his beauty; and he speaks to the child, but never gets any reply except a smile. Suddenly, at a certain point of the road the child begins to grow tall, to grow tremendous; his stature reaches the sky, and in a terrible voice that shakes everything like an earth-quake, he announces that though he may be Love, he is also Death, and that only the fool imagines him to be Love alone. There is a bit both of old and of new philosophy in this; and I remarked when reading it that in Indian my-thology there is a similar representation of this double at-tribute of divinity, love and death, creation and destruc-

tion, represented by one personage.   But we had better read
the scene which I have been trying to describe, the meeting
with the child:

> That well-nigh wept for wonder that it smiled,
> And was so feeble and fearful, with soft speech
> The youth bespake him softly; but there fell
> From the sweet lips no sweet word audible
> That ear or thought might reach;
> No sound to make the dim cold silence glad,
> No breath to thaw the hard harsh air with heat,
> Only the saddest smile of all things sweet,
> Only the sweetest smile of all things sad.
>
> And so they went together one green way
> Till April dying made free the world for May;
> And on his guide suddenly Love's face turned,
> And in his blind eyes burned
> Hard light and heat of laughter; and like flame
> That opens in a mountain's ravening mouth
> To blear and sear the sunlight from the south.
> His mute mouth opened, and his first word came;
> "Knowest thou me now by name?"
> And all his stature waxed immeasurable,
> As of one shadowing heaven and lightening hell;
> And statelier stood he than a tower that stands
> And darkens with its darkness far-off sands
> Whereon the sky leans red;
> And with a voice that stilled the winds he said:
> "I am he that was thy lord before thy birth,
> I am he that is thy lord till thou turn earth;
> I make the night more dark, and all the morrow
> Dark as the night whose darkness was my breath:
> O fool, my name is sorrow;
> Thou fool, my name is death."

By the term "darkness" in the third line from the end of
the above quotation, we must understand the darkness and
mystery out of which man comes into this world, and comes
only to die.   This monstrous symbolism may need some
explanation, before you see how very fine the meaning is.

Love, that is the attraction of sex to sex, with all its emotions, heroisms, sacrifices, and nobilities, cannot be understood by the young. To them, love is only the physical and the moral charm of the being that is loved. In man the passion of love becomes noble and specialised by the development in him of moral, æsthetic, and other feelings that are purely human. But the attraction of sex, that is behind all this, is a universal and terrible fact, a tremendous mystery, whose ultimate nature no man knows or ever will know. Why? Because if we knew the nature and origin of the forces that create, we could understand the whole universe, and ourselves, and everything that men now call mystery. But all that we certainly do know is this, that we come into the world out of mystery and go out of the world again back into mystery, and that no mortal man can explain the Whence, the Why, or the Whither. The first sensations of love for another being are perhaps the most delicious feelings known to men; the person loved seems for the time to be more beautiful and good than any one else in the world. This is what the poet means by describing the first appearance of love as a beautiful, tender child, innocent and dumb. But later in life the physical illusion passes away; then one learns the relation of this seeming romance to the awful questions of life and death. The girl beloved becomes the wife; then she becomes the mother; but in becoming a mother, she enters into the very shadow of death, sometimes never to return from it. Birth itself is an agony, the greatest agony that humanity has to bear. We come into the world through pains of the most deadly kind, and leave the world later on in pain; and what all this means, we do not know. We are only certain that the Greeks were not wrong in representing love as the brother of death. The Oriental philosophers went further; they identified love with death, making them one and the same. One cannot help thinking of the Indian statue representing the creative power, holding in his hand the symbol of life, but wearing around his neck a necklace of human skulls.

The poem that introduces the first volume of Swinburne's poems, as published in America, gave its name to the book, so that thousands of English readers used to call the volume by the name of this poem, "Laus Veneris," which means the praise of Venus. I do not think that there is a more characteristic poem in all Swinburne's work; it is certainly the most interesting version in any modern language of the old mediæval story. Without understanding the story you could not possibly understand the poem, and as the story has been famous for hundreds of years, I shall first relate it.

After Christianity had made laws forbidding people to worship the old gods, it was believed that these gods still remained wandering about like ghosts and tempting men to sin. One of these divinities especially dreaded by the Christian priests, was Venus. Now in the Middle Ages there was a strange story about a knight called Tannhauser, who, riding home one evening, saw by the wayside a beautiful woman unclad, who smiled at him, and induced him to follow her. He followed her to the foot of a great mountain; the mountain opened like a door, and they went in, and found a splendid palace under the mountain. The fairy woman was Venus herself; and the knight lived with her for seven years. At the end of the seven years he became afraid because of the sin which he had committed; and he begged her, as Urashima begged the daughter of the Dragon King, to let him return for a little time to the world of men. She let him go; and he went to Rome. There he told his story to different priests, and asked them to obtain for him the forgiveness of God. But each of the priests made answer that the sin was so great that nobody except the Pope of Rome could forgive it. Then the knight went to the Pope. But when the Pope heard his confession, the Pope said that there was no forgiveness possible for such a crime as that of loving a demon. The Pope had a wooden

staff in his hand, and he said, "Sooner shall this dry stick
burst into blossom than you obtain God's pardon for such
a sin." Then the knight, sorrowing greatly, went back to
the mountain and to Venus. After he had gone, the Pope
was astonished to see that the dry staff was covered with
beautiful flowers and leaves that had suddenly grown out
of it, as a sign that God was more merciful than his priests.
At this the Pope became sorry and afraid, and he sent out
messengers to look for the knight. But no man ever saw
him again, for Venus kept him hidden in her palace under
the mountain. Swinburne found his version of the story
in a quaint French book published in 1530. He represents, not the incidents of the story itself, but only the feelings of the knight after his return from Rome. There is
no more hope for him. His only consolation is his love
and worship for her; but this love and worship is mingled
with fear of hell and regret for his condition. Into the
poem Swinburne has put the whole spirit of revolt of which
he and the Pre-Raphaelite school were exponents. A few
verses will show you the tone. The knight praises Venus:

> Lo, this is she that was the world's delight;
> The old grey years were parcels of her might;
>   The strewings of the ways wherein she trod
> Were the twain seasons of the day and night.
>
> Lo, she was thus when her clear limbs enticed
> All lips that now grow sad with kissing Christ,
>   Stained with blood fallen from the feet of God,
> The feet and hands whereat our souls were priced.
>
> Alas, Lord, surely thou art great and fair.
> But lo her wonderfully woven hair!
>   And thou didst heal us with thy piteous kiss;
> But see now, Lord; her mouth is lovelier.
>
> She is right fair; what hath she done to thee?
> Nay, fair Lord Christ, lift up thine eyes and see;
>   Had now thy mother such a lip—like this?
> Thou knowest how sweet a thing it is to me.

This calling upon God to admire Venus, this asking Christ whether his mother was even half as beautiful as Venus, was to religious people extremely shocking, of course. And still more shocking seemed the confession in the latter part of the poem that the knight does not care whether he has sinned or not, since, after all, he has been more fortunate than any other man. This expression of exultation after remorse appeared to reverent minds diabolical, the thought of a new Satanic School. But really the poet was doing his work excellently, so far as truth to nature was concerned; and these criticisms were as ignorant as they were out of place. The real fault of the poem was only a fault of youth, a too great sensuousness in its descriptive passages. We might say that Swinburne himself was, during those years, very much in the position of the knight Tannhauser; he had gone back to the worship of the old gods because they were more beautiful and more joyous than the Christian gods; we may even say that he never came back from the mountain of Venus. But all this poetry of the first series was experimental; it was an expression of the Renaissance feeling that visits the youth of every poet possessing a strong sense of beauty. Before the emotions can be fully corrected by the intellect, such poets are apt to offend the proprieties, and even to say things which the most liberal philosopher would have to condemn. It was at such a time that in another poem Swinburne spoke of leaving

> The lilies and languors of virtue
> For the raptures and roses of vice,

—lines that immediately became famous. It was also at such a time that he uttered the prayer to a pagan ideal:

> Come down and redeem us from virtue.

But on the other hand, if all poets were to wait for the age of wisdom before they began to sing, we should miss a thousand beautiful things of which only youth is capable, wherefore it were best to forgive the eccentricities for the sake of the incomparable merits. For example, in the very poem from which these quotations have been made, we have such splendid verses as these, referring to the worship of Venus in the time of Nero:

> Dost thou dream, in a respite of slumber,
>   In a lull of the fires of thy life,
> Of the days without name, without number,
>   When thy will stung the world into strife;
> When, a goddess, the pulse of thy passion
>   Smote kings as they revelled in Rome,
> And they hailed thee re-risen, O Thalassian,
>   Foam-white, from the foam?

Thalassian means the sea-born, derived from the Greek word Thalatta, the sea. Here Swinburne might be referring to the times of the Triumvirate, when Cleopatra succeeded in bewitching the great captain Cæsar and the great captain Antony, and set the world fighting for her sake. Then we have a reference to the great games in Rome, the splendour and the horror of the amphitheatre:

> On sands by the storm never shaken,
>   Nor wet from the washing of tides;
> Nor by foam of the waves overtaken,
>   Nor winds that the thunder bestrides;
> But red from the print of thy paces,
>   Made smooth for the world and its lords,
> Ringed round with a flame of fair faces,
>   And splendid with swords.

The floor of the amphitheatre was covered with sand, which absorbed the blood of the combatants. But you will ask what had the games to do with the goddess? All the Roman festivities of this kind were, to a certain extent, considered as religious celebrations; they formed parts of holiday ceremony.

> There the gladiator pale for thy pleasure,
>   Drew bitter and perilous breath;

> There torments laid hold on the treasure
>   Of limbs too delicious for death;
> When thy gardens were lit with live torches;
>   When the world was a steed for thy rein;
> When the nations lay prone in thy porches,
>   Our Lady of Pain.
>
> When with flame all around him aspirant,
>   Stood flushed, as a harp-player stands,
> The implacable beautiful tyrant
>   Rose-crowned, having death in his hands;
> And a sound as the sound of loud water
>   Smote far through the flight of the fires,
> And mixed with the lightning of slaughter
>   A thunder of lyres.

The reference here in the third, fourth, and fifth lines of the first of the above stanzas is to the torture of the Christians by Nero in the amphitheatre. By "limbs too delicious for death" the poet refers to the torture of young girls. The "live torches" refers to Nero's cruelty in having hundreds of Christians wrapped about with combustible material, tied to lofty poles, and set on fire, to serve as torches during a great festival which he gave in the gardens of his palace. The second stanza represents him as the destroyer of Rome. It is said that he secretly had the city set on fire in a dozen different places, in order that he might be thereby enabled to imagine the scene of the burning of Troy, as described by Homer. He wanted to write a poem about it; and it is said that while the city was burning, he watched it from a high place, at the same time composing and singing a poem on the spectacle. The "flight of fires" refers of course to the spreading of fire through Rome. The "lightning of slaughter" means the flashing of swords in the work of killing, and is explained by the legend that Nero sent soldiers to kill anybody who tried to put out the fire. Anything was possible in the times of which Swinburne sings; for the world was then governed by emperors who were not simply wicked but mad. But what I wish to point out is that while a poet can write verses so splendid in sound and colour as those that I have quoted, even such a composition as "Dolores" must be preserved, with all its good and bad, among the treasures of English verse.

In spite of his radicalism in the matter of religion and of ethics, the Bible has had no more devoted student than Swinburne; he has not only appreciated all the beauties of its imagery and the strength of its wonderful English, but he has used for the subjects of not a few of his pieces, and his more daring pieces, Biblical subjects. The extraordinary composition "Aholibah" was inspired by a study of Ezekiel; unfortunately this is one of the pieces especially inappropriate to the classroom. "A Litany" will suit our purpose better. It consists of a number of Biblical prophecies, from Isaiah and other books of the Old Testament, arranged into a kind of dramatic chorus. God is made the chief speaker, and he is answered by his people. This is a kind of imitation of a certain part of the old church-service, in which one band of singers answers another, such singing being called "antiphonal," and the different parts, "antiphones." There is very little English verse written in the measure which Swinburne has adopted for this study, and I hope that you will notice the peculiar rhythmic force of the stanzas. We need quote only a few.

> All the bright lights of heaven
>   I will make dark over thee;
> One night shall be as seven
>   That its skirts may cover thee;
> I will send on thy strong men a sword,
>   On thy remnant a rod:
> Ye shall know that I am the Lord,
>   Saith the Lord God.

And the people answer:

> All the bright lights of heaven
>   Thou hast made dark over us;

> One night has been as seven,
>   That its skirt might cover us;
> Thou hast sent on our strong men a sword,
>   On our remnant a rod;
> We know that thou art the Lord,
>   O Lord our God.

But this submission is not enough; for the Lord replies:

> As the tresses and wings of the wind
>   Are scattered and shaken,
> I will scatter all them that have sinned,
>   There shall none be taken;
> As a sower that scattereth seed,
>   So will I scatter them;
> As one breaketh and shattereth a reed,
>   I will break and shatter them.

The antiphone is:

> As the wings and the locks of the wind
>   Are scattered and shaken,
> Thou hast scattered all them that have sinned;
>   There was no man taken,
> As a sower that scattereth seed,
>   So hast thou scattered us;
> As one breaketh and shattereth a reed,
>   Thou hast broken and shattered us.

Observe that, simple as this versification looks, there is nothing more difficult. With the simplest possible words, the greatest possible amount of sound and force is here obtained. There are many other stanzas, and a noteworthy fact is that very few words of Latin origin are used. Most of the words are Anglo-Saxon; perhaps that is why the language is so sonorous and strong. But when the poet does use a word of Latin origin, the result is simply splendid:

> Ye whom your lords loved well,
>   Putting silver and gold on you,
> The inevitable hell
>   Shall surely take hold on you;

> Your gold shall be for a token,
>   Your staff for a rod;
> With the breaking of bands ye are broken,
>   Saith the Lord God.

The use of the Latin adjective "inevitable" here gives an extraordinary effect, the main accent of the line coming on the second syllable of the word. But, as if to show his power, in the antiphonal response the poet does not repeat this effect, but goes back to the simple Anglo-Saxon with astonishing success:

> We whom the world loved well,
>   Laying silver and gold on us,
> The kingdom of death and of hell
>   Riseth up to take hold on us;
> Our gold is turned to a token,
>   Our staff to a rod;
> Yet shalt thou bind them up that were broken,
>   O Lord our God!

Here the substitution of these much simpler words gives nearly as fine an effect of sound and a grander effect of sense because of the grim power of the words themselves.

Besides studies in Biblical English, the poet has made a number of studies in the Old Anglo-Saxon poets, most of whom were religious men who liked sad and terrible subjects. In the poem entitled "After Death" we have an example of this Anglo-Saxon feeling combined with the plain strength of a later form of language, chiefly Middle English, with here and there a very quaint use of grammar. It was common in Anglo-Saxon poetry to depict the horrors of the grave. Here we have a dead man talking to his own coffin, and the coffin answers him horribly:

> The four boards of the coffin lid
> Heard all the dead man did.
>
> .   .   .   .   .   .
>
> "I had fair coins red and white,
> And my name was as great light;

"I had fair clothes green and red,
And strong gold bound round my head.

"But no meat comes in my mouth,
Now I fare as the worm doth;

"And no gold binds in my hair,
Now I fare as the blind fare.

"My live thews were of great strength,
Now am I waxen a span's length;

"My live sides were full of lust,
Now they are dried with dust."

The first board spake and said:
"Is it best eating flesh or bread?"

The second answered it:
"Is wine or honey the more sweet?"

The third board spake and said:
"Is red gold worth a girl's gold head?"

The fourth made answer, thus:
"All these things are as one with us."

The dead man asked of them:
"Is the green land stained brown with flame?

"Have they hewn my son for beasts to eat,
And my wife's body for beasts' meat?

"Have they boiled my maid in a brass pan,
And built a gallows to hang my man?"

The boards said to him:
"This is a lewd thing that ye deem.

"Your wife has gotten a golden bed;
All the sheets are sewn with red.

"Your son has gotten a coat of silk,
The sleeves are soft as curded milk.

"Your maid has gotten a kirtle new,
All the skirt has braids of blue.

"Your man has gotten both ring and glove,
Wrought well for eyes to love."

The dead man answered thus:
"What good gift shall God give us?"

The boards answered anon:
"Flesh to feed hell's worm upon."

I doubt very much whether a more terrible effect could be produced by any change of language. The poem is an excellent illustration of the force of the Old English, without admixture of any sort. Do not think that this is simple and easy work; perhaps no other living man could have done it equally well. It is not only in these simple forms, however, that Swinburne shows us the results of his Old English studies. Two of the most celebrated among his early poems, "The Triumph of Time" and the poem on the swallow, "Itylus," are imitations of very old forms of English verse, though the language is luxurious and new. I have already given you a quotation from the former poem, describing the poet's love of the sea. I now cite a single stanza of "Itylus."

Swallow, my sister, O sister swallow,
  How can thine heart be full of the spring?
  A thousand summers are over and dead.
What hast thou found in the spring to follow?
What hast thou found in thine heart to sing?
  What wilt thou do when the summer is shed?

Probably Swinburne found this measure in early Middle English poetry; it was used by the old poet Hampole in his "Prick of Conscience." After it had been forgotten for five hundred years, Swinburne brought it to life again. Something very close to it forms the splendid and beautiful chorus of "Atalanta in Calydon:"

When the hounds of spring are on winter's traces,
  The mother of months in meadow or plain
Fills the shadows and windy places
  With lisp of leaves and ripple of rain;
And the brown bright nightingale amorous
  Is half assuaged for Itylus,
For the Thracian ships and the foreign faces,
  The tongueless vigil, and all the pain.

Here as in all other cases, however, the poet has far surpassed his model. The measures which he revived take
new life only because of the extraordinary charm which
he has put into them.

Passing suddenly from these lighter structures, let us observe the great power which Swinburne manifests in another kind of revival, the sixteen syllable line. This is
not a modern measure at all. It was used long ago, but
was practically abandoned and almost forgotten except by
scholars when Swinburne revived it. Nor has he revived
it only in one shape, but in a great many shapes, sometimes
using single lines, sometimes double, or again varying the
accent so as to make four or five different kinds of verse
with the same number of syllables. The poem on the
Armada is a rich example of this re-animation and variation of the long dead form. In this poem Swinburne describes the god of Spain as opposed to the god of England,
and the most forceful lines are those devoted to these con-
ceptions. Observe the double rhymes.

Ay, but *we* that the wind and *sea* gird round with shelter of storms
  and *waves,*
Know not *him* that ye worship, *grim* as dreams that quicken from
  dead men's *graves:*
God is *one* with the sea, the *sun,* the land that nursed us, the love
  that *saves.*

Love whose *heart* is in ours, and *part* of all things noble and all
  things *fair;*
Sweet and *free* as the circling *sea,* sublime and kind as the foster-
  ing *air;*

Pure of *shame* as is England's *name*, whose crowns to come are as crowns that *were*.

Now we have, quite easily, a change in the measure. We have sixteen syllables still, but the whole music is changed.

But the Lord of darkness, the God whose love is a flaming fire,
The master whose mercy fulfils wide hell till its tortures tire,
He shall surely have heed of his servants who serve him for love, not hire.

The double rhymes are not used here. Later on, after the English victory and the storm, they are used again, for the purpose of additional force. The address is to the Spaniards and to their gods.

Lords of *night*, who would breathe your *blight* on April's morning and August's *noon*,
God your *Lord*, the condemned, the *abhorred*, sinks hellward, smitten with deathlike *swoon*,
Death's own *dart* in his hateful *heart* now thrills, and night shall receive him *soon*.

God the *Devil*, thy reign of *revel* is here forever eclipsed and *fled;*
God the *Liar*, everlasting *fire* lays hold at last on thee, hand and *head*.

Page after page of constantly varying measures of this kind will be found in the poem—a poem which notwithstanding its strong violence at times, represents the power of the verse-maker better than almost any other single piece in the work of his later years.

From what extracts we have already made, I think you will see enough of the value and beauty of Swinburne's diction to take in it such interest as it really deserves. We might continue the study of this author for a much longer time. But the year is waning, the third term, which is very short, will soon be upon us; and I wish to turn with you next week to the study of Browning.

CHAPTER V

STUDIES IN BROWNING

ROBERT BROWNING very much reminds us in some respects of the American thinker, Emerson. The main doctrine of Emerson is Individualism; and this happens also to be the main doctrine of Browning. By Individualism, Emerson and Browning mean self-cultivation. Both thought that the highest possible duty of every man was to develop the best powers of his mind and body to the utmost possible degree. Make yourself strong—that is the teaching. You are only a man, not a god; therefore it is very likely that you will do many things which are very wrong or very foolish. But whatever you do, even if it be wrong, do it well—do it with all your strength. Even a strong sin may be better than a cowardly virtue. Weakness is of all things the worst. When we do wrong, experience soon teaches us our mistake. And the stronger the mistake has been, the more quickly will the experience come which corrects and purifies. Now you understand what I mean by Individualism —the cultivation by untiring exercise of all our best faculties, and especially of the force and courage to act.

This Individualism in Emerson was founded upon a vague Unitarian pantheism. The same fact is true of Browning's system. According to both thinkers, all of us are parts of one infinite life, and it is by cultivating our powers that we can best serve the purpose of the Infinite Mind. Leaving out the words "mind" and "purpose," which are anthropomorphisms, this doctrine accords fairly well with evolutional philosophy; and both writers were, to a certain degree, evolutionists. But neither yielded much to the melancholy of nineteenth century doubt. Both were optimists. We may say that Browning's philosophy is an optimistic pantheism, inculcating effort as the very first and highest duty of life. But Browning is not especially a philosophical poet. We find his philosophy flashing out only at long intervals. Knowing this, we know what he is likely to think under certain circumstances; but his mission was of another special kind.

His message to the world was that of an interpreter of life. His art is, from first to last, a faithful reflection of human nature, the human nature of hundreds of different characters, good and bad, but in a large proportion of cases, decidedly bad. Why? Because, as a great artist, Browning understood very well that you can draw quite as good a moral from bad actions as from good ones, and his unconscious purpose is always moral. Such art of picturing character, to be really great, must be dramatic; and all of Browning's work is dramatic. He does not say to us, "This man has such and such a character"; he makes the man himself act and speak so as to show his nature. The second fact, therefore, to remember about Browning is that artistically he is a dramatic poet, whose subject is human nature. No other English poet so closely resembled Shakespeare in this kind of representation as Browning.

There is one more remarkable fact about the poet. He always, or nearly always, writes in the first person. Every one of his poems, with few exceptions, is a soliloquy. It is not he who speaks, of course; it is the "I" of some other person's soul. This kind of literary form is called "monologue." Even the enormous poem of "The Ring and the Book" is nothing but a gigantic collection of monologues, grouped and ordered so as to produce one great dramatic effect.

In the case of Browning, I shall not attempt much illustration by way of texts, because a great deal of Browning's form could be not only of no use to you, but would even be mischievous in its influence upon your use of language. In Browning every rule of rhetoric, of arrangement, is likely to be broken. The adjective is separated by vast distances from the noun; the preposition is tumbled after the word to which it refers; the verb is found at the end of a sentence of which it should have been the first word. When Carlyle first read the poem called "Sordello," he said that he could not tell whether "Sordello" was a man or a town or a book. And the obscurity of "Sordello" is in some places so atrocious that I do not think anybody in the world can unravel it. Now, most of Browning's long poems are written in this amazing style. The text is, therefore, not a good subject for literary study. But it is an admirable subject for psychological study, emotional study, dramatic study, and sometimes for philosophic study. Instead of giving extracts, therefore, from very long poems, I shall give only a summary of the meaning of the poem itself. If such summary should tempt you to the terrible labour of studying the original, I am sure that you would be very tired, but after the weariness, you would be very much surprised and pleased.

Providing, of course, that you would understand; and I very much doubt whether you could understand. I doubt because I cannot always understand it myself, no matter how hard I try.

One reason is the suppression of words. Browning leaves out all the articles, prepositions, and verbs that he can. I met some years ago a Japanese scholar who had mastered almost every difficulty of the English language except the articles and prepositions; he had never been abroad long enough to acquire the habit of using them properly. But it was his business to write many letters upon technical subjects, and these letters were always perfectly correct, except for the extraordinary fact that they contained no articles and very few prepositions. Much of Browning's poetry reads just in that way. You cannot say that there is anything wrong; but too much is left to the imagination. Therefore he has been spoken of as writing in telegraph language.

Not to make Browning too formidable at first, let us begin with a few of his lighter studies, in very simple verse. I will take as the first example the poem called "A Light Woman." This is a polite word for courtesan, "light" referring to the moral character. The story, told in monologue, is the most ordinary story imaginable. It happens in every great city of the world almost every day, among that class of young men who play with fire. But there are two classes among these, the strong and the weak. The strong take life as half a joke, a very pleasant thing, and pass through many dangers unscathed simply because they know that what they are doing is foolish; they never consider it in a serious way. The other class of young men take life seriously. They are foolish rather through affection and pity than through anything else. They want a woman's love, and they foolishly ask it from women who cannot love at all—not, at least, in ninety cases out of a hundred. They get what seems to them affection, however, and this deludes them. Then they become bewitched; and the result is much sorrow, perhaps ruin, perhaps crime, perhaps suicide. In Browning's poem we have a representative of each type. A strong man, strong in character, has a young friend who has been fascinated by a woman of a dangerous class. He says to himself, "My friend will be ruined; he is bewitched; it is no use to talk to him. I will save him by taking that woman away from him. I know the kind of man that she would like; she would like such a man as I." And the rest of the cruel story is told in Browning's verses too well to need further explanation.

> So far as our story approaches the end,
>   Which do you pity the most of us three?—
> My friend, or the mistress of my friend
>   With her wanton eyes, or me?
>
> My friend was already too good to lose,
>   And seemed in the way of improvement yet,

When she crossed his path with her hunting-noose,
 And over him drew her net.

When I saw him tangled in her toils,
 A shame, said I, if she adds just him
To her nine-and-ninety other spoils,
 The hundredth for a whim!

And before my friend be wholly hers,
 How easy to prove to him, I said,
An eagle's the game her pride prefers,
 Though she snaps at a wren instead!

So I gave her eyes my own eyes to take,
 My hand sought hers as in earnest need,
And round she turned for my noble sake,
 And gave me herself indeed.

The eagle am I, with my fame in the world,
 The wren is he, with his maiden face.
You look away, and your lip is curled?
 Patience, a moment's space!

For see, my friend goes shaking and white;
 He eyes me as the basilisk:
I have turned, it appears, his day to night,
 Eclipsing his sun's disk.

And I did it, he thinks, as a very thief:
 "Though I love her—that, he comprehends—
One should master one's passions (love, in chief),
 And be loyal to one's friends!"

And she—she lies in my hand as tame
 As a pear late basking over a wall;
Just a touch to try, and off it came;
 'Tis mine,—can I let it fall?

With no mind to eat it, that's the worst!
 Were it thrown in the road, would the case assist?
'Twas quenching a dozen blue-flies' thirst
 When I gave its stalk a twist.

And I,—what I seem to my friend, you see:
    What I soon shall seem to his love, you guess:
What I seem to myself, do you ask of me?
    No hero, I confess.

'Tis an awkward thing to play with souls,
    And matter enough to save one's own:
Yet think of my friend, and the burning coals
    He played with for bits of stone!

One likes to show the truth for the truth;
    That the woman was light is very true:
But suppose she says,—Never mind that youth!
    What wrong have I done to you?

Well, anyhow, here the story stays,
    So far at least as I understand;
And, Robert Browning, you writer of plays,
    Here's a subject made to your hand!

Now let us see how much there is to study in this simple-seeming poem. It will give us an easy and an excellent example of the way in which Browning must be read; and it will require at least an hour's chat to explain properly. For, really, Browning never writes simply.

Here we have a monologue. It is uttered to the poet by a young man with whom he has been passing an hour in conversation. We can guess from the story something about the young man; we can almost see him. We know that he must be handsome, tall, graceful, and strong; and full of that formidable coolness which the sense of great strength gives—great strength of mind and will rather than of body, but probably both. Let us hear him talk. "You see that friend of mine over there?" he says to the poet. "He hates me now. When he looks at me his lips turn white. I can't say that he is wrong to hate me, but really I wanted to do him a service. He got fascinated by that woman of whom I was speaking; she was playing with him as a cat plays with a mouse or with a bird before killing it.

Well, I thought to myself that my friend was in great danger, and that it was better for me to try to save him.   You see, he is not the kind of man that a woman of that class could fancy; he is too small, too feeble, too gentle; they like strong men only, men they are afraid of.   So, just for my friend's sake, I made love to her one day, and she left him immediately and came to me.   I have to take care of her now, and I do not like the trouble at all.   I never cared about the woman herself; she is not the kind of woman that I admire; I did all this only to save my friend.   And my friend does not understand.   He thinks that I took the woman from him because I was in love with her; he thinks it quite natural that I should love her (which I don't); but he says that even in love a man ought to be true to his friends."

At this point of the story the young man sees that the poet is disgusted by what he has heard, but this does not embarrass him; he is too strong a character to be embarrassed at all, and he resumes: "Don't be impatient—I want to tell you the whole thing.   You see, I have destroyed all the happiness of my friend merely through my desire to do him a service.   He hates me, and he does not understand.   He thinks that I was moved by lust; and everybody else thinks the same thing.   Of course it is not true.   But now there is another trouble.   The woman does not understand.   She thinks that I was really in love with her; and I must get rid of her as soon as I can.   If I tell her that I made love to her only in order to save my friend, she will say, 'What had that to do with your treatment of me?   I did not do you any harm; why should you have amused yourself by trying to injure and to deceive me?'   If she says that, I don't know how I shall be able to answer.   So it seems that I have made a serious mistake; I have lost my friend, I have wantonly wronged a woman whose only fault toward me was to love me, and I have made for myself a bad reputation in society. People cannot understand the truth of the thing."

This is the language of the man, and he perhaps thinks that he is telling the truth. But is he telling the truth? Does any man in this world ever tell the exact truth about himself? Probably not. No man really understands himself so well as to be able to tell the exact truth about himself. It is possible that this man believes himself to be speaking truthfully, but he is certainly telling a lie, a half-truth only. We have his exact words, but the exact language of the speaker in any one of Browning's monologues does not tell the truth; it only suggests the truth. We must find out the real character of the person, and the real facts of the case, from our own experience of human nature. And to understand the real meaning behind this man's words, you must ask yourselves whether you would believe such a story if it were told to you in exactly the same way by some one whom you know. I shall answer for you that you certainly would not.

And now we come to the real meaning. The young man saw his friend desperately in love with a woman who did not love that friend. The woman was beautiful. Looking at her, he thought to himself, "How easily I could take her away from my friend!" Then he thought to himself that not only would this be a cause of enmity between himself and his friend, but such an action would be severely judged by all his acquaintances. Could he be justified? When a man wishes to do what is wrong, he can nearly always invent a moral reason for doing it. So this young man finds a moral reason. He says, "My friend is in danger; therefore I will sacrifice myself for him. It will be quite gratifying both to my pride and to my pleasure to take that woman from him; then I shall tell everybody why I did it. My friend would like to kill me, of course, but he is too weak to avenge himself." He follows this course, and

really tries to persuade himself that he is justified in following it.   When he says that he did not care for the woman,
he only means that he is now tired of her.   He has indulged
his lust and his vanity by the most treacherous and brutal
conduct; yet he tries to tell the world that he is a moral man,
a martyr, a calumniated person.   Such is the real meaning
of his apology.

Nevertheless we cannot altogether dislike this young
man.   He is selfish and proud and not quite truthful, but
these are faults of youth.   On the other hand we can feel
that he is very gifted, very intelligent, and very brave, and,
what is still better, that he is ashamed of himself.   He has
done wrong, and the very fact that he lies about what he
has done shows us that he is ashamed.   He is not all bad.
If he does not tell us the whole truth, he tells a great deal
of it; and we feel that as he becomes older he will become
better.   He has abused his power, and he feels sorry for
having abused it; some day he will probably become a very
fine man.   We feel this; and, curiously, we like him better
than we like the man whom he has wronged.   We like him
because of his force; we despise the other man because of
his weakness.   It would be a mistake to do this if we did
not feel that the man who has done wrong is really the
better man of the two.   What he has done is not at all to
be excused, but we believe that he will redeem his fault
later on.   This type is an English or American type—perhaps it might be a German type.   There is nothing Latin
about it.   Its faults are of the Northern race.

But now let us take an unredeemable type, the purely
bad, the hopelessly wicked, a type not of the North this
time, but purely Latin.   As the Latin races have been civilised for a very much longer time than the Northern races,
they have higher capacities in certain directions.   They are
physically and emotionally much more attractive to us.
The beauty of an Italian or French or Spanish woman is
incomparably more delicate, more exquisite, than the beauty

of the Northern women.   The social intelligence of the Italian or Spaniard or Frenchman is something immeasurably superior to the same capacity in the Englishman, the Scandinavian, or the German.   The Latins have much less moral stamina, but imaginatively, æsthetically, emotionally, they have centuries of superiority.   The Northern races were savages when these were lords of the world.   But the vices of civilisation are likely to be developed in them to a degree impossible to the Northern character.   If their good qualities are older and finer than ours, so their bad qualities will be older and stronger and deeper.   At no time was the worst side of man more terribly shown than during the Renaissance.   Here is an illustration.   We know that for this man there is no hope; the evil predominates in his nature to such an extent that we can see nothing at all of the good except his fine sense of beauty.   And even this sense becomes a curse to him.

MY LAST DUCHESS

That's my last Duchess painted on the wall,
Looking as if she were alive.   I call
That piece a wonder, now: Frà Pandolf's hands
Worked busily a day, and there she stands.
Will't please you sit and look at her? I said
"Frà Pandolf" by design, for never read
Strangers like you that pictured countenance,
The depth and passion of its earnest glance.
But to myself they turned (since none puts by
The curtain I have drawn for you, but I)
And seemed as they would ask me, if they durst,
How such a glance came there; so, not the first
Are you to turn and ask thus.

Let us paraphrase the above.   It is a duke of Ferrara who speaks.   The person to whom he is speaking is a marriage-maker, a *nakodo* employed by the prince of a neighbouring state.   For the duke wishes to marry the daughter of that prince.   When the match-maker comes, the duke draws a

curtain from a part of the wall of the room in which the
two men meet, and shows him, painted upon the wall, the
picture of a wonderfully beautiful woman.   Then the duke
says to the messenger: "That is a picture of my last wife.
It is a beautiful picture, is it not?   Well, it was painted by
that wonderful monk, Frà Pandolf.   I mention his name
on purpose, because everybody who sees that picture for the
first time wants to know why it is so beautiful, and would
ask me questions if they were not afraid.   I have shown it
to several other people; but nobody, except myself, dares
draw the curtain that covers it.   Yes, Frà Pandolf painted
it all in one day; and the expression of the smiling face still
makes everybody wonder.   You wonder; you want to know
why that woman looks so charming, so bewitching in the
picture."

Now listen to the explanation.   It is worthy of the greatest of the villains of Shakespeare:

                              Sir, 'twas not
Her husband's presence only, called that spot
Of joy into the Duchess' cheek: perhaps
Frà Pandolf chanced to say, "Her mantle laps
Over my lady's wrist too much," or, "Paint
Must never hope to reproduce the faint
Half-flush that dies along her throat": such stuff
Was courtesy, she thought, and cause enough
For calling up that spot of joy.   She had
A heart—how shall I say?—too soon made glad,
Too easily impressed: she liked whate'er
She looked on, and her looks went everywhere.
Sir, 'twas all one!   My favour at her breast,
The dropping of the daylight in the West,
The bough of cherries some officious fool
Broke in the orchard for her, the white mule
She rode with round the terrace—all and each
Would draw from her alike the approving speech,
Or blush, at least.   She thanked men—good! but thanked
Somehow—I know not how—as if she ranked
My gift of a nine-hundred-years-old name
With anybody's gift.

The explanation at least shows us the sweet and childish character of the woman, which the speaker tries to describe as folly: "It was not her gladness at seeing me, her husband, that made her smile so beautifully, that brought the rosy dimple to her cheek. Probably the painter said something to flatter her, and she smiled at him. She was ready to smile at anything, at anybody, she was altogether too easily pleased; she liked everything and everybody that she saw, and she took a pleasure in looking at everything and at everybody. Nothing made any difference to her. She would smile at the jewel which I gave her, but she would also smile at the sunset, at a bunch of cherries, at her mule, at anything or anybody. Any matter would bring the dimple to her cheek, or the blush of joy. I do not blame her for thanking people, but she had a way of thanking people that seemed to show that she was just as much pleased by what a stranger did for her, as by the fact that she had become the wife of a man like myself, head of a family nine hundred years old." Notice how the speaker calls the man who gave his wife a bough with cherries upon it "an officious fool." We can begin to perceive what was the matter. He was insanely jealous of her, without any cause; and she, poor little soul! did not know anything about it. She was too innocent to know. The duke does not want anybody else to know, either; he is trying to give quite a different explanation of what happened:

> Who'd stoop to blame
> This sort of trifling? Even had you skill
> In speech—(which I have not)—to make your will
> Quite clear to such an one, and say, "Just this
> Or that in you disgusts me; here you miss,
> Or there exceed the mark"—and if she let
> Herself be lessoned so, nor plainly set
> Her wits to yours, forsooth, and made excuse,
> —E'en then would be some stooping; and I choose
> Never to stoop. Oh sir, she smiled, no doubt,

> Whene'er I passed her; but who passed without
> Much the same smile?

This means, "A man like me cannot afford to degrade himself by showing what he feels under such circumstances; a man like me cannot say to a woman, 'I am greatly vexed and pained when I see you smile at any one except myself.' If I were to speak to her about the matter at all, she might think I was jealous. Of course she would insult me by making excuses, by saying that she did not know, which would be nothing less than daring to oppose her judgment to mine. To speak about my feelings in any case would require a skill in the use of language such as only poets or such vulgar people possess. I am a prince, not a poet, and I shall never disgrace myself by telling anybody, especially a woman, that I do not like this or I do not like that. So I said nothing. Perhaps you think that she did not smile when she saw me. That would be a mistake; she always smiled when I passed. But she smiled at everybody else in exactly the same way." He found the smile unbearable at last, and the poet lets him tell us the rest in a very few words:

> This grew; I gave commands;
> Then all smiles stopped together.

In other words, he caused her to be killed; told somebody to cut her throat, probably, or to give her a drink of poison, all without having ever allowed her to know how or why he had been displeased with her. And he is not a bit sorry. No, looking at the dead woman's picture, in company with the marriage-maker, he coolly expresses his admiration for it as a work of realistic art—as much as to say, "You can see for yourself how beautiful she was; but that did not prevent me from killing her." Listen to his atrocious chatter:

> There she stands
> As if alive. Will't please you rise? We'll meet
> The company below, then. I repeat,

The Count your master's known munificence
Is ample warrant that no just pretence
Of mine for dowry will be disallowed;
Though his fair daughter's self, as I avowed
At starting, is my object.   Nay, we'll go
Together down, sir. . . . Notice Neptune, though,
Taming a sea-horse, thought a rarity,
Which Claus of Innsbruck cast in bronze for me!

Evidently both had seated themselves in front of the picture.   The count says, "Now she is as if alive; and we shall go downstairs together.   As for the matter of the new marriage, you can tell your master that I am quite sure so generous a man will not make any objection to my just demands for a dowry—though, of couise, it is his daughter that I principally want."   Here the messenger bows, to allow the duke to go first downstairs.   He answers: "No, we can go down together this time."   On the way, probably at a turn of the grand staircase, the count points to a fine bronze statue, representing the god of the sea, and asks the man to admire it.   That is all.

This is a Renaissance character, and a very terrible one. But it is also very complicated.   We must think a little before we can even guess the whole range and depth of this man's wickedness.   Even then we can only guess, because he lets us know only so much about him as he wishes us to know.   Every word that he says is carefully measured in its pride, in its falsehood, in its cruelty, in its cunning. Just this much he tells us: "I had a beautiful wife, but you must not think that I can be influenced by beauty. Look at the picture of her.   You would worship a woman like that.   But I cut her throat.   Why did I do it?   Just because I did not like her way of smiling; she was too tender-hearted to love.   And I would do the same thing tomorrow to any one who displeased me.   Some people will think that I am jealous; let them think so.   But you had better tell the girl who now expects to become my wife what kind of person I am."

How much of this is the truth?   Probably more than
half.   Undoubtedly the man was jealous, and he wishes to
deceive us in regard to the whole extent of that jealousy.
He has no shame or remorse for crime, but he has shame of
appearing to be weak.   Jealousy is a weakness; therefore
he does not like to be suspected of being weak in that way.
He gives a strong suggestion that he must not have future
cause for jealousy—nothing more.   But the fact that he
most wishes to have understood is that his wife must be a
wicked woman, a vulture among vultures.   He does not
want a dove.   And he hated his first wife much more because she was good and gentle and loving, than because she
smiled at other people.   You may ask, why should he hate
a woman for being good?   The answer is simple.   In the
courts of such princes as the Borgias, a good woman could
only do mischief.   She could not be used for cunning and
wicked purposes.   She would have refused to poison a
guest, or to entice a man to make love to her only in order
to get that man killed; and as you will discover if you read
the terrible history of the Italian republics, all these things
had to be done.   Morality was a hindrance to such men.
Power remained only to cunning and strength; all kind-
heartedness was regarded as criminal weakness.   When you
have become familiar with the real history of Ferrara, you
will perceive the terrible truth of this poem.

The most unpleasant fact still remains to be noticed.
The wickedness of this man is not a wickedness of ignorance.   It is a wickedness of highly cultivated intelligence.
The man is an artist, a judge of beauty, a connoisseur.   To
suppose that cultivation makes a naturally wicked man better is a great educational mistake, as Herbert Spencer
showed long ago.   Education does not make a man more
moral; it may give him power to be more immoral.   Italian
history furnishes us with the most extraordinary illustrations of this fact.   Some of the wickedest of the Italian
princes were great poets, great artists, great scholars, and

great patrons of learning.   Among the monsters, we have, for example, the terrible Malatesta of Rimini, whose life was given to us some years ago by the French antiquarian Yriarte.   He wrote the most delicate and tender poetry, and he committed crimes so terrible that they cannot be named.   When he laid his hand, however lightly, upon a horse, the animal began to tremble from head to foot.   Yet he could love, and be the most devoted of gallants.   Again, you know the case of Benvenuto Cellini, a splendid artist and an atrocious murderer, who actually tells us the pleasure that he felt in killing.   And there were the Borgias, all of them, father, daughter, and brothers, who committed every crime and never knew remorse, yet who were beautiful and gifted lovers of art and poetry.   So in this case Browning is true to life when he shows us the duke pointing out the beauty of pictures and statues, even in the same moment that he is uttering horrors.   There is a strange mixture of the extremes of the bad and of the good in the higher types of the Italian race—a mingling that gives us much to think about in regard to moral problems.   Probably that is why a very large number of Browning's studies are of the dark side of Italian character.

Now we can take a lighter subject.   It is not black, it is only gloomy, and the interest of it will chiefly be found in the extraordinary moral comment made by Browning. This is one of the few studies which is not all written in the first person.   It is called "The Statue and the Bust." It is a tale or tradition of Florence.

The legend is that a certain duke of Florence, by name Ferdinand, attempted to captivate the young bride of a Florentine nobleman named Riccardi.   But Riccardi, a very keen man, observed what was going on; and he said to his wife very quietly and firmly, "This is your room in my house; you shall stay in this room and never leave it during the rest of your life, never leave it until you are carried to the graveyard."   So she had to live in that room.   But the duke, who was a very handsome man, got a splendid bronze statue of himself on horseback erected in the public street opposite the window of the lady's room, so that she could always look at him.   Then she had a bust of herself made and placed above the window, so that the duke could see the bust whenever he rode by.   That is all the story— but not all the story as Browning tells it.   Browning tells us the secret thoughts and feelings of the imprisoned wife and of the duke.   At first the two intended to run away to- gether.   It would have been an easy matter.   The woman would only have had to dress herself like a boy, and drop from the window, and get help from the duke to reach his palace.   The duke thought to himself, "I can get this woman whenever I wish; but it will be better to wait a little while; then we can manage to live as we please without making too much trouble."   So they both waited till they became old.   Then the woman called an artist and said:

> "Make me a face on the window there,
> Waiting as ever, mute the while,
> My love to pass below in the square!
>
> "And let me think that it may beguile
> Dreary days which the dead must spend
> Down in their darkness under the aisle,
>
> "To say, 'What matters it at the end?
> I did no more while my heart was warm
> Than does that image, my pale-faced friend.' "

She thinks to console herself a moment by saying, "What is life worth?   When I was young and beautiful and im- pulsive, I did no more harm or good, no more right or wrong, than the bust that resembles me.   It is a comfort to think that I did nothing wrong."   But is that enough?

> "Where is the use of the lip's red charm,
> The heaven of hair, the pride of the brow,
> And the blood that blues the inside arm—

> "Unless we turn, as the soul knows how,
> The earthly gift to an end divine?
> A lady of clay is as good, I trow."

Somehow or other she feels that it is no consolation not to
have done wrong.   She wonders what was the use of being
so beautiful, if she could not make use of that beauty.   The
bust itself lived just as much as she did.   And all this is
true; but she is nearer to living than the duke.   What does
he say?

> "Set me on horseback here aloft,
> Alive, as the crafty sculptor can,
>
> "In the very square I have crossed so oft:
> That men may admire, when future suns
> Shall touch the eyes to a purpose soft,
>
> "While the mouth and the brow stay brave in bronze—
> Admire and say, 'When he was alive
> How he would take his pleasure once!'"

Nothing else; he only wants to be admired after his death,
to have people say, looking at his statue, "What a splendid
looking man he must have been, how the women must have
loved him!"   And they both died, and were buried in the
church near where they lived; and the English poet Browning went to that church, and heard the story, and thought
about it, and gives us the moral of it.   It is a startling moral
and needs explanation.   I think you will be shocked when
you first hear it, but you will not be shocked if you think
about it.   The following verses are the poet's own reflections:

> So!   While these wait the trump of doom,
> How do their spirits pass, I wonder,
> Nights and days in the narrow room?
>
> Still, I suppose, they sit and ponder
> What a gift life was, ages ago,
> Six steps out of the chapel yonder.

> Only they see not God, I know,
> Nor all that chivalry of his,
> The soldier-saints who, row on row,
>
> Burn upward each to his point of bliss—

He condemns them. Why? Because they did not do anything. Anything? You do not mean to say that they
ought to have committed adultery?

> I hear your reproach—"But delay was best,
> For their end was a crime." —Oh, a crime will do
> As well, I reply, to serve for a test,
>
> As a virtue golden through and through,
> Sufficient to vindicate itself
> And prove its worth at a moment's view!
>
> Must a game be played for the sake of pelf?
> .   .   .   .
> The true has no value beyond the sham:
> As well the counter as coin, I submit,
> When your table's a hat, and your prize, a dram.
>
> Stake your counter as boldly every whit,
> Venture as truly, use the same skill,
> Do your best, whether winning or losing it,
>
> If you choose to play—is my principle!
> Let a man contend to the uttermost
> For his life's set prize, be it what it will!
>
> The counter our lovers staked was lost
> As surely as if it were lawful coin;
> And the sin I impute to each frustrate ghost
>
> Was the unlit lamp and the ungirt loin,
> Though the end in sight was a crime, I say.

In order to understand the full force of this strange ethical
philosophy, you must remember that the word "counter" is

here a gambling term; it is used for the round buttons or disks of bone or ivory, not in themselves money, but representing money to be eventually received or paid. Remembering this, we can simplify Browning; this is what he says:

"These people were the most contemptible of sinners; they deliberately threw their lives away. They were afraid to commit a sin. To wish to commit a sin and to be afraid to commit it, is much worse than committing it. All their lives those two dreamed and purposed and desired a sin; they wanted to commit adultery. If they had committed the crime, there would have been some hope for them; there is always hope for the persons who are not afraid. When a young man begins to doubt what his parents and teachers tell him about virtue, it is sometimes a good thing for him to test this teaching by disobeying it. Human experience has proclaimed in all ages that theft and murder and adultery and a few other things can never give good results. It is not easy to explain the whole why and wherefore to a young person who is both self-willed and ignorant. But let him try for himself what murder means, or theft means, or adultery means, and after he has experienced the consequences, he will begin to perceive what moral teaching signifies. If he is not killed, or imprisoned for life, he will very possibly become wise and good at a later time. Now in regard to those two lovers, they wanted to have an experience; and the experience might have been so valuable to them that it would have given them a new soul—but they were afraid; they were criminals without profit; and their great sin was that of being too cowardly to commit sin. Never will God forgive such weakness as that!" Of course all great religions teach that the man who wishes to do wrong does the wrong in wishing as truly as if he did it with his body; there is only a difference of degree. Now Browning goes a little further than such religious teaching; he tells us that only wishing under certain circumstances may be incomparably worse than doing, because the doing brings about its punishment in ninety-nine cases out of a hundred, and the punishment becomes a moral lesson, forcing the sufferer to think about the moral aspect of what he has done. That is why Browning says, "A sin will do to serve for a test." But only to wish to do, and not do, leaves a person in the state of inexperience. There is an old proverb, which is quite true: "Any man can become rich who is willing to pay the price." With equal truth it might be said, "You can do anything that you please in this world, if you are willing to pay the price, but the price of acts and thoughts is fixed by the Eternal Powers, and you must not try to cheat them."

Philosophers will tell you that our moral laws are not always perfect, that man cannot make a perfect code invariably applicable to all times and circumstances. This is true. But it is also true that there is a higher morality than human codes, and when human law fails to give justice, a larger law occasionally steps in to correct the failure. Browning delights in giving us examples of this kind, extraordinary moral situations, wrong by legal opinion, right by the larger law of nature, which is sometimes divine. A startling story which he tells us, entitled "Iàn Iànovitch," will show us how he treats such themes. Iàn, the hero of the story, is a wood-cutter, who works all day in his native village, to support a large family. He is the most highly respected of the young peasants, the strong man of the community, a good father and a good husband. One day, while he is working out of doors in the bitter cold, a sledge drawn by a maddened and dying horse enters the village, with a half dead woman on it. The woman is the wife of Iàn's best friend, and she has come back alone, although she had taken her three children with her on the homeward journey. Iàn helps her into the house, gives her something warm to drink, caresses her, comforts her, and asks at last for her story. The sledge had been pursued by wolves, and the wolves had eaten the three children, one after another. Iván listens very carefully to the mother's relation of how the three children were snatched out of the sledge by the wolves. As soon as she has told every one in her own way, Iván takes his sharp axe, and with one blow cuts the woman's head off. To the other peasants he simply observes, "God told me to do that; I could not help it." Of course Iván knew that the woman had lied. The wolves had not taken the children away from her: she had dropped one child after another out of the sledge in order to save her own miserable life.

At the news of the murder, the authorities of the village all hurry to the scene. There is the dead body without its head, and the blood flowing, or rather crawling like a great red snake over the floor. The lord of the village declares that Iván must be executed for this crime. The Stàrosta, or head man, takes the same view of the situation. But, just as Iván is about to be arrested, the old priest of the village, the Pope as the peasants call him, a man more than a hundred years of age, comes into the assembly and speaks. He is the only man who has a word to say on behalf of Iván, but what he says is extraordinary in its force and primitive wisdom. All of it would be too long to quote. I give you only the conclusion, which immediately results in Iván's being acquitted both by law and by public opinion.

"A mother bears a child: perfection is complete
So far in such a birth.   Enabled to repeat
The miracle of life,—herself was born so just
A type of womankind, that God sees fit to trust
Her with the holy task of giving life in turn.

.   .   .   .

How say you, should the hand God trusted with life's torch
Kindled to light the word—aware of sparks that scorch,
Let fall the same?   Forsooth, her flesh a fire-flake stings:
The mother drops the child!   Among what monstrous things
Shall she be classed?"

Of course the old Pope is speaking from the Christian point

of view when he says that perfection is complete in a birth; he refers to the orthodox belief that the soul of man is created a perfect thing of its kind, a perfect spiritual entity, to be further made or marred by its own acts and thoughts. The mother does not give birth only to a body, but to a soul also, expressly made by God to fit that body. She is allowed to repeat the miracle of creation thus far; as mother she is creator, but only in trust. She has made the vessel of the soul; her most sacred duty is to guard that little body from all harm. A mother who would even let her child fall to escape pain herself would be incomparably more ignoble than the most savage of animals. The rule is that during motherhood even the animal-mother for the time being becomes the ruling power; the male animal then allows her to have her own way in all things.

"Because of motherhood, each male
Yields to his partner place, sinks proudly in the scale:
His strength owned weakness, wit—folly, and courage—fear,
Beside the female proved male's mistress—only here.
The fox-dam, hunger-pined, will slay the felon sire
Who dares assault her whelp: the beaver, stretched on fire,
Will die without a groan: no pang avails to wrest
Her young from where they hide—her sanctuary breast.
What's here then? Answer me, thou dead one, as I trow,
Standing at God's own bar, he bids thee answer now!
Thrice crowned wast thou—each crown of pride, a child—thy charge!
Where are they? Lost? Enough: no need that thou enlarge
On how or why the loss: life left to utter 'lost'
Condemns itself beyond appeal. The soldier's post
Guards from the foe's attack the camp he sentinels:
That he no traitor proved, this and this only tells—
Over the corpse of him trod foe to foe's success.
Yet—one by one thy crowns torn from thee—thou no less
To scare the world, shame God—livedst! I hold he saw
The unexampled sin, ordained the novel law,
Whereof first instrument was first intelligence
Found loyal here. I hold that, failing human sense,
The very earth had oped, sky fallen, to efface
Humanity's new wrong, motherhood's first disgrace.

Earth oped not, neither fell the sky, for prompt was found
A man and man enough, head-sober and heart-sound,
Ready to hear God's voice, resolute to obey.

. . . .

                                I proclaim
Ivàn Ivànovitch God's servant!"

On hearing this speech the peasantry are at once convinced; the Russian lord orders the proclamation to be made
that the murderer is forgiven, and the head man of the
village goes to Ivàn's house to bring the good news. He
expects to find Ivàn on his knees at prayer, very much afraid
of the police and coming punishment. But on opening the
door the head man finds Ivàn playing with his five children,
and making for them a toy-church out of little bits of wood.
It has not even entered into the mind of Ivàn that he did
anything wrong. And when they tell him, "You are free,
you will not be punished," he answers them in surprise,
"Why should I not be free? Why should you talk of my
not being punished?" To this simple mind there is nothing to argue about. He has only done what God told him
to do, punished a crime against Nature.

The story is a strange one; but not stranger than many
to be found in Browning. None of his moral teachings are
at discord with any form of true religion, yet they are mostly
larger than the teachings of any creed. Perhaps this is why
he has never offended the religious element even while
preaching doctrines over its head. The higher doctrines
thus proclaimed might be anywhere accepted; they might
be also questioned; but no one would deny their beauty and
power. We may assume that Browning usually considers
all incidents in their relation to eternal law, not to one place
or time, but to all places and to all times, because the results
of every act and thought are infinite. This doctrine especially is quite in harmony with Oriental philosophy, even
when given such a Christian shape as it takes in the beautiful verses of "Abt Vogler."

Abt Vogler was a great musician, a great improvisor. Here let me explain the words "improvise" and "improvisation," as to some of you they are likely to be unfamiliar, at least in the special sense given to them in this connection. An improvisation in poetry means a composition made instantly, without preparation, at request or upon a sudden impulse.   In Japanese literary history, I am told, there are some very interesting examples of improvisation.   For example, the story of that poetess who, on being asked to compose a poem including the mention of something square, something round, and something triangular, wrote those celebrated lines about unfastening one corner of a mosquito-curtain in order to look at the moon.   Among Europeans improvisation is now almost a lost art in poetry, except among the Italians.   Some Italian families still exist in which the art of poetical improvisation has been cultivated for hundreds of years.   But in music it is otherwise.   Improvisation in music is greatly cultivated and esteemed. Most of our celebrated musicians have been great improvisors.   Those who heard such music would regret that it could not be reproduced, not even by the musician himself. It was a beautiful creation, forgotten as soon as made, because never written down.

Now you know what Browning means by improvisation in his poem "Abt Vogler."   The musician has been improvising, and the music, made only to be forgotten, is so beautiful that he himself bitterly regrets the evanescence of it.   We may quote a few of the verses in which this regret is expressed; they are very fine and very strange, written in a measure which I think you have never seen before.

Would that the structure brave, the manifold music I build,
   Bidding my organ obey, calling its keys to their work,
Claiming each slave of the sound, at a touch, as when Solomon
      willed
   Armies of angels that soar, legions of demons that lurk,

Man, brute, reptile, fly,—alien of end and of aim,
  Adverse, each from the other heaven-high, hell-deep removed,—
Should rush into sight at once as he named the ineffable Name,
  And pile him a palace straight, to pleasure the princess he
    loved!

The musician is comparing the music that he makes to magical architecture; he refers to the Mohammedan legends of Solomon. Solomon knew all magic; and all men, animals, angels, and demons obeyed him. God has ninety-nine names by which the faithful may speak of him, but the hundredth name is secret, the Name ineffable. He who knows it can do all things by the utterance of it. When Solomon pronounced it, all the spirits of the air and of heaven and of hell would rush to obey him. And if he wanted a palace or a city built, he had only to order the spirits to build it, and they would build it immediately, finishing everything between the rising and the setting of the sun. That is the story which the musician refers to. He has the power of the master-musician over sounds; but the sounds will not stay.

Would it might tarry like his, the beautiful building of mine,
  This which my keys in a crowd pressed and importuned to raise!
Ah, one and all, how they helped, would dispart now and now
    combine,
  Zealous to hasten the work, heighten their master his praise!
And one would bury his brow with a blind plunge down to hell,
  Burrow awhile and build, broad on the roots of things,
Then up again swim into sight, having based me my palace well,
  Founded it, fearless of flame, flat on the nether springs.

The musician wishes that his architecture of sound could remain, as remained the magical palace that Solomon made the spirits build to please Queen Balkis. He remembers how beautiful his music was; he remembers how the different classes of notes combined to make it, just as the different classes of spirits combined to make the palace of Solomon. There the deep notes, the bass chords, sank down thundering like demon-spirits working to make the foundation in the very heart of the earth.   And the treble notes seemed to soar up like angels to make the roof of gold, and to tip all the points of the building with glorious fires of illumination.   Truly the palace of sounds was built, but it has vanished away like a mirage; the builder cannot reproduce it.   Why not?   Well, because great composition of any kind is not merely the work of man; it is an inspiration from God, and the mystery of such inspired composition is manifested in music as it is manifested in no other art. For the harmonies, the combinations of tones, are mysteries, and must remain mysterious even for the musician himself. Who can explain them?

But here is the finger of God, a flash of the will that can,
    Existent behind all laws, that made them, and lo, they are!
And I know not if, save in this, such gift be allowed to man
    That out of three sounds he frame not a fourth sound, but a star.
Consider it well; each tone of our scale in itself is naught:
    It is everywhere in the world—loud, soft, and all is said:
Give to me to use!   I mix it with two in my thought:
    And there!   Ye have heard and seen: consider and bow the head!

But for the same reason that they are mysteries and cannot be understood because they relate to the infinite, they are eternal.   That is the consolation.   The musician need not regret that the music composed in a moment of divine inspiration cannot be remembered; he need not regret that it has been forgotten.   Forgotten it is by the man who made it; forgotten it is by the people who heard it; forgotten it is therefore by all mankind.   Nevertheless it is eternal, because the Universal Soul that inspired it never forgets anything.   I think that the verse in which this beautiful thought is expressed—the verse that contains the whole of Browning's religion, is the most beautiful thing in all his work.   But you must judge for yourselves:

All we have willed or hoped or dreamed of good shall exist:
    Not its semblance, but itself; no beauty, nor good, nor power

Whose voice has gone forth, but each survives for the melodist
  When eternity affirms the conception of an hour.
The high that proved too high, the heroic for earth too hard,
  The passion that left the ground to lose itself in the sky,
Are music sent up to God by the lover and the bard;
  Enough that he heard it once; we shall hear it by and by.

By the phrase "when eternity affirms the conception of an hour," the poet means when we ourselves, in a future and higher state of being, shall see the worth of our good acts and thoughts proved by the fact that they survive along with us. Eternity affirms them—that is, recognises them as worthy of immortality by suffering them to exist. This line gives us the key to the philosophy of the rest. It is quite in harmony with Buddhist philosophy. Browning holds that all good acts and thoughts are eternal, whether men in this world remember them or not. But what of the bad acts and thoughts? Are they also eternal? Not in the same sense. Evil acts and thoughts do indeed exert an influence reaching enormously into the future, but it is an influence that must gradually wane, it is a Karma that must become exhausted. As for regretting that nobody sees or knows the good that we do, that is very foolish. The good will never die; it will be seen again—perhaps only in millions of years, yet this should make no difference. To the dead the time of a million years and the time of a moment may be quite the same thing.

But you must not suppose that Browning lives much in the regions of abstract philosophy. He is human in the warmest way, and very much alive to impressions of sense. Not even Swinburne is at times more voluptuous, but the voluptuous in Browning is always natural and healthy as well as artistic. I must quote to you some passages from the wonderful little dramatic poem entitled "In a Gondola." You know that a gondola is a peculiar kind of boat which in Venice takes the place of carriages or vehicles of any kind. In the city of Venice there are no streets to speak of, but canals only, so that people go from one place to another only by boat. These boats or gondolas of Venice are not altogether unlike some of the old-fashioned Japanese pleasure-boats; they have a roof and windows and rooms, and it is possible to travel in them without being seen by anybody. In the old days of Venice, many secret meetings between lovers and many secret meetings of conspirators were held in such boats. The poet is telling us of the secret meeting of two lovers, at the risk of death, for if the man is seen he will certainly be killed. At the end of the poem he actually is killed; the moment he steps on shore he is stabbed, because he has been watched by the spies of a political faction that hates him. But this is not the essential part of the poem at all. The essential part of the poem is the description of the feelings and thoughts of these two people, loving in the shadow of death; this is very beautiful and almost painfully true to nature. We get also not a few glimpses of the old life and luxury of Venice in the course of the narrative. As the boat glides down the long canals, between the high ranges of marble palaces rising from the water, the two watch the windows of the houses that they know, and talk about what is going on inside.

> Past we glide, and past, and past!
>   What's that poor Agnese doing
> Where they make the shutters fast?
>   Grey Zanobi's just a-wooing
> To his couch the purchased bride:
>   Past we glide!
>
> Past we glide, and past, and past!
>   Why's the Pucci Palace flaring
> Like a beacon to the blast?
>   Guests by hundreds, not one caring
> If the dear host's neck were wried:
>   Past we glide!

It is the man who is here looking and talking and criticising. The woman is less curious; she is thinking only of love,

and what she says in reply has become famous in English
literature; we might say that this is the very best we have
in what might be called the "literature of kissing."

> The moth's kiss, first!
> Kiss me as if you made believe
> You were not sure, this eve,
> How my face, your flower, had pursed
> Its petals up; so, here and there
> You brush it, till I grow aware
> Who wants me, and wide open burst.
>
> The bee's kiss, now!
> Kiss me as if you entered gay
> My heart at some noonday,
> A bud that dares not disallow
> The claim, so all is rendered up,
> And passively its shattered cup
> Over your head to sleep I bow.

Of course you know all about the relation of insects to
flowers—how moths, beetles, butterflies, and other little
creatures, by entering flowers in order to suck the honey,
really act as fertilisers, carrying the pollen from the male
flower to the female flower. It is the use of this fact from
natural history that makes these verses so exquisite. The
woman's mouth is the flower; the lips of the man, the visiting insect. "Moth" is the name which we give to night
butterflies, that visit flowers in the dark. What the woman
says is this in substance: "Kiss me with my mouth shut
first, like a night moth coming to a flower all shut up, and
not knowing where the opening is." The second comparison of the bee suggests another interesting fact in the relation between insects and flowers. A bee or wasp, on finding
it difficult to enter a flower from the top, so as to get at the
honey, will cut open the side of the flower, and break its
way in. The woman is asking simply, "Now give me a
rough kiss after the gentle one." All this is mere play, of
course, but by reason of the language used it rises far above

the merely trifling into the zones of supreme literary art.
Later on, we have another comparison, made by the man,
which I think very beautiful. The thought, the comparison itself, is not new: from very ancient times it has been
the custom of lovers to call the woman they loved an angel.
I fancy this custom is reflected in the amatory literature of
all countries; it exists even in Japanese poetry. But really
it does not matter whether a comparison be new or old;
its value depends upon the way that a poet utters it.
Browning's lover says:

> Lie back; could thought of mine improve you?
> From this shoulder let there spring
> A wing; from this, another wing;
> Wings, not legs and feet, shall move you!
> Snow-white must they spring, to blend
> With your flesh, but I intend
> They shall deepen to the end,
> Broader, into burning gold,
> Till both wings crescent-wise enfold
> Your perfect self, from 'neath your feet
> To o'er your head, where, lo, they meet
> As if a million sword-blades hurled
> Defiance from you to the world!

This is a picture painted after the manner of the Venetian
school; we seem to be looking at something created by the
brush of Titian or Tintoretto. I am not sure that it will
seem to you as beautiful as it really is, for it is intended to
appeal to the imagination of persons who have actually
seen the paintings of the Italian masters, or at least en-
gravings of them. Angels were frequently represented by
those great artists as clothed with their own wings, the
wings, white below, gold above, meeting over the head like
two new moons joining their shining tips. What the poet
means by "sword-blades" are the long narrow flashing
feathers of the angel-wings, which, joined all together, look
like a cluster of sword-blades. But one must have seen

the pictures of the Italian masters to appreciate the skill of this drawing in words. Here I may remind you that Dante, in his vision of Paradise, uses colours of a very similar sort—blinding white and dazzling gold appear in the wings of his angels also.

The above examples of the merely artistic power of Browning will suffice for the moment; great as he always is when he descends to earth, he is most noteworthy in those other directions which I have already pointed out, and which are chiefly psychological. I want to give you more examples from the poems of the psychological kind, partly because they are of universally recognised value in themselves, and partly because it is these that make the distinction between Browning and his great contemporaries. One of these pieces, now quoted through the whole English-speaking world, is "A Grammarian's Funeral." This poem is intended to give us the enthusiasm which the students of the later Middle Ages felt for scholarship, the delight in learning which revived shortly before the Renaissance. I suppose that many of you recollect the first enthusiasm for Western studies in Japan; people then studied too hard, tried to do even more than they could do. So it was in Europe at the time of the revival of learning; men killed themselves by overstudy. In this poem Browning makes us listen to the song sung by a company of university students burying their dead teacher; they are carrying him up to the top of a high mountain above the mediæval city, there to let him sleep forever above the clouds and above the vulgarities of mankind. The philosophy in it is very noble and strong, though it be only the philosophy of young men.

> Let us begin and carry up this corpse,
>   Singing together.
> Leave we the common crofts, the vulgar thorpes
>   Each in its tether
> Sleeping safe on the bosom of the plain,
>   Cared-for till cock-crow:

Look out if yonder be not day again
   Rimming the rock-row!
That's the appropriate country; there, man's thought,
   Rarer, intenser,
Self-gathered for an outbreak, as it ought,
   Chafes in the censer.
Leave we the unlettered plain its herd and crop;
   Seek we sepulture
On a tall mountain, citied to the top,
   Crowded with culture!
All the peaks soar, but one the rest excels,
   Clouds overcome it;
No! yonder sparkle is the citadel's
   Circling its summit.
Thither our path lies; wind we up the heights;
   Wait ye the warning?
Our low life was the level's and the night's;
   He's for the morning.
Step to a tune, square chests, erect each head,
   'Ware the beholders!
This is our master, famous, calm and dead,
   Borne on our shoulders.

Some little description will be necessary before we can go further with the poem. It was dark, before daybreak, when the students assembled for the funeral, and it is still rather dark when the funeral procession starts up the mountain. This appears from the lines, "Look out if yonder be not day again rimming the rock-row"—meaning, see if that is not daylight up there at the top of the mountains. It is not full day, but they can see, far up, the lights of the citadel. The poet wants to give us the feeling of a fortified city of the Middle Ages. You must understand that multitudes of cities, especially in France and in Germany, were then built upon mountain tops, so that they could be better fortified and defended against attack. Part of such a city would be of course on sloping ground. But the very highest place was always reserved, inside the city, for military purposes. Outside the city were walls and ditches and towers. Inside the city there was a smaller city or citadel, also surrounded by ditches and walls and towers, and occupying the highest place possible. An enemy, after capturing the city proper, would still have the citadel to capture, always a very difficult military feat. Now you will understand better the suggestions of immense height in the poem. The students are going up above the citadel to bury their teacher. They say that the place is appropriate because the air at that height is, like intellectual thought, cold and pure and full of electricity, the symbol of mental energy and moral effort. You may notice that the students are still somewhat rough in their ways. It was a rough age; they do not intend to submit to any interference on the way, nor even to any curiosity, so the ignorant "beholders" are bidden to be very careful.

At this point the poem gives us the students' account of their teacher's life. They are singing a song about it, and you must understand that all the lines in parentheses do not necessarily mean interruptions of the narrative, though some of them do. A little careful reading will make everything clear; then you will perceive how very fine the spirit of the whole thing is.

> Sleep, crop and herd! sleep, darkling thorpe and croft,
>   Safe from the weather!
> He, whom we convoy to his grave aloft,
>   Singing together,
> He was a man born with thy face and throat,
>   Lyric Apollo!
> Long he lived nameless: how should Spring take note
>   Winter would follow?
> Till lo! the little touch, and youth was gone!
>   Cramped and diminished,
> Moaned he, "New measures, other feet anon!
>   My dance is finished?"
> No, that's the world's way: (keep the mountain-side,
>   Make for the city!)
> He knew the signal, and stepped on with pride
>   Over men's pity;
> Left play for work, and grappled with the world

> Bent on escaping:
> "What's in the scroll," quoth he, "thou keepest furled?
>   Show me their shaping,
> Theirs who most studied man, the bard and sage,—
>   Give!" so he gowned him.
> Straight got by heart that book to its last page:
>   Learned, we found him.

When his first students met him, they met him as a youthful and a learned man; these latest students found him old, bald, scarcely able to see—and yet he had not allowed himself any rest.   In spite of the fact that he felt death was coming, he continued to study day and night, he read all the books then existing, and when he had read them all, he said only, "Now I have got to the beginning of my real studies.   The material is in my hands; now I shall use it." Sickness or health made no difference to him.   This life he thought of only as the commencement of eternity.

> He said, "What's Time?   Leave Now for dogs and apes!
>   Man has Forever!"
> Back to his books then; deeper drooped his head:
>   *Calculus* racked him:
> Leaden before, his eyes grew dross of lead:
>   *Tussis* attacked him.

In vain did his friends and pupils beg him to take a little rest, but he never would; he said that he must learn everything he could before dying.

> So, with the throttling hands of death at strife,
>   Ground he at grammar;
> Still, through the rattle, parts of speech were rife;
>   While he could stammer
> He settled *Hoti's* business—let it be!—
>   Properly based *Oun*—
> Gave us the doctrine of the enclitic *De*,
>   Dead from the waist down.

"Hoti" is the Greek word "that"; "Oun" is the word "then," also "now"; it has other kindred meanings.   "De" has the meaning of "toward" when enclitic; but there is another Greek word "de" meaning "but." The reference in the poem is to the rule for distinguishing the Greek "de" meaning "toward" from the Greek "de" meaning "but." "Calculus" is the disease commonly called "stone in the bladder." "Tussis" is a cough.

And now the singers have brought the body to the burial-place at the top of the mountain, and their song ends with this glorious burst:

> Well, here's the platform, here's the proper place:
> Hail to your purlieus,
> All ye highfliers of the feathered race,
> Swallows and curlews!
> Here's the top-peak; the multitude below
> Live, for they can, there;
> This man decided not to Live but Know—
> Bury this man there?
> Here—here's his place, where meteors shoot, clouds form,
> Lightnings are loosened,
> Stars come and go! Let joy break with the storm,
> Peace let the dew send!
> Lofty designs must close in like effects:
> Loftily lying,
> Leave him—still loftier than the world suspects,
> Living and dying.

We may turn from this fine poem without further comment to a piece entitled "The Patriot." There is a bit, and a very bitter bit, of the true philosophy of life in it. Nothing is so fickle, so uncertain, so treacherous as popularity. Thousands of men who tried to get the applause of the multitude, the love of the millions, and thought that they had succeeded, found out at a later day how quickly that applause could be turned into roars of hate, how quickly that seeming admiration could be changed into scorn. This fact about the instability of human favour is well known to every clear headed person who enters into what is called the social struggle; but it is more often illustrated in poli-

tics.   The political aspect of the matter is the most remarkable, and has therefore been chosen by Browning.   I
do not know to what particular person he may be making
reference—perhaps he was thinking of Rienzi.   But in all
periods of history the fact has been about the same.   You
will remember, no doubt, the case of Pericles in the history of Athens, and of many others.   You may remember
also how the French Revolution devoured its own children,
how the men that were one day almost worshipped by the
people like gods, would be dragged to the guillotine the
day after.   And even in the history of this country I think
you must remember not a few examples of how uncertain
popular favour must always be.   In this case the victim
speaks, some man who once had been regarded as the saviour of the people, but who is now regarded as their enemy,
and who is going to be executed as a common criminal, simply because he happened to be unfortunate.   He remembers the past, and contrasts it with the cruel present:

> It was roses, roses, all the way,
>   With myrtle mixed in my path like mad:
> The house-roofs seemed to heave and sway,
>   The church-spires flamed, such flags they had,
> A year ago on this very day.
>
> The air broke into a mist with bells,
>   The old walls rocked with the crowd and cries.
> Had I said: "Good folk, mere noise repels—
>   But give me your sun from yonder skies!"
> They had answered, "And afterward, what else?"

Here I may say that in Western countries from very ancient times it has been the custom to cover with flowers the
road along which some great conqueror or other honoured
person was to come.   The ancients used especially roses and
myrtles, but even to-day it is often the custom to throw
flowers on the ground before the passing of a sovereign or
other great person.   "Like mad" is an idiom used to ex-

press extreme action of any sort; "to laugh like mad," would be to laugh unreasonably and extravagantly. The reference to the apparent movement of the roofs of the houses pictures the crowding of people on the house-tops to see the hero, a custom still kept up. And the reference to the effect of the bells as making "mist," indicates the excessive volume of sound; for it is said that the firing of cannon or the making of any other great noise will often cause rain to fall. The idea is that the people rang the bells so hard that the rain fell, and these were what we call "joy-bells."

"If on that day of my triumph," he says, "I had asked them to give me the sun, they would have answered out of their hearts, Certainly—and what else?" Now it is very different indeed.

> Alack, it was I who leaped at the sun
>   To give it my loving friends to keep!
> Nought man could do, have I left undone:
>   And you see my harvest, what I reap
> This very day, now a year is run.
>
> There's nobody on the house-tops now—
>   Just a palsied few at the windows set;
> For the best of the sight is, all allow,
>   At the Shambles' Gate—or, better yet,
> By the very scaffold's foot, I trow.
>
> I go in the rain, and, more than needs,
>   A rope cuts both my wrists behind;
> And I think, by the feel, my forehead bleeds,
>   For they fling, whoever has a mind,
> Stones at me for my year's misdeeds.

What he says is this: "I did not ask them for anything for myself; it was I who wanted to give them the sun, or anything else that they wished for. Every possible sacrifice that any man could make I made for these people, and you see what my reward is to-day—just one year from the time when they honoured and revered me. Nobody now

stands on the house tops to look at me; all have gone to
the execution ground to see me die, except a few old people
who cannot walk, and who stay at the windows to see me
pass, with my hands tied behind my back.   People are
throwing stones at me, and I think my face is bleeding."
The last allusion is to a very cruel custom only of late
years abolished in England by better police regulations.   In
the old times, when a prisoner was being taken to the gallows, people would often strike him, or throw stones at him
as he went by, and nobody attempted to protect him.   To-
day this is not done, simply because the police do not allow
it, but the natural cruelty of a mob is perhaps just as great
as it ever was.

> Thus I entered, and thus I go!
>   In triumphs people have dropped down dead.
> "Paid by the world, what dost thou owe
>   Me?"—God might question; now instead,
> 'Tis God shall repay: I am safer so.

These are the man's last thoughts.   "I came into this
city a hero, as I told you; now I am going out of it, to be
executed like a vulgar criminal.   How much better would
it have been if I had died on the day when all the people
were honouring me!   I have heard that men have fallen
dead from joy in the middle of such a triumph as I then
had.   But would it have been better if I had died happy like
that?   Perhaps it would not.   God is said to demand a
strict account in the next world from any human being who
has been too happy in this.   If I had died that day, God
might have said to me, You have had your reward from the
world; have you paid to me what you owed in love and
duty?   But now the world kills me; it is from God only
that I can hope for justice.   He is terrible, but I can trust
him better than this people; I am safer with him!"
   I am not sure what Browning refers to in speaking of

those who have been known to drop dead in the middle of a triumph. But perhaps he is referring to the story of the Sicilian, Diagoras, which is one of the most beautiful of all Greek stories, and is fortunately quite true. Diagoras had been the greatest wrestler among the Greeks, the greatest athlete of his time, and was loved and honoured by all men of Greek blood. He had seven sons. When he was a very old man these seven sons went to contend at the great Olympic games (if I remember correctly). There were but seven prizes for all the feats of strength and skill; and these seven prizes were all won by the seven sons of Diagoras— that is to say, they had proved themselves the best men of the whole world at that time, even the boy son winning the prize given only to boys. Then the people demanded to know the name of the father of those young men, and the sons lifted him upon their shoulders to show him to all the people. The people shouted so that birds flying above them, fell down; and the old man in the same moment died of joy, as he was thus supported upon the shoulders of his sons. The Greeks said that this was the happiest death that any man ever died. Perhaps Browning was referring to this story; but I am not sure.

Kings have sometimes been accused of ingratitude, but on the whole, kings have shown more gratitude than mobs; a sovereign is apt to remember that it is good policy to repay loyalty and to encourage affection. Browning gives us a few magnificent specimens of loyal feeling toward sovereigns, feeling which it is pleasant to know was not repaid with ingratitude. I am referring to his "Cavalier Tunes," little songs into which he has managed to put all the fiery love and devotion of the English gentlemen who fought for the king against Cromwell and his Puritans, and who fought, luckily for England, in vain at that time. Right or wrong as we may think their cause, it is impossible not to admire the feeling here expressed. I shall quote the second song first. You must imagine that all these gentlemen are drinking the health of the king, with songs and cheers, even at the time when the king's cause seems hopeless.

GIVE A ROUSE!

King Charles, and who'll do him right now?
King Charles, and who's ripe for fight now?
Give a rouse: here's, in hell's despite now,
King Charles!

(*Single voice*)

Who gave me the goods that went since?
Who raised me the house that sank once?
Who helped me to gold I spent since?
Who found me in wine you drank once?

(*Chorus, answering*)

King Charles, and who'll do him right now?
King Charles, and who's ripe for fight now?
Give a rouse: here's, in hell's despite now,
King Charles!

(*Single voice*)

To whom used my boy George quaff else,
By the old fool's side that begot him?
For whom did he cheer and laugh else,
While Noll's damned troopers shot him?

(*Chorus, answering*)

King Charles, and who'll do him right now?
King Charles, and who's ripe for fight now?
Give a rouse: here's, in hell's despite now,
King Charles!

The father is reminding his friends of the brave death of his own son, who died shouting for the king and laughing at his executioners. I do not think that there is a more spirited song in English literature than this. Perhaps you may observe that the measure in the third stanza does not run smoothly like the measure of the other stanzas; it hesitates a little. But this is a great stroke of art, for it indicates the suppressed emotion of the father speaking of his dead son. The other song, the first of the three given by Browning, represents the feeling of an earlier time in the civil war, probably the time when the aristocracy and gentry first gathered together to defend the king. There is a splendid swing in it. Both songs are a little rough, because the spirit of the age was rough; the finest gentleman used to swear in those days, and to use words which we now consider rather violent. I may remark, however, that even to-day in the upper ranks of the English army and navy, something of the same scorn of conventions still remains; generals and admirals will swear occasionally in battle, just as these gentlemen of an older school swore as they advanced against the Puritan armies.

MARCHING ALONG

Kentish Sir Byng stood for his King,
Bidding the crop-headed Parliament swing:
And, pressing a troop unable to stoop
And see the rogues flourish and honest men droop,
Marched them along, fifty-score strong,
Great-hearted gentlemen, singing this song.

God for King Charles! Pym and such carles
To the Devil that prompts 'em their treasonous parles!
Cavaliers, up! Lips from the cup,
Hands from the pasty, nor bite take nor sup
Till you're—
(*Chorus*)   Marching along, fifty-score strong,
         Great-hearted gentlemen, singing this song.

Hampden to hell, and his obsequies' knell
Serve Hazelrig, Fiennes, and young Harry as well!
England, good cheer! Rupert is near!
Kentish and loyalists, keep we not here,
(*Chorus*)   Marching along, fifty-score strong,
         Great-hearted gentlemen, singing this song.

Then God for King Charles! Pym and his snarls
To the Devil that pricks on such pestilent carles!
Hold by the right, you double your might;
So, onward to Nottingham, fresh for the fight,
(*Chorus*)   March we along, fifty-score strong,
         Great-hearted gentlemen, singing this song.

The names in this poem are all of them great names of the Civil War. Hampden, you know, was Parliamentary leader in the movement against the king. He was killed in battle, and his place as leader was taken by Pym. The other names are of members of the Long Parliament—except Rupert. Rupert, or Prince Rupert, as he is more generally known, was the leader of the Royal cavalry, one of the most brilliant cavalry leaders of history. He was never beaten seriously until he met Cromwell's Puritan cavalry. A reference may be necessary in regard to Nottingham. There was no fight exactly at Nottingham; but it was at Nottingham that the cavalry gathered round the king's standard before the battle of Edgehill, near Banbury, a drawn battle, not decided either way.

So much for the references. As for the song itself, something remains to be said. I think that the two songs are about the most spirited in English literature. They are so for many reasons, especially because of the fiery emotion which the poet has flung into them, and because of their absolute truth to the feeling of the seventeenth century, both as to form and as to tone. But I wonder whether any of you have noticed what it is that gives such uncommon force to the verses. To a great degree, it is the use of triple rhymes. In both songs the rhymes are triple, while the measure is short, and the result is something of that rough strength which characterises the old Northern poetry. For instance:

> Hold by the *right*, you double your *might*,
> So onward to Nottingham, fresh for the *fight*.

> King Charles, and who'll do him *right* now?
> King Charles, and who's ripe for *fight* now?
> Give a rouse: here's in hell's *despite* now,
> 　King Charles!

You see that very great effects may be produced by very simple means. In "Marching Along," the "swing" or "lilt" is partly due to the fact that the three rhymes follow each other not in regular but in irregular succession, a rhymeless measure alternating between the second and the third rhymes, as will be plainly seen if we write the verses in another form:

Kentish Sir *Byng*
Stood for his *king*,
Bidding the crop-headed
Parliament *swing*.

But I want to explain the spirit rather than the workmanship of Browning; and I have turned aside here to the subject of measure only because the instances happened to be very extraordinary. The beauty of the work is really in the glow and strength of the loyal feeling that peals through it.

Do not suppose, however, that the poet picks out by preference the noble or the attractive side of human feeling in any form of society, for his subject. Quite the contrary. Most often he paints the ugly side, even in speaking of kings and courts, nobles and princes. In the splendid poem "Count Gismond," which I dictated last year, you may have seen one very beautiful side of knightly character, but there were horrible phases of human nature exhibited in the story. Browning made the shadows very heavy, with the result that the lights appeared more dazzling. Sometimes we have no lights—all is shadow, and sometimes a shadow of hell. Such is the case in the horrible poem called "The Laboratory," depicting the feelings of a jealous court-lady, as she stands in the laboratory of a chemist who is selling her a poison with which she intends to poison her rival in the favour of the king. The story is laid in the time of Louis XIV, probably, when such things did actually occur in France. A still blacker shadow, a still more infernal picture of humanity's dark side, is "The Heretic's Tragedy," portraying the wicked feelings of a superstitious person while watching a heretic being burned alive. Another frightful

thing is "The Confessional," a story of the Inquisition in
Spain, showing how the inquisitors succeeded in seizing, con-
victing, and burning alive a young man, by taking advantage of the innocence of his sweetheart, who was made to
betray him through confession without knowing it.   Another piece that is ugly psychologically, is "Cristina and
Monaldeschi."   Cristina was a queen of Sweden, and one of
the most learned women of her time, but very masculine;
she liked to wear men's clothes and to follow the amuse-
ments of men.   She abdicated her throne, merely in order
to feel more free in her habits.   It is believed that she secretly loved her private secretary, and that he was dishon-
ourable enough to tell other people of his relation to her.
At all events, one day she ordered him to come into her
room, and after upbraiding him with treachery to her, she
had him killed in her presence.   The fact shocked Europe
a great deal at the time.   Browning tries to make us understand Cristina's feeling, and he forces us to sympathise a
little with her anger.   There are multitudes of poems of
this class in Browning.   He wants us to know all the
strange possibilities of the human soul, bad or good, and he
never hesitates because a subject may be shocking to weak
nerves.   It is just because he does not care about public
feeling, ignorant public opinion, upon these matters, that
he manages to give us such exact truth; he is not afraid.
For a little bit of truth thus exemplified—this is not ugly
—let us take a little piece entitled "Which?"   Here is another picture of the manners of the old French court, a very
corrupt court and very luxurious.   You must read Taine's
"Ancien Régime" to understand what its morals were.   But
let us turn to the little picture.   Three great ladies are talking with a priest about love—a fashionable priest, a priest
of the old age, ready to make love or to say mass just according as it suited his private interest.   A very good priest
could scarcely have existed in the court; one had to be very
clever and very subtle to live there.   The conversation of

these four persons gives us a hint of the feeling of the age. Only one woman really seems to say what she thinks; and she says what she thinks only because she is the most clever of the three.

> So, the three Court-ladies began
>   Their trial of who judged best
> In esteeming the love of a man:
> Who preferred with most reason was thereby confessed
> Boy-Cupid's exemplary catcher and cager;
> An Abbé crossed legs to decide on the wager.
>
> First the Duchesse: "Mine for me—
>   Who were it but God's for Him,
> And the King's for—who but he?
> Both faithful and loyal, one grace more shall brim
> His cup with perfection: a lady's true lover,
> He holds—save his God and his king—none above her."
>
> "I require"—outspoke the Marquise—
>   "Pure thoughts, ay, but also fine deeds:
> Play the paladin must he, to please
> My whim, and—to prove my knight's service exceeds
> Your saint's and your loyalist's praying and kneeling—
> Show wounds, each wide mouth to my mercy appealing."
>
> Then the Comtesse: "My choice be a wretch,
>   Mere losel in body and soul,
> Thrice accurst! What care I, so he stretch
> Arms to me his sole saviour, love's ultimate goal,
> Out of earth and men's noise—names of 'infidel,' 'traitor,'
> Cast up at him? Crown me, crown's adjudicator!"
>
> And the Abbé uncrossed his legs,
>   Took snuff, a reflective pinch,
> Broke silence: "The question begs
> Much pondering ere I pronounce. Shall I flinch?
> The love which to one and one only has reference
> Seems terribly like what perhaps gains God's preference."

The answer of the priest, giving the victory to the Comtesse, is clever and double-edged. He probably knows everything that goes on in the court: he knows how many lovers the Duchesse has had, and the Marquise. He knows that their talk about religion and loyalty as the perfections of man, are not quite sincere. Indeed, the Marquise is much more sincere than the Duchesse; but if she were altogether sincere, she would have recognised that her wish—her expressed wish, at least—must appear as pure pride, not anything else. But the Comtesse tells a bitter truth by pointing out that if it is a question of real love, the place and station of the man can signify nothing at all; love should be a thing of the heart, not a thing of rank and fashion. And the priest, in supporting her claim and in saying that a true love can have reference only to one person, really suggests to his audience, whose love relations have doubtless been very numerous, what he thinks to be the opinion of God on the subject. But "perhaps," as the priest utters the word, is terrible irony. "Perhaps gains God's preference," means "I know, of course, that in the society to which we belong, love only for one's husband is not considered fashionable; yet the opinions of God may not be the same as the opinions of our society. It would not be polite of me to say directly that your opinions and God's opinions are different, but I just hint it." It was a very queer age. Taine, in his history of the time, tells a story about a nobleman who, on entering his wife's room suddenly and finding her making love to another man, took off his hat and saluted her, saying, "Oh, my dear, how can you be so careless! Suppose it had not been your husband who opened the door!" You must understand all this, to understand the mockery of the poem. Then, again, you must understand the desire of the Comtesse even for the love of a "wretch," a mere losel, as meaning that here is a woman who deserves to be loved, but is not loved by her husband, and who has learned that real love has a value in this world beyond all value of rank or money or influence.

If you ask me why I have talked so much about so short

a poem, the answer is that nearly all of Browning's short poems mean a great deal, and force us to think and to talk about them. The reason is that the characters in these poems are really alive; they impress us exactly as living persons do, and excite our curiosity in precisely the same way. Accordingly, notwithstanding their many faults of construction and obscure English, they have something of the greatness of Shakespeare's dramas.

It is now time to turn to the study of the greatest of all Browning's poems. Perhaps I should not call it a poem. It is rather an immense poetic drama. As printed in this single volume it represents four hundred and seventy-seven pages of closely printed small text. It is, therefore, even considered as a dramatic composition, many times larger than any true drama. But no true drama, except Shakespeare's, is more real or more terrible. Besides, it is a purely psychological drama. There is no scenery, no narrative in the ordinary sense. Everything is related in the first person. The whole is divided into twelve parts, each of which is a monologue. Nearly all of the monologues are spoken by different persons. The first monologue is the author's own, in which he tells us the meaning of the title and the story of the drama.

It is a true story of Italian life in the seventeenth century, the chief incident having really occurred in the year 1698. The poet one day found in an old Italian book shop a little book for sale, which was the history of a celebrated criminal trial. Besides the book, which included the speeches of the lawyers on both sides, and the evidence given before the court, there was a good deal of old manuscript—papers probably prepared by some lawyer of the time in connection with the case. Browning was able to buy the whole thing for eight pence; that small sum furnished him with material for the most enormous poem in the English language. When he read the facts of the trial, he said he could actually see all the characters as plainly

as if they were alive, and could even hear them speak.
He soon formed in his mind the plan for his poem; but
it was a peculiar plan.   The plan is indicated by the title
of "The Ring and the Book."   In Italy there is a great
deal of beautiful light gold work made—for rings especially,
which looks so delicate that at first sight you cannot understand how it was made.   In a gold ring there are leaves
and flowers and fruits and insects, so lightly made that even
if you let the ring fall they would be injured or destroyed.
Gold is very soft.   In order to cut the gold in this way, the
goldsmith uses a hard composition with which he covers
the gold work, and after the carving and engraving have
been done, this composition is melted off, so that only the
pure gold is left, with all the work upon it.   Browning says
that he made his book somewhat in the same way that the
Italian goldsmith makes his ring—by the use of an alloy.
The facts of history and of law represent the gold in this
case, and the poet mixes them with an alloy of imagination, emotion, sympathy, which helps him to make the whole
story into a perfectly rounded drama, a complete circle, a
Ring.   This is the meaning of the title.

I shall first tell you the story briefly, according to the
historical facts.   About the year 1679 there was a family
in Rome of the name of Comparini.   The family consisted
only of husband and wife; but it happened that the fact
of their being without children proved a legal obstacle in
the way of obtaining some money which they greatly desired.   The wife, Violante, knew that her husband was too
honest to wish to cheat the law, so she determined to try
to get the money without letting him know her deceit in the
matter.   She pretended to have given birth, unexpectedly,
to a child, but the child had really been bought from a woman
of loose life—it was a very pretty female child, and was
called Francesca Pompilia.   Little Pompilia was supposed
to be the real child of the Comparini; and the much desired

money thus passed into their hands.   This is the first act of the tragedy.

Pompilia grew up into a wonderfully beautiful girl; and when she was thirteen years old, many people wished to marry her.   Guido Franceschini, Count of Arezzo, noticed the girl's beauty, and heard that she was rich.   He determined to marry her if possible, chiefly for the sake of her money.   He was a wicked old man, between fifty and sixty years of age, ugly, cunning, and poor.   But he had immense influence, both among the nobility and among the church dignitaries, on account of his family relations; and he was himself of high rank.   The marriage was negotiated successfully.   Pompilia, a child of thirteen, could not naturally have wished to marry this horrible old man, but she had been taught to obey her parents as she obeyed Almighty God, and when she was told to marry him she married him without one word of complaint.   By this marriage the wicket Count got into his hands all the property of the Comparini family, but it had been promised that the parents of the girl were to live in the palace of the Count, and to be taken care of for the rest of their lives.   Nevertheless, as soon as the Count had everything in his hands, he turned the old parents out of his house, in a state of absolute destitution; he had taken from them their daughter and all their money, everything that they had in the world.   This is the second act of the tragedy.

Naturally the Comparini family were very angry.   The mother of the girl was so angry that she told her husband all about the trick which she had played in passing off Pompilia for her own child.   Pompilia, you know, was not her real child at all.   This changed the legal aspect of the matter.   Old Comparini went to the Count and said, "You took our money, and thought that you were taking our daughter.   But you must give back that money.   The girl is not our daughter; the money does not belong to her: it will have to be given back to the government that we deceived." This is the third act of the tragedy.

The Count was equal to the occasion. He understood the law; but he understood it much better than the Comparini people. So long as he kept Pompilia as his wife, he knew that he could keep the money. If he divorced her, on the ground that she was of vulgar origin, then he would have to give up the money. But this was not the only alternative. There was a third possibility. If Pompilia committed adultery, then he could either kill her or get rid of her and keep the money notwithstanding. Pompilia was a weak child only thirteen years old. He was a wicked and terrible man, with half a century of experience, diabolical cunning, diabolical cruelty, and ferocious determination. He could make her commit adultery. That would be the simplest possible solution of the difficulty. But, strange to say, this terrible man could not conquer that delicate child of thirteen. First he tried to appeal to her passions, to excite her imagination in an immoral way. But her heart was too pure to be corrupted. There was in her no spur of lust. She was a simple good pure wife, too pure for any wicked ideas to be planted in her mind. Then he tried force, atrocious cruelty, horrible menace, always without letting her know what he really intended. What he really intended was to force her to run away from him. She could not run away except in the company of a protector. If she ran away with a protector, then he could kill both her and the man and claim that he had detected the two in adultery. After having tortured the girl hideously, in every moral and immoral way, he did succeed in getting her to ask for protection. She first asked protection from priests and bishops. The priests and bishops were afraid of the Count, and told her, like the cowards that they were, that they could not help her. She wanted to become a nun. The nuns were afraid of the Count, and refused her prayer. At last she did find one priest, a brave man, who was willing to save her if possible. He said, "You must run away with me, though it will look very bad; there is no other way to help you." She ran away with him. Within twenty-four hours the pair were overtaken by the Count and his company of armed men. The opportunity to kill Pompilia and her "lover" had come; but the so-called "lover," although only an honest poor priest, showed fight, and protected Pompilia against the Count and all his followers. The priest refused to surrender Pompilia except to the Church. The Church arrested both. Pompilia was put into a convent for safe keeping. The priest was tried for adultery, and acquitted. But he had done wrong by breaking the law of the Church even for a good purpose; therefore he was sentenced to banishment for a certain number of years. This is the fourth act of the tragedy.

The Count finds that all his plans have failed. He has not been able to convict his wife of adultery, although he has been able to injure her reputation in the opinion of the public. He cannot get rid of her, and keep her money too, except by killing her. But she is in the convent. While he is thinking what to do, another event happens which upsets all his calculations. Pompilia gives birth to a child of which he certainly is the father. The money question, the legal aspect of it, is still more complicated by the birth of the child. At once the Count determines to kill Pompilia and her parents, out of revenge. He knows that on certain days she goes to visit her parents. He watches for such an occasion, and with the help of some professional murderers, he kills the Comparini, and stabs Pompilia twenty-two times with a dagger. He imagined that this could be done so as to remain undiscovered; he thought that the crime could not be proved upon him. But poor Pompilia is very hard to kill. Although her slender body was thus stabbed through and through by a powerful man, she did not die at once; her wonderful youth kept her alive long enough to tell the police what had happened. The

Count and his hired murderers were arrested and thrown into prison. This is the fifth act of the tragedy.

It is one thing to find the author of a crime, and put him into prison; it is a very different thing to convict and punish him. The Count was very powerful with the army, with the nobility, with the Church; everybody in his native city was more afraid of him than of the devil. Nothing is so hard to get in this world as justice. The Count's powerful friends and relations all united to defend him. Dukes and great captains, cardinals and bishops and abbots and priests, rich merchants, influential statesmen, all combined to secure his acquittal. They obtained the services of great lawyers. They used money and threats to corrupt witnesses or to terrify them. Yet there was one thing necessary to secure his acquittal—evidence that the deed, which he cannot deny, was justified by adultery. An attempt was made to blacken the character of the murdered wife. But this evidence was overthrown in the court, and the judges pronounced sentence of death. Thereupon all the Count's friends made an appeal to the Pope; the Pope can save the Count, if pressure be brought of a sufficient sort upon his judgment. But the Pope happened to be a good man, and a keen man. He examines the evidence. He sees the truth. He understands the innocence and beauty of the character of the murdered Pompilia; he comprehends also the innocence and the courage of the priest who tried to defend her. He sends word to the prison that the Count must be executed immediately. So justice is obtained, at least so far as the punishment of murder can be called justice. But what becomes of the money? The nuns of the convent in which Pompilia died, they get the money by very discreditable means, and they keep it. The terrible Franceschini family cannot try to get that money from the convent; for the convent means the power of the Church; and the power of the Church is even more terrible than the power of the Franceschini. Of course the Pope knows nothing of this matter; the Pope is the finest character in the whole story. Historically this Pope was Innocent XII, but his character, as drawn in the study of Browning, is much more like the character of one of his predecessors, Innocent XI.

Now I have told you the story, or rather the history of the real tragedy, which happened something more than two hundred years ago. You can imagine how complicated the whole thing is, from the very short summary which I have made. Now if you had to treat a story like this dramatically, how would you do it? where would you begin? in what way could you hope to make artistic order out of such confusion? The task might have puzzled even Shakespeare. It puzzled Browning for more than a year before he felt how the thing was possible to manage. When I tell you the way in which he treated the whole material of the case, I think you will perceive that only a genius could have thought of the way.

As I have said, Browning divides his poem into twelve parts; and each part is a monologue. I shall now give you in paragraphs as brief as possible, the subject of each monologue. You had better follow the order of the book, using Roman numerals at the beginning of each paragraph, and putting the title of the book in Italic letters:

I. *The Ring and the Book.* Interpretation of the title, and history of the crime and the trial as told in the ancient legal documents. This monologue represents the author's speaking only.

II. *Half-Rome.* Public opinion is always divided upon any extraordinary event. Browning here tries to give us one side of public opinion in the year 1698, upon the Franceschini murder. The monologue represents the ideas of a man of the society of that time.

III. *The Other Half Rome.* This monologue represents the contrary opinion on the subject. But it is a curious fact that neither form of public opinion even approaches the truth. Both sides are absolutely mistaken, and very unjust to poor Pompilia.

IV. *Tertium Quid* (i.e., "a third somebody" or "party"). This opinion is quite different from that of the two halves of Rome, but it is equally far from the truth.

V. *Count Guido Franceschini.* Notice that although the three forms of opinion previously expressed all contradict each other, and all are untrue, nevertheless every one of them seems true while you read it. So does the story of Count Guido Franceschini, the murderer, in his own defence. Although you have been prejudiced against him from the beginning, when you first read his side of the story you cannot help thinking that it is a very reasonable and very true story. He says in substance that he made a great mistake in marrying so young a girl, that she disliked him, that he did everything in his power to obtain her affection and to make her happy, that she ran away from his house with a monk, that even after that he was willing to make every allowance for her, but that at last it was impossible for him, without losing all self-respect, not to punish her crimes, and those of her infamous parents. He makes an excellent speech, this Count Guido Franceschini.

VI. *Giuseppe Caponsacchi.* This is the good priest, the true loyal man that tried to save Pompilia. He tells his story with perfect truthfulness and simplicity, and you know that it is true. But at the same time you feel that no one can believe it. The evidence is against the priest. Although he is innocent, everybody laughs at his protestations of innocence.

VII. *Pompilia.* This is the most horrible part of the book. It is a monologue by Pompilia telling of the cruelty and the atrocious wickedness of her husband. It makes your blood run cold to read it, but you know that nobody would believe that story in a court of justice. It is too terrible, too unnatural. Those who hear it only think that Pompilia is a very cunning wicked woman, trying to make people hate her husband, in order to excuse her own adultery.

VIII. *Dominus Hyocinthus de Archangelis, Pauperum Procurator.* The speech of the lawyer for the defence, very cautious, very learned, very cunning. It was in those days the custom to argue such cases partly in Latin, and the papers were made out in Latin. "Dominus," "lord," was the Latin title of lawyer. "Pauperum Procurator" means the advocate or counsel of the poor; persons without money enough to procure legal services in the ordinary way, might be furnished with a lawyer employed by the state.

IX. *Juris Doctor Johannes-Battista, &c.* The speech of the lawyer on the other side, equally learned, equally cunning, and equally cautious. The reader is forced to the conclusion that neither of these lawyers really understands the truth of the case. Both are telling untruth, and both are afraid of the truth. But you will notice that the lawyer who should speak in favour of Pompilia really does her more harm than the lawyer whose duty it is to speak against her. This is the result of cowardice and self-interest on both sides.

X. *The Pope.* A beautiful study of character. For the first time we learn the truth in this tenth monologue, so that we feel it is all there, and not to be mistaken by any one who hears it.

XI. *Guido.* Horrible. The murderer's confession of his own character.

XII. *The Book and the Ring.* Conclusion, and moral commentary.

I believe there is only part of this whole drama that has been seriously called into question by critics—the last line of the eleventh monologue, where Guido cries out, "Pompilia, will you let them murder me?" The question is whether the poet is right in representing this terrible man in such a passion of fear that he calls to his dead wife to help him. Certainly it is a general rule that the man ca-

pable of studied cruelty to women and children—to the
weak, in short—is a coward at heart. But there are exceptions to this rule, and a great many remarkable Italian exceptions. Again many tribes of savages contradict the rule,
being at once brave and cruel. I think that the criticism
in this case may have been largely inspired by the history
of certain Italian families, who were cruel indeed, but fe-
rociously brave as well. However, Browning studied the
facts for his characters very closely, and he may be right
in representing Guido as a coward. He has been proved
to be both treacherous and avaricious by the evidence in the
case, and although prudence may sometimes be mistaken for
cowardice, there were some facts brought out by witnesses
that seem to show the man to have been as much of a coward
as he was a miser.

Now observe the immense psychological work that this
treatment of the story involves—the study of nine or ten
completely different characters, no one of whom could re-
semble a character of the nineteenth century, not at least
in the matter of thought and speech. To create these was
almost as wonderful as to call the dead of two hundred
years ago out of their graves, a veritable necromancy. This
work alone would make the book a marvellous thing. But
the book is more than marvellous; it is in the highest degree philosophically instructive. Almost anything that
happens in this world is judged somewhat after the fashion
of the judgments delivered in the "Ring and the Book."
For example, let us suppose an episode in Tokyo to-day,
rather than an episode in Italy two hundred years ago, a
case of killing. At first when the mere fact of the killing
is known, there is a great curiosity as to the reason of it,
and different newspapers publish different stories about it,
and different people who knew both parties express different opinions as to the why and how. You may be sure
that none of these accounts is perfectly true—they could
not be true, because those from whom the accounts come

have no perfect knowledge of the antecedents of the crime. But presently the case comes before the criminal court, with lawyers on both sides, to prosecute and to defend. Each does his duty the very best he can, one trying to convict, one trying to secure acquittal. But do these know the real story from beginning to end? Probably not. It is very seldom indeed that a lawyer can learn the inside, the psychological, history of a crime. He learns only the naked facts, and he must theorise largely from these facts. Finally the judge pronounces judgment. Does the judge know all about the matter? Almost certainly not. His duty is fixed by law in rigid lines, and he cannot depart from those lines; he can sentence only according to the broad conclusions which he draws from the facts. And after the whole thing is over, still the real secrets of the two parties, of the criminal and the victim, remain forever unknown in a majority of cases. Now what does this prove? It proves that human judgment is necessarily very imperfect, and that nothing is so difficult to learn as the absolute truth of motives and of feelings, even when the truth of the facts is unquestionable. Browning's book tells us more than this; it shows us that in some cases, where power and crime are on one side, and poverty and virtue upon the other, the chances against truth being able to make itself heard are just about a thousand to one. Of course the world is a little better to-day than two hundred years ago; murder is less common, justice is less corrupt. But allowing for these things, the chances of a man persecuted by a rich corporation, without reason, perhaps with monstrous cruelty, to obtain even a hearing, would be scarcely better than those of Pompilia in the story of "The Ring and the Book."

So much for the teaching. There is more than teaching, however; there are studies of character truly Shakespearian. Pompilia is quite as sweet a woman as Shakespeare's Cordelia. Her sweetness is altogether shown by a multitude of details, little words and thoughts and feelings, that we find scattered through her account of her terrible sufferings. The author never interrupts his speakers; he makes them describe themselves. In the case of the Pope, we are brought into the presence of a very superior intellect—one-sided, perhaps, but immensely strong in the direction of moral judgment; the mind of an old man whose entire life has been spent in the finest study of human nature from an ethical point of view, of human nature in its manifestations of good and evil. Nothing but this long experience helps him to see exactly how matters stand. The evidence brought before him is hopelessly confused, and where not confused, the facts are against Pompilia and strongly in favour of the murderer. Moreover, the murderer is powerful in the Church, with all the influence of clergy and nobility upon his side. But the old man can see through the entire plot; he cuts it open, gets to the heart of it, perceives everything that was hidden. What is the lesson of his character? I think it is this, that a pure nature obtains, simply by reason of its unselfishness and purity, certain classes of perceptions that very cunning minds never can obtain. Very cunning people are peculiarly apt to make false judgments, because they are particularly in the habit of looking for selfish motives. They judge other hearts by their own. A pure nature does not do this; it considers the motive in the last rather than the first place, preferring to judge kindly so long as the evidence allows it. Intellectual training cannot always compensate for purity of character.

The studies of Guido himself, which are very horrible, are especially studies of the man of the Renaissance. We have had other studies of this kind in other poems of Browning, some of which I have already quoted to you. But there is a special moral in this study of Guido, the moral that a really wicked man must hate a really good woman, simply for the reason that she is good. Then we have in the two lawyers, two pictures of conflicting selfish interests, of selfishness and falsehood combined to defeat the truth, not because truth is necessarily unpleasant to the lawyer, but because he wants to make no enemies by exposing it. This is the way of the world to-day, and although these men speak the language of the sixteenth or seventeenth century, their feelings are those of the shrewd and selfish modern man of society, the man who has no courage in the face of wrong, if his pocket happens to be in danger. We like only three characters in the whole drama—Pompilia, the Pope, and Caponsacchi. Yet there is nothing very remarkable about Caponsacchi, except in the way of contrast. He is the one character who, although his life and interests and reputation are at stake, boldly risks everything simply for a generous impulse. Happily he is not extraordinary; if he were, one would lose faith in so terrible a world. Happily we know that wherever and whenever a great wrong is done, there will always be a Caponsacchi to speak out and to do all that is possible against it. But Caponsacchi is crushed; and even the Pope is obliged to punish him for doing what is noble. This is one of the moral problems of the composition. The man who wants to do right, and cannot do right except by disobedience to law, may be loved for doing right, but he must be punished nevertheless for breaking the law. Does this mean that he is punished for doing right? I think we should not look at it in that way. The truth is that the observance of discipline must be insisted upon even in exceptional cases, because it regards the happiness of millions. We cannot allow men to decide for themselves when discipline should be broken. Caponsacchi is thus a martyr in the cause of individual justice. He has to pay, justly, the penalty of setting a dangerous example to thousands of others. But he is not on that account less estimable and lovable, and even the Pope, in punishing him, gives him words of warm praise.

The consideration of this huge poem ought also to tempt some of you at a later day to try some application of its method to some incident of real life. I do not now mean in poetry, but in prose. If you know enough about human nature to make the attempt, there is no better way of telling a story. It was a pure invention on the part of Browning, and we may call it a new method. But of course one must have a very great power of reading character to be able to do anything of the same kind.

This is the most colossal attempt in psychology made by Browning, but a large number of his longer poems are worked out in precisely the same manner as single monologues. "The Bishop Orders his Tomb," another Italian study, gives us all the ugly side of the Renaissance character—its selfishness, lust, hypocrisy, and ambition, together with that extraordinary sense of art which gave a certain greatness even to very bad men. "Bishop Blougram's Apology" (which is said to be a satire upon a famous English Cardinal) is quite modern, but it is almost equally ugly. It shows us a very powerful mind arguing, with irresistible logic and merciless cleverness, in an absolutely unworthy cause. The bishop has heard a young free thinker observe that the bishop could not believe the doctrines of the church, he was too clever a bishop for that. So he calls the young man to him, and utterly crushes him by a very clever lecture, in which he proves that belief or unbelief are equally foolish, that right and wrong are interchangeable, that black may be white or white black, that common sense and a knowledge of the world represent the highest wisdom, and that the free thinker is an absolute fool because he tells the world that he is a free thinker. We know that the bishop is morally wrong the whole way through, that every statement which he makes is wrong; yet it would take a clever man to prove him wrong. The logic is too well managed. Few psychological studies are comparable to this. "Mr. Sludge, 'the Medium,'" said

to be a satire upon the great Scottish spiritualist and humbug, Home, shows us another kind of quackery; a man who
lives by imposture explains to us how he can practise imposture with a good moral conscience, and under the belief
that imposture is a benefit to mankind. He talks so well
that he obliges even the person who has detected his imposture to lend him or give him a considerable sum of
money—in short, he can trick even those who know his
trickery. But see how different these beings are from each
other, and how different the studies of their character must
necessarily prove. Yet Browning seems never to find any
difficulty in painting the mind of a man, whether good or
bad, whether of to-day or of the Middle Ages. "Par-
acelsus," for example, is a mediæval character; Browning
makes him tell us the story of his researches into alchemy
and magic, makes him impart to us the secret ambition that
once filled him, and the consequences of disappointment and
of failure. "Sordello," again, is of the thirteenth century;
you will find his name in the great poem of Dante. Sordello was a poet and troubadour, who tried to succeed
socially and politically by the exercise of a brilliant talent,
and almost did succeed. Browning's poem on him is the
whole story of a human soul; only, it is the man himself who tells it. And the moral is that suffering and sorrow bring wisdom. How various and how wonderful is
this range of character-study! Yet I have mentioned only
a few out of scores and scores of compositions. I cannot
insist too much upon this quality of versatility in Browning, this display of Shakespearian power. In all Tennyson you will find scarcely more than twenty really distinct characters; and some of these are but half drawn.
In Rossetti you will find scarcely more than half a dozen,
mostly women. In Swinburne there is no character whatever, except the poet's own, outside of that grand singer's
dramatic work. But in Browning there are hundreds of
distinct characters, and there is nothing at all vague about

them; they speak, they move, they act with real and not with artificial life. Sometimes a character may occupy a hundred pages, sometimes it may be drawn in half a dozen lines, but the drawing is equally distinct and equally true. And there is scarcely any kind of human nature of which we have no picture. Even the lowest type of savage is drawn, the primitive savage, for "Caliban upon Setebos" gives us the thoughts and feelings of such a savage about God—God being figured in the savage mind, of course, as only a much stronger and larger kind of savage, possessing magical power.

In all his poems, as I said, Browning is essentially dramatic. Quite rightly has he grouped several collections of short poems under titles which suggest this fact, such as "Dramatic Idyls," "Dramatis Personæ," "Men and Women." Sometimes the poet himself is the only speaker and actor, giving us his own particular feelings of the moment; but in the most noteworthy cases of this kind he is talking, not to the reader, but to ghosts. For instance, "Parleyings with Certain People of Importance in Their Day," are imaginary conversations which Browning holds with the ghosts of men long dead—writers, philosophers, statesmen, priests. It is in this collection that you will find the remarkable verses on the great poem of Smart, which revived Smart's work for modern readers after a hundred years of oblivion. I cannot find time to tell you about the other personages of these imaginary conversations; but I may mention that Mandeville is the subject of a special conversation, and that you will find the whole germ of Mandeville's philosophy in this composition. But let us turn to some consideration of Browning's work in the true dramatic form—in plays, tragedies or comedies, and in translations of plays from the Greek.

It would require several lectures to give a summary of Browning's plays; and they do not always represent his best genius. For it is a curious fact that this man who, as a simple poet, was the greatest of English dramatists after Shakespeare, was rarely quite successful when he attempted the true dramatic form. He was great in the monologue; he was not great upon the stage. Some of his plays were acted, such as "Strafford" and "The Blot on the 'Scutcheon"; but they did not prove to be worthy of great success. "In a Balcony," which could not be put upon the stage at all, is much better; and perhaps it is better because it consists only of two monologues, or rather of a conversation between two persons; for the part taken by the other actors is altogether insignificant. "The Return of the Druses" and "Luria," like Tennyson's dramas, are excellent poetry, but they are not suited for the stage. The best of all Browning's dramas, the only one that I really want you to read, is "A Soul's Tragedy." I may say a word about the plot of this. It is a story of friendship between two young men, patriots and statesmen. In a political crisis one of the young men stabs a political enemy, and has fled from the country. But before fleeing, he trusts all his interests and his property to his friend, and asks the friend also to take care of his betrothed. What does the friend do? Exposed to great temptation, he betrays his trust. He sees a chance to obtain political power by pretending to be the man who really stabbed the politician on the other side—the tyrant of an hour. The people acclaim him as their saviour, make him dictator. Then he goes further in his treachery, by making love to his friend's sweetheart. At last a Roman statesman, Ogniben, appears upon the scene, with power to crush the revolution, or to do anything that he pleases. But Ogniben is a terribly clever man, and he does not want blood-shed; he knows the character of the new dictator, and determines to play with him, as a cat with a mouse. First he flatters him enough to make him betray all his weaknesses, his vanities, his fears. Then, at quite the unexpected moment, he summons the young man who had run away, I mean the friend betrayed, and brings him face to face with the treacherous dictator. The result is of course a moral collapse; that is the real Soul's Tragedy. I am giving only a thin skeleton of the plot. But you ought to read this play, if only for the wonderful studies of character in it, not the least remarkable of which is the awful Ogniben, far-seeing, cunning beyond cunning, strong beyond force, who can unravel plots with a single word and pierce all masks of hypocrisy with a single glance; but whom you feel to be, in a large way, generous and kindly, and so far as possible, just. I think not only that this is Browning's greatest play, but that as a play it is psychologically superior to anything else which has been done in Victorian drama. It is not fit for the stage, and it is not even very great as poetry—indeed half of it or more is prose, and rather eccentric prose; but it offers wonderful examples of analytical power not surpassed in any other contemporary poet or dramatist.

About Browning's translations from the Greek poets, I scarcely know what to say. Most critics of authority acknowledge that Browning has made the most faithful metrical translation of the "Agamemnon" of Æschylus. But they also declare that in spite of its exactness, the Greek spirit and feeling have entirely vanished under Browning's treatment. My own feeling about the matter is that you would do much better to read the prose translation of Æschylus. Yet I could not say this in regard to Browning's translation of the "Alkestis" of Euripides, which you will find embodied in the text of "Balaustian's Adventure." Balaustian is a Greek dancing girl. She is taken prisoner with many Athenian people at the time of the disastrous Greek expedition to Syracuse, which you must have read about in history. To please her captors, she repeats for them the wonderful verses of Euripides, by which they are so much affected that they pardon both her and her companions. This incident is founded upon fact, and Browning uses it very well to introduce his translation.

Perhaps the genius of Euripides was closer to the genius of Browning than that of Æschylus; for this translation is incomparably better from an emotional point of view than the other. It is very beautiful indeed; and even after having read the Greek play in a good prose translation, I think that you would find both pleasure and profit in reading Browning's verses.

The important thing now for you to get clearly into your minds is one general fact about this enormously various work of Browning. Suppose somebody should ask you what is different in the work of Browning from that of all other modern poets, what would you be able to answer? But unless you can answer, the whole value of this lecture would be lost upon you. Browning himself has excellently answered, in a little verse which forms the prologue to the second series of the Dramatic Idyls.

> "You are sick, that's sure,"—they say:
> "Sick of what?"—they disagree.
> " 'Tis the brain,"—thinks Doctor A;
> " 'Tis the heart,"—holds Doctor B.
> "The liver—my life I'd lay!"
> "The lungs!" "The lights!" Ah me!
> So ignorant of man's whole
> Of bodily organs plain to see—
> So sage and certain, frank and free,
> About what's under lock and key—
>   Man's soul!

That is to say, even the wisest doctors cannot agree about the simple fact of a man's sickness, notwithstanding the fact that they have studied anatomy and physiology and osteology, and have examined every part of the body. Yet, although the wisest men of science are obliged to confess that they cannot tell you everything about the body, which can be seen, even ignorant persons think that they know everything about the soul of a man, which cannot be seen at all, and about the mind of a man, to which only God himself has the key. Now all the purpose of Browning's work and life has been to show people what a very wonderful and complex and incomprehensible thing human character is—therefore to show that the most needful of all study is the study of human nature. He is especially the poet of character, the only one who has taught us, since Shakespeare's time, what real men and women are, how different each from every other, how unclassifiable according to any general rule, how differently noble at their best, how differently wicked at their worst, how altogether marvellous and infinitely interesting. His mission has been the mission of a great dramatic psychologist. And if anybody ever asks you what was Robert Browning, you can answer that he was the great Poet of Human Character—not of character of any one time or place or nation, but of all times and places and peoples of which it was possible for him to learn anything.

Here we must close our little studies of Victorian poets —that is to say, of the four great ones. I hope that you will be able to summarise in your own mind the main characteristic of each, as I have tried to indicate in the case of Browning. Remember Tennyson as the greatest influence upon the language of his mother country, because of his exquisiteness of workmanship and his choice of English subjects in preference to all others. He is the most English of all the four. Remember Rossetti as being altogether different in his personality and feeling—a man of the Middle Ages born into the nineteenth century, and in the nineteenth century still the poet of mediæval feeling. And think of Swinburne—the greatest musician of all, the most perfect master of form and sound in modern poetry—as an expounder of Neo-Paganism, of another Renaissance in the world of literature.

CHAPTER VI

WILLIAM MORRIS

WILLIAM MORRIS suffers by comparison with the more exquisite poets of his own time and circle. Nevertheless he is quite great enough to call for a special lecture. I am not sure whether I shall be able to make you much interested in him; but I shall certainly try to give you a clear idea of his position in English poetry as something entirely distinct, and very curious.

A few words first about the man himself—in more ways than one the largest figure among the Romantics. He was the great spirit of the Pre-Raphaelite coterie; he was the most prolific poet of the century; and he was in all respects the nearest in his talent and sentiment to Sir Walter Scott. All these reasons make it necessary to speak of him at considerable length.

He was born in 1834 and died in 1896, so that he is very recent in his relation to English poetry. There was nothing extraordinary in the incidents of his life at school or in his university career. In this man the extraordinary gift was altogether of the mind. Without the eccentricity of genius, he was also without the highest capacity of genius; but in his life as well as in his poetry he was always correct and always charming in a certain gentle and dreamy way. He had the stature and strength of a giant, perfect health, and immense working capacity, and did very well whatever he tried to do. Fortunately for his inclinations, he was the son of a rich man and never knew want; so that when he took to literature as a profession, he never had to think about pleasing the public, nor to care how much money his books might bring. After leaving Oxford University he devoted his life to art and literature, becoming equally well known as a painter and a poet. At a later day he established various businesses for an æsthetic purpose. For example, he thought that the early Italian printers and Venetian printers had done much better work and produced much more wonderful books than any modern printer; and he founded a press for the purpose of producing modern books in the same beautiful way. Then he thought that a reform in the matter of house furniture was possible. The furniture of the sixteenth and seventeenth centuries had been good, solid, costly, and beautiful; but the later furniture had become both cheap and ugly. Morris's artistic interests had led him to study furniture a great deal; he became familiar with the furniture of the Middle Ages, of the Elizabethan Age, and of later times, as scarcely any man of the day had become. It occurred to him that the best and most beautiful forms of mediæval and later furniture might be reintroduced, if anybody would only take pains to manufacture them. The ordinary manufacturers of furniture would not do this. Morris and a few friends established a factory, and there designed and made furniture equal to anything in the past. This undertaking was successful, and it changed the whole fashion of English house furnishing. Only a decorative artist like Morris would have been capable of imagining and carrying out such a plan; and it was carried out so well that almost every rich house in England now possesses some furniture designed by him.

Thus you will see that he must have been a very busy man, occupied at once with poetry, with romance (for he wrote a great many prose romances), with artistic printing, with house furniture, with designs for windows of stained glass, and with designs for beautiful tiling—also with a very considerable amount of work as a decorative artist. All this would appear almost too much for any one person to attempt. But it was rendered easy to Morris by the simple fact that the whole of his various undertakings happened to be influenced by exactly the same spirit and motive, the artistic feeling of the Middle Ages, and of the period ending with the eighteenth century. Whether Morris was making books of poetry or books of prose, whether he was translating sagas from the Norse or writing stories in imitation of the early French romances, whether he was casting Italian forms of type for the making of beautiful books or designing furniture for some English palace, whatever he was doing, he had but one thought, one will—to reproduce the strange beauty of the Middle Ages. There was almost nothing modern about the man. The whole of his writings, comprising a great many volumes, contained scarcely ten pages having any reference to modern things. Even the language that he used has been correctly described by a great critic as eighteenth century English, mixed with Scandinavian idioms and forms. Thus there were two men among the Pre-Raphaelites who actually did not belong to their own century—Rossetti and Morris. Both were painters as well as poets, and though the former was the greater in both arts, the practical influence of Morris counted for much more in changing English taste both in literature and in æsthetics.

We have chiefly to consider his writing, and, of that writing, especially the poetry. As a poet I have already mentioned him as having points of resemblance with Sir Walter Scott. But he also had even more points of resemblance with Chaucer. He was like Scott in the singular ease and joyous force of his creative talent. Scott could sit down and write a romance in verse beautifully, correctly, without any more difficulty than other men write prose. Byron, you know, used to write his poetry straight off, without even taking the trouble to correct it; as a consequence it is now becoming forgotten. But Scott took very great trouble to make his verse quite correct, without trying to be exquisite, and his verse will always count as good, stirring English poetry. Morris had almost exactly the same talent, the talent that can give you a three-volume story either in verse or prose, just as you may prefer. And he wrote in verse on a scale that astonishes, a scale exceeding that of any modern poet. To find his equal in production we must go back to the poets of those romantic Middle Ages which he so much loved, the poets who wrote vast epics or romances in thirty or forty thousand lines. Eleven volumes of verse and fifteen volumes of prose represent Morris's production; and the extraordinary thing is that all his production is good. It does not reach the very highest place in literature; no man could write so much and make his work of the very highest class. But it is good as to form, good as to feeling, much beyond mediocrity at all times; and sometimes it rises to a level that is only a little below the first class.

I am not going to give selections from his larger works, so I can only mention here what the large works signify and how he is related to Chaucer through one of them. The most successful, in a popular sense, of all his poems is the "Earthly Paradise," originally published in five volumes, now published in four—and the volumes are very thick. This vast composition is much on the plan of the "Canterbury Tales"; and Morris and Chaucer both followed the same method, and were filled with the same sense of beauty. Both found in the legends of the Middle Ages and in the myths of antiquity, material for their art in the shape of stories; and as these stories had no inter-relation, belonging even to widely different epochs of human civilisation, it was necessary to imagine some general plan according to which all could be brought harmoniously together, like jewels, upon a single tray. This plan of uniting heterogeneous masses of fiction or legends into one artistic circle was known to the East long before it was known in Europe; the great Indian collections of stories, such as the Panchatantra and the Kathâ-sarit-sâgara, are perhaps the oldest examples; and the huge Sanskrit epics show something of the same design, afterwards adopted by Arabian and Persian story-tellers. But Chaucer was the first to make the attempt with any success in English literature. His plan was to have the stories told by pilgrims travelling on their way to Canterbury, every man or woman of the company being obliged to tell one or two stories. The plan was so good that it has been followed in our own day; Longfellow's "Tales of a Wayside Inn" are constructed upon precisely the same principle. But Chaucer made a plan so large that he had not the strength nor the time to carry it to completion; Morris, upon a scale nearly as large, brought his work to a happy conclusion with the greatest ease. He makes a company of exiled warriors tell the stories of a foreign court, as results of their experience or knowledge obtained in many different countries. There are twenty-four stories, twelve mediæval or romantic and twelve classical; and each pair of these corresponds with one of the twelve months, the first two stories being told in January, the second two in February, and so forth. The division neatly partitions the great composition into twelve books, with the regular prologues and epilogues added. The English are not apt to trouble themselves to read very long poems these days; but Morris was able actually to revive the mediæval taste for long romances. Tens of thousands of his books were sold, notwithstanding their costliness, and the result was altogether favourable for the new development of romantic feeling, not only in literature, but in art and decoration. One might suppose that such composition was enough to occupy a lifetime, but Morris threw it off quite lightly and set to work upon a variety of poetical undertakings nearly as large. He translated Homer and Virgil into the same kind of flowery verse; and he put the grand Scandinavian epic of Sigurd the Volsung into some of the finest long-lined poetry produced in modern times. This epic seems to me the better work of the two long productions by which Morris is best known; later on some lines from it may be quoted. But Morris was scarcely less attracted by Greek myths than by the old literature of Scandinavia; and he also produced a long epic poem upon the story of Jason and Medea, the story of the Golden Fleece. Nevertheless, I can much better illustrate to you what Morris is in literature and what his influence and his objects were, by means of his still earlier and shorter poems. There are several volumes of these, now published in more compact form under the titles of "Poems by the Way" and "Love is Enough" and "The Defense of Guinevere." From the last, originally dedicated to Rossetti, I will make some quotations that will show you how Morris tried to revive the Middle Ages.

One of the most remarkable things in the late Mr. Froude's charming account of a voyage which he made to Norway, is his statement of a sudden conviction that there came to him about the character of the ancient Vikings. He felt assured, he said, that the modern Norwegian and the ancient Norwegian were very much the same; that modern customs, religion, and education had produced only differences of surface; and that if we could go back against the stream of time to the age of the sea kings, we should find that they were exactly like the men of to-day in all that essentially belongs to race character. Now Morris, while studying mediæval romances and loving them for their intrinsic curious beauty, came to a very similar conclusion. It is true, he thought, that the Middle Ages were much more cruel, more ignorant, more savage than the ages before them or after them; but after all, the men and women of those times must have felt about many things just like modern men and women. Why should we not feel enough of this to study their fashions, joys, and feelings under the peculiar conditions of their terrible society? And this is what he did. You may say that, except for some difference in the home speech, the talk of these people in the poems of Morris is the talk of modern men and women. There is some difference as to sentiment. But you cannot say that it is not natural, not likely; in fact, the seeming pictures often have such force that you cannot forget them. That is a test of truth.

They are very brief pictures, like sudden glimpses caught during a flash of lightning: a glimpse into an arena where two men are about to fight to the death in presence of their king, according to the code of the day; a knight riding through a flooded country in order to take a castle by surprise; a woman driven to madness by the murder of her lover; a woman at the stake about to be burned alive, when the sound of the hoofs of the lover's horse is heard, as he gallops to her rescue; ladies in the upper chamber of a castle, weaving and singing; the capture of a robber and his vain pleading for life; also some fairy tales of weird and sensuous beauty, told as people of the Middle Ages must have felt them. To me one of the most powerful pictures is the story of "The Haystack in the Floods." We are not told how the tragedy began, nor how it ended; and this is great art to tell something without beginning and without end, so well that the reader is always thereafter wondering what the beginning was and what the end might have been. The poem begins with the words:

> Had she come all the way for this
> To part at last without a kiss?
> Yea, had she borne the dirt and rain
> That her own eyes might see him slain
> Beside the haystack in the floods?

We know from this only that the woman referred to is a woman of gentle birth, accustomed to luxurious things, so that it was very difficult for her to travel in rainy weather and cold, and that she thought it was a great sacrifice on her part to do so even for a lover. If she thought this, we have a right to suspect that she is a wanton—though we are not quite sure about it. The description of her does not explain anything further than the misery of the situation.

> Along the dripping leafless woods,
> The stirrup touching either shoe,
> She rode astride as troopers do;
> With kirtle kilted to her knee,
> To which the mud splashed wretchedly;
> And the wet dripp'd from every tree
> Upon her head and heavy hair,
> And on her eyelids broad and fair;
> The tears and rain ran down her face.

The delicate woman has also the pain of being lonesome on her ride; for the lover, the knight, cannot ride beside her, cannot comfort her; he has to ride far ahead in order to see what danger may be in the road.   He is running away with her; perhaps he is a stranger in that country; we shall presently see.

Suddenly, nearby in the middle of a flooded place the enemy appears, a treacherous knight who is the avowed lover of the woman and the enemy of the man.   She counts the number of spears with him—thirty spears, and they have but ten.   Fighting is of no use, the woman says, but Robert (now we know for the first time the name of her companion) is not afraid—believes that by courage and skill alone he can scatter the hostile force, and bring his sweetheart over the river.   She begs him not to fight; her selfishness shows her character—it is not for him she is afraid, but for herself.

> But, "O," she said,
> "My God!   My God!   I have to tread
> The long way back without you; then
> The court at Paris; those six men,
> The gratings of the Chatelet; . . ."

And worse than the gratings of the Chatelet is the stake, at which she may be burned, or the river into which she may be thrown, if her lover is killed; there is only one way to secure her own safety—that is to accept the love of another man whom she hates, the wicked knight Godmar, who is now in front of them with thirty spearsmen. Evidently this is no warrior woman, no daughter of soldiers; she may love, but like Cleopatra she is afraid of battle. Her lover Robert, like a man, does not answer her tearful prayers, but gives the command to his men to shout his war-cry, and boldly charges forward. Then, triple sorrow! his men stand still; they refuse to fight against three times their number, and in another moment Robert is in the power of his enemy, disarmed and bound. Thereupon Godmar with a wicked smile observes to the woman:

> "Now, Jehane,
> Your lover's life is on the wane
> So fast, that, if this very hour
> You yield not as my paramour,
> He will not see the rain leave off."

He does more than threaten to kill her lover; he reminds her of what he can further do to her. She has said that if he takes her into his castle by force, she will kill either herself or him (we may doubt whether she would really do either); and he wants a voluntary submission. He talks to her about burning her alive; how would she like that? And the ironical caressing tone of his language only makes it more implacable.

> "Nay, if you do not my behest;
> O Jehane! though I love you well,"
> Said Godmar, "would I fail to tell
> All that I know." "Foul lies," she said.
> "Eh! lies, my Jehane? by God's head
> At Paris folks would deem them true!
> Do you know, Jehane, they cry for you,
> Jehane the brown! Jehane the brown!
> Give us Jehane to burn or drown!—
> Eh—gag me Robert!—sweet my friend,

> This were indeed a piteous end
> For those long fingers, and long feet,
> And long neck, and smooth shoulders sweet;
> An end that few men would forget,
> That saw it—So, an hour yet;
> Consider, Jehane, which to take
> Of life or death!"

She considers, or rather tries to consider, for she is almost too weary to speak, and very quickly falls asleep in the rain on the wet hay.   An hour passes.   When she is awakened, she only sighs like a tired child, and answers, "I will not." Perhaps she could not believe that her enemy and lover would do as he had threatened; and in spite of the risk of further angering him, she approaches the prisoner and tries to kiss him farewell.   Immediately,

> With a start
> Up Godmar rose, thrust them apart;
> From Robert's throat he loosed the bands
> Of silk and mail; with empty hands
> Held out, she stood and gazed, and saw,
> The long bright blade without a flaw
> Glide out from Godmar's sheath, his hand
> In Robert's hair; she saw him bend
> Back Robert's head; she saw him send
> The thin steel down; the blow told well,
> Right backward the knight Robert fell,
> And moaned as dogs do, being half dead,
> Unwittingly, as I deem: so then
> Godmar turn'd grinning to his men,
> Who ran, some five or six, and beat
> His head to pieces at her feet.

The knight groans involuntarily, in the death struggle only, and probably the sound of his pain pleases Godmar, but in order to make sure that he cannot recover again, he makes a sign to his followers to finish the work of murder; so they beat in his skull—an ugly thing for a woman to see done.   There were rough-hearted men in those days who could see a woman burned alive and laugh at her suffering. You have read, I think, the terrible story about Black Fulk, who made a great holiday on the occasion of burning his young wife alive, and took his friends to see the show, himself putting on his best holiday attire. This Godmar seems to be nearly as harsh a brute, judging from what he next has to say.

> Then Godmar turn'd again and said:
> "So, Jehane, the first fitte is read!
> Take note, my lady, that your way
> Lies backward to the Chatelet!"
> She shook her head and gazed awhile
> At her cold hands with rueful smile,
> As though this thing had made her mad.
>
> This was the parting that they had
> Beside the haystack in the floods.

Notice the brutal use of the word "fitte" (often spelled fytte). This was an old name for the divisions of a long poem, romance, or epic. Later the Italian term "canto" was substituted for it. Godmar refers to the woman's love as her romance, her poem: "Now the first canto of our love-romance has been read—only the first, remember!" The second fitte will be perhaps the burning of the woman when she is brought back to the castle prison from which she fled. It all depends upon circumstances. If she has really become mad, she may escape. The poem ends here, leaving us in doubt about the rest. We can only imagine the termination. I think that she has not really become mad, that she is too selfish and weak to bear or even to feel the real emotional shock of the thing; and that when they are half way to the prison she is likely to yield to Godmar's will. If she does so, he will probably keep her in his castle until he tires of her, and finds it expedient to end her existence with as little scruple as he showed in killing Robert. But, as an actual fact, it is difficult to be sure of anything, because we know neither the beginning nor the end of the affair. We have only a glimpse of the passion, suffering, selfishness, cruelty—then utter darkness. And this method of merely glimpsing the story causes it to leave a profound impression upon the imagination. Please do not forget this, because it is the most important art in any kind of narrative literature, whether of poetry or of prose.

A second example of the same device is furnished by another terrible poem called "The Judgment of God." The Judgment of God is an old name for trial by single combat. It was a superstitious law, a foolish and wicked law, but it served a purpose in the Middle Ages, and it afforded an opportunity for many noble and courageous deeds. Browning took up this subject in his stirring poem of "Count Gismond." The law was this: when one knight was accused by another of some evil, cruel, or treacherous act, he was allowed to challenge the man who brought the charge against him to fight to the death—*a l'outrance*, as the old term expressed it. The combat took place in the presence of the lord or king and before a great assembly, according to fixed rules. If the man who brought the charge lost the fight, then it was thought that he had proved himself a liar. If the person accused won the battle, then he was declared to be innocent. For it was thought that God would protect the truth in such cases; and therefore these combats were called the "judgment of God." Nevertheless you will perceive that a very skilful knight might be able to kill a great number of accusers, and lawfully "prove" himself innocent of a hundred crimes. That was a great defect of the system.

The "Judgment of God" is a monologue, quite as good in its way as many of the short monologues of Browning. It is the knight against whom accusation has been brought that tells us the feelings and impressions of the moment that he enters the lists to fight. In this case we are more moved to sympathy than in the former stories, because we know that the man, whether otherwise bad or good, has saved a woman from the stake, and killed the lords who were about to burn her. So we are inclined to think of him as a hero. We have just one sudden vision of a man's mind, as he stands in the face of death, with no sympathy about him except that of his old father, who comes to give him advice about fighting, because he is to be matched against a very skilful knight.

> "Swerve to the left, son Roger," he said,
>   "When you catch his eyes through the helmet-slit,
> Swerve to the left, then out at his head,
>   And the Lord God give you joy of it!"

The old man knows how to fight, has probably won many a battle, and he has observed the way that the light is falling. So he tells his son, "When you begin to fight, don't turn to the right—turn to the left; then you will be able to see his eyes through the helmet, and immediately that you see them, strike straight for his head, and may God help you to kill him." He has just heard these words from his father when the prologue begins.

> The blue owls on my father's hood
>   Were a little dimm'd, as I turned away;
> This giving up of blood for blood
>   Will finish here somehow to-day.
>
> So when I walked from out the tent,
>   Their howling almost blinded me;
> Yet for all that I was not bent
>   By any shame. Hard by, the sea
>
> Made a noise like the aspens where
>   We did that wrong, but now the place
> Is very pleasant, and the air
>   Blows cool on any passer's face.
>
> And all the throng is gather'd now
>   Into the circle of these lists—

Yea, howl out, butchers! tell me how
    His hands were cut off at the wrists;

And how Lord Roger bore his face
    A league above his spear point, high
Above the owls, to that strong place
    Among the waters—yea, yea, cry!

The owls on the crest are the emblem of the family.
The knight has been waiting in his tent according to rule,
until the signal is given; and his father and his retainers
probably helped to arm him there. He feels no emotion
except at the moment of bidding his father good-bye, and
then he knows that there are tears in his own eyes, because
the owl crest on his father's hood suddenly appears dim.
Then, as the signal is given, he walks out of the tent into
the lists, only to hear a roar of hatred and abuse go up
from all the circles of seats. The friends of the dead are
evidently in great force, and he has no friend except his
father and his retainers. And they shout at him, his enemies, telling him what he has done—how he cut off the
hands of the knight and cut off his head and carried it upon
the top of a spear for three miles, carried it above his own
banner to his own castle. This was indeed considered an
unknightly thing in those days, for such was the treatment given to common people in war, not to knights or men
of rank.

Then he sees the man with whom he must fight, waiting
for him, all in armour, with white linen over his arm, to
indicate that he is fighting for the cause of truth. At
this Roger can very well laugh; and he remarks that the
face of the champion's lady looks even whiter than the
linen upon her lord's arm. She has reason, perhaps, to be
afraid for him. And though he has not much time for
thinking, Roger remembers his own beloved, waiting for
him, remembers even how he first met her. Addressing her
in thought, he says:

And these say: "No more now my knight,
 Or God's knight any longer"—you
Being than they so much more white,
 So much more pure and good and true,

Will cling to me forever—there,
 Is not that wrong turn'd right at last
Through all these years, and I wash'd clean?
 Say, yea, Ellayne; the time is past,

Since on that Christmas-day last year
 Up to your feet the fire crept;
And the smoke through the brown leaves sere
 Blinded your dear eyes that you wept;

Was it not I that caught you then
 And kiss'd you on the saddle-bow?
Did not the blue owl mark the men
 Whose spears stood like the corn a-row?

Evidently she has reason to love him and his house; did
he not save her from the fire?—did he not come with his
spearmen and crush her enemies, and take her away upon
his horse to safety? And was not that enough to atone
for whatever other wrong he might have done? But he
has only a moment in which to think all this, for the trumpet
is about to sound for the fight, and there are other things
to think about. One of these is that his antagonist is a
very good man, difficult to overcome; the other is that
there is danger for him even if he conquers, because there
are so many present who hate him.

This Oliver is a right good knight,
 And needs must beat me, as I fear,
Unless I catch him in the fight,
 My father's crafty way—John, here!

Bring up the men from the south gate,
 To help me if I fall or win,
For even if I beat, their hate
 Will grow to more than this mere grin.

If the reader could imagine the result of the combat, the real effect of the poem in its present form would be lost. No man can imagine it. The challenged knight acknowledges his antagonist to be a better man—indeed, he says that he can only hope to conquer him by the cunning trick taught him by his old father. But the really dangerous man never underrates the capacity of an enemy; and we may suspect that the forces are at least even. So, as I have said, no man can guess the result of the battle, and the reader is forced to keep wondering what happened. He will always wonder, but he will never be able to feel convinced. And to leave the mind of the reader thus interested and unsatisfied is a great stroke of literary art. The same book contains a number of mediæval pieces of the same sort, showing how very unimportant it is whether you begin a story in the middle or whether you leave it without an end. The greatest French story-tellers of modern times have made almost popular the form of art in fiction to which I refer. Take, for example, the late Guy de Maupassant, many of whose short stories have, I am told, been translated into Japanese. No one modern prose writer ever succeeded better in telling a story without any beginning or without any end. Positively no beginning and no end is necessary, in many cases; and remember, this method of representing only the middle of things is exactly true to life. We never see or hear of the whole of any incident that happens under our eyes. We see only a fact, without knowing what caused it to come about, and without knowing what will be the consequences of it. Outside of our own homes we do not see much of other people's lives, and never the whole of any one's life.

Among other pieces in the book I should call your attention to "The Little Tower," "Sir Peter Harpdon's End," "The Wind," "The Eve of Crecy," "In Prison," and "The Blue Closet." They are very different in idea, but I think that you will find them all extremely original. "The Little

Tower" has no beginning and no end. It only describes faithfully the feelings of a knight riding over an inundated country, swimming his horse along the side of bridges under water, and thinking to himself of the joy of capturing an enemy's castle by surprise, killing the lord and burning the lady. It is brutal in a certain way, but supremely natural. The story of "Sir Peter Harpdon's End" is not a monologue; it is a very dramatic narrative in which a number of men of different character play their parts. It has no beginning, but the end is plainly suggested—and this shows the tender side of human nature in the Middle Ages. Sir Peter is brave, kindly, and true. Therefore, when he has his enemy at his mercy, instead of killing him, he only cuts off his ears. As a consequence he is afterwards himself destroyed; the obvious moral of the narrative is that a merciful heart was a dangerous possession in those times. The good men were easily trapped by playing upon their feelings of pity or sympathy. "The Wind" represents the madness of a very old knight, alone in his castle. The sound of the wind makes him think of the voices of the dead whom he knew, and brings him back to the memories of his youth, and of a woman that he loved. And at last the ghosts of forgotten friends enter and glide about him. This has no beginning and no end, and it remains very strongly impressed upon the memory. We should like to know the story of that woman, the story of the madness of the old man, but we shall never know. "The Eve of Crecy" represents the state of mind of a young French knight just before the fatal battle, when the flower of the French chivalry was destroyed by a mere handful of English soldiers driven to bay. You may remember that before the battle the English prepared themselves very thoroughly and made fervent prayers to heaven for success. But the French spent the night in carousing and jesting, never dreaming that they could lose the fight. Here Morris shows us one of the young noblemen thinking only about his sweetheart, some girl of noble rank whom he hopes to win. He is going to do great deeds the next day, then the king will smile upon him, and he will not be afraid to ask the father of that girl to permit him to become his son-in-law. And so the poem abruptly breaks off. The end here we can guess—a corpse riddled with English arrows, and trampled under the feet of thousands of horses. "In Prison," among the others, represents the emotions of a knight confined in a mediæval dungeon. "The Blue Closet" is a fantasy, a wild mediæval fairy tale, put into a dramatic form that reminds one singularly of the later work of Maeterlinck. It is, however, a noteworthy composition as poetry, and attained immediate popularity among all those who looked for beauties of colour and sound rather than reflections of life.

Those notes will give you an idea of the variety of the book. And the mediæval pieces are worth thinking about, if any of you should care to attempt authorship in a similar direction, whether in poetry or in prose. There was a period in Japanese feudalism, a period of constant civil wars and baronial quarrels, which would have produced a very similar condition of things to that described in certain of these poems, and I even think that more startling effects could be produced by a judicious handling of Japanese themes in the same way, that is, without attempting any beginning or suggesting any end.

But observe that I am not holding up these poems to you as great masterpieces of verse. I mean only that they suggest how great masterpieces might be made. And please to note especially one phase of the art of them, its psychological quality. Morris was not so great a psychologist as Browning, who came nearest to Shakespeare in this respect of all English poets. But Morris has considerable ability in this way, and the most striking effects in his short poems are produced by making us understand the feelings of persons in particular moments of pain or terror or heroic effort. For example, how natural and horrible is the soliloquy of Guinevere in the long poem with which the book opens. You know that Tennyson did not follow the original account of Malory in regard to the more cruel episodes of the old story. He felt repelled by such an incident as the preparations for burning the queen alive. In the real story she is about to be burned when Lancelot comes and saves her, not without killing half the knights present and some of his own relations into the bargain. But Morris saw in this episode an opportunity for psychological work, and took it, just as Browning might have done. He makes the queen express her thought:

> . . . "I know
> I wondered how the fire, while I should stand,
> And burn, against the heat, would quiver so,
> Yards above my head."

This startles, because it is true. The quotations which I gave you from "The Haystack in the Floods" contain several passages of an equally impressive sort. We can best revive the past in literature not by trying to describe the details of custom and of costume then prevalent, but by trying to express faithfully the feelings of people who lived long ago. And this can be managed most effectively either by monologue or dialogue.

The only other collection of short poems written by Morris is now compressed into a companion volume entitled "Poems by the Way." All of it is later work, but it is not more successful than the youthful productions which we have been considering. Nevertheless it excels in greater variety. You have here dramatic pieces of several kinds, ballads and translations of ballads, fairy tales and translations of fairy tales, mediæval and Norse stories, and strangely mixed with these a number of socialist poems —for Morris believed in the theories of socialism, in the possibility of an ideal communism.

The bulk of the pieces in the volume, however, are Scandinavian, and the general tone of the book is Northern. Morris was a tremendous worker in the interest of Scandinavian literature. He loved the mediævalism of the pagan Norse even more than the corresponding period of the Christian and chivalrous South. He helped the work of those great Oxford professors who brought out the Corpus Poeticum Boreale, translating in conjunction with one of them several ancient Sagas. And as a poet he did a great deal to quicken English interest in Norse literature, as we shall see later on. In this book we have only short pieces, but they are good, and a number of them have the value of almost literal translations. As for the style, a good example is furnished by the story of the killing of the Hallgerd (or Hallgerda) by Hallbiorn the Strong. The story is taken from an old Icelandic history, and is undoubtedly true. Hallbiorn wedded a daughter of a man called Odd, on account of his odd character. She was very beautiful. Her father insisted that Hallbiorn should spend the whole next season, winter, with him, and said that he might take his bride away in the spring for the summer. During the winter Hallgerda had a secret intrigue with a blood relation called Snæbiorn. The husband did not know, he only felt a little suspicious at times. When the summer came, and he asked Hallgerda to go with him to the house which he had built for her, she did not answer. He asked her twice, still she did not answer. The third time she refused. Then he killed her. Then Snæbiorn, her lover, attacked him, and after a terrible fight in which eight or nine men were killed, Hallbiorn was cut down. Snæbiorn then left the country vowing that he would never speak to man again, and settled in Greenland, where he died. The incidents are not wonderful, but the simple and terrible way in which they are told by the Icelandic chronicle makes them appeal greatly to the imagination. And Morris did

justice to the style of the old Landnámabok, as it is called.
The following lines relate to the tragedy only:

> . . . But Hallbiorn into the bower is gone
> And there sat Hallgerd all alone.
> She was not dight to go nor ride,
> She had no joy of the summer-tide,
> Silent she sat and combed her hair,
> That fell all round about her there.
> The slant beam lay upon her head
> And gilt her golden locks to red.
> He gazed at her with hungry eyes
> And fluttering did his heart arise.
> "Full hot," he said, "is the sun to-day,
> And the snow is gone from the mountain-way,
> The king-cup grows above the grass,
> And through the wood do the thrushes pass."
> Of all his words she hearkened none
> But combed her hair amidst the sun.
> "The laden beasts stand in the garth,
> And their heads are turned to Helliskarth."
> The sun was falling on her knee,
> And she combed her gold hair silently.
> "To-morrow great will be the cheer
> At the Brothers' Tongue by Whitewater."
> From her folded lap the sunbeam slid;
> She combed her hair, and the word she hid.
> "Come, love; is the way so long and drear
> From Whitewater to Whitewater?"
> The sunbeam lay upon the floor;
> She combed her hair and spake no more.
> He drew her by the lily hand:
> "I love thee better than all the land."
> He drew her by the shoulders sweet,
> "My threshold is but for thy feet."
> He drew her by the yellow hair,
> "Oh, why wert thou so deadly fair?
> Oh, am I wedded to death?" he cried,
> "Is the Dead-strand come to Whitewater side?"

In order to know how terrible all this is, we must under-

stand the character of the Norse woman. Like the will
of the man, her will is iron; she cannot be broken, she cannot be made to bend, except by love, and when she refuses
to bend there is nothing to be done but to kill her. All
the facts stated here in rhymed verse are even more terrible and more simple in the prose chronicle. Throughout
Norse history we repeatedly hear of women being killed
under like circumstances. These ferocious men would not
beat or abuse their women; that would have been no use.
But they insisted upon being obeyed; to refuse obedience
was to court death. In the present true story, however,
the refusal to obey means much more than to court death;
it means a bold confession by the bride that she has loved
and still loves another man than her husband, and that is
the reason of his sudden and terrible question, "Oh, am I
wedded to death? Is the Dead-strand come to this place?"
The Dead-strand or Corpse-strand was, in Norse mythology,
the name of a part of Hel, the region of the dead, the
Hades of old Norse, so his question really means, "Have
the evil dead come here for us both?" for good men and
women did not go to the Dead-strand. Now hear her
answer. When he speaks at last, she sings in his face her
secret lover's favourite song, which is just the same thing
as to say, "I am glad to be killed for my lover's sake."
And to kill a Norse woman meant, of course, death for the
man who slew her, for her kindred were bound to avenge
her. So she is defying him in every way.

> The sun was fading from the room,
> But her eyes were bright in the change and the gloom,
> "Sharp Sword," she sang,—"and death is sure,
> But over all doth love endure."
> She stood up shining in her place
> And laughed beneath his deadly face.
> Instead of the sunbeam gleamed a brand,
> The hilts were hard in Hallbiorn's hand.

The last line contains a phrase from old Northern war

poetry. To say that the hilt of a man's sword was hard in his hand, signifies that he was a terrible swordsman, accustomed to mighty blows. But Morris here makes a little departure from the original chronicle. He makes Hallbiorn pass his sword through the woman's body. As a matter of fact he did nothing of the kind; he simply cut her head off at a single blow. Very dramatic, however, is his telling of the subsequent flight of Hallbiorn, and the pursuit by Snæbiorn. Hallbiorn's men are surprised at the fact that he does not hold his ground, for they know nothing of what happened in the house, and one of them says, "Where shall we sleep to-night?" Hallbiorn answers grimly, "Under the ground." Then his retainers know for the first time that they are going to be attacked. The attacking party consists of twelve men. Hallbiorn's retainers urge their master to hasten forward; it is still possible, they think, to escape. But he stops his horse and leaps down, exclaiming:

"Why should the supper of Odin wait?
Weary and chased I will not come
To the table of my father's home."

That is a fine expression about the supper of Odin, referring to the hope of every brave man to enter, at his death, into Valhalla, the hall of Odin, and to sup with the gods. And to enter there one had to be killed in battle. So you can see the fierce humour of Hallbiorn's remark that he does not want to come late to the supper of the gods, and to keep the feast waiting. Snæbiorn does not speak. Hallbiorn only laughs. He kills five men; then one of his feet is cut off, but he rushes forward upon the bleeding stump, and kills two more before he is overpowered. It was a terribly savage world, the old Norse world; but we like to read about it, and we cannot help loving the splendid courage of the men and women who passed their lives among such tragedies, fearing nothing but loss of honour.

Several other Norse subjects have been treated by Morris with equal success; and one is remarkable for the strange charm of a refrain used in it, a refrain from the Norse. It is called "The King of Denmark's Sons," and it is the story of a fratricide. King Gorm of Denmark had two sons, Knut and Harald:

> Fair was Knut of face and limb,
> As the breast of the Queen that suckled him;
> But Harald was hot of hand and heart
> As lips of lovers ere they part.

In history Knut was called the beloved. All men loved him, he was the heir; and the old king loved him so much that he one day said, "If any one, man or woman, ever tells me that my son Knut is dead, that person has spoken the word which sends him or her to Hel." But this great love only made the younger brother jealous. Harald was a Viking; he voyaged southward and eastward, ravaging coasts in the Mediterranean or desolating provinces nearer home. His name was a terror in England at one time. But his father never praised him as he praised his brother. So one day at sea he attacked his brother, overcame all resistance, and killed him. Then he went home and told his mother what had been done. But who dare tell the King? The mother imagined a plan. During the night she decked the palace hall all in black, taking away every ornament. So in the morning, when the King entered the hall, he asked, "Who has dared to do this?" the Queen answered, "We, the women of the palace have done it." "Then," said the King, "tell me that my son Knut is dead!" "You yourself have said the word," the Queen made answer. And therewith the old king died as he sat in his chair; and the wicked son became king. This is the simple history, and Morris has not departed from historic truth in his version of it. The refrain excellently suits the ballad

measure chosen; from the very first stanza, the tone of it
suggests all the tragedy that is going to follow.

> In Denmark gone is many a year,
> *So fair upriseth the rim of the sun,*
> Two sons of Gorm the King there were,
> *So grey is the sea when the day is done.*

Sunrise symbolises happiness, joy; grey is the colour of
melancholy; and nothing is so lonesome, so sad looking,
as the waste of the sea when it turns to grey in the twilight. The refrain reminds one of a famous line by an
American poet, Bryant, who certainly never saw this ballad:

> Old ocean's grey and melancholy waste.

Besides the above Norse subjects, I might call your attention to the following titles: "The Folk-Mote by the
River," "Knight Aagen and Maiden Else," "Hafbur and
Signy," "The Raven and the King's Daughter." All these
are well worth reading. So are the purely fairy tales.
Northern fairy tales had a great charm for Morris. He
chose them as subjects, perhaps because he saw a way of
putting into them a new charm, a charm not suited for child
readers, but attractive to the adult public. I suppose you
know that fairy tales, as written for children, are written so
as to appeal chiefly to the imagination, and to those simple
emotions of which children are capable. But originally
such stories were told for the amusement of grown up people, and a great deal of love sentiment figures in some of
them. Morris remembering this, took several charming
stories and infused them with a new artistic sensuousness,
making love the motive and the principal sentiment. In
the other volume of which I spoke, the old story of "Rapun-
zel" is treated in this way; in the volume now under consideration we have the story "Goldilocks and Goldilocks."

It is the wildest, the most impossible kind of fairy tale (so, for that matter, is Coleridge's "Christabel"), but he gave it a very human charm by putting delightful little bits of human nature into it—such as the passage where the enchanted maiden, who never saw a man before, meets the handsome knight for the first time:

> But the very first step he made from the place
> He met a maiden face to face.
>
> Face to face, and so close was she,
> That their lips met soft and lovingly.
>
> Sweet-mouthed she was, and fair he wist;
> And again in the darksome wood they kissed.
>
> Then first in the wood her voice he heard,
> As sweet as the song of the summer bird.
>
> "O thou fair man with the golden head, ·
> What is the name of thee?" she said.
>
> "My name is Goldilocks," said he,
> "O sweet-breathed, what is the name of thee?"
>
> "O Goldilocks the Swain," she said,
> "My name is Goldilocks the Maid."
>
> He spake, "Love me as I thee,
> And Goldilocks one flesh shall be."
>
> She said, "Fair man, I wot not how
> Thou lovest, but I love thee now."

And they go on talking together, like two children, in their eighteenth century English—she full of wonder at the beauty of the stranger of another sex, he full of loving pity for her supreme innocence. And then all kinds of magical dangers and troubles come to separate them, but love conquers all. The story is known by many children, but not as Morris tells it. His principal purpose is to picture a character of perfect innocence and perfect trust; and he does this so delightfully that we cease to care whether the tale is a fairy one or not. It stirs most agreeably something which is true in everybody's heart; we love what is beautiful in the character of the child or the supremely innocent young girl.

As a single work in one key, the greatest production of Morris is the "Story of Sigurd"; indeed, we might call it the masterpiece of the poet, but for the fact that it is not original in the true sense. It is little more than a magnificent translation in swinging verse of the Volsunga Saga. But in more ways than one, it has become a literary work of extreme importance. It was through this metrical version that the Volsunga Saga first became known to English readers in a general way. Since then we have had prose translations.

I want to speak about this Saga, because the subject is of extreme literary importance. To-day you can scarcely open a literary periodical or any volume of essays on literary subjects without finding there some reference to the famous Northern story. It is one version of an epic which in various forms belongs to the whole Northern race; and one of the forms best known is the Nibelungenlied of Germany. Through German musical art the latter form of the story has in our own time become universally known in all great cities of the West, for Wagner made it the subject of a magnificent composition; the greatest of all modern operas, dramatically at least, is certainly his musical presentation of the epic cycle.

A word now about the place of this story in European literature. Mediæval Europe produced four great epics. Each of these represents the beginning of a vast national literature. The great English epic is the story of Beowulf, and I am sorry to say that it is not the best. The great French epic is the story of Roland. The great Spanish epic is the story of the Cid. And the great German epic is the Nibelungenlied or Nibelunge Nôt, as it has also been called. Of these four the German epic is the grandest. Its date is not exactly known. But the best critics assert that it cannot be older than the middle of the twelfth century, and not later than the middle of the thirteenth. Therefore the date must be somewhat between 1150–1250.

But the German epic is by no means the oldest form of the story. The older forms are Norse. There are poetical fragments of the story to be found in the ancient Scandinavian literature (you can find them in the library in the Corpus Poeticum Boreale), and there is a splendid prose version of the story in the old Icelandic—this is the Volsunga Saga, from which Morris took his poetical materials. Between the versions of the German and the North, there are great differences of narrative, but perhaps not great differences of merit. If we could have the whole of the old Norse epic, we should perhaps find it even grander than the German. But only fragments have been preserved of the poetry, and we can only imagine from the prose Saga how magnificent the lost poetry may have been. And now a word about the story itself.

When Herbert Spencer, some years ago, criticised certain English translations issued by the Japanese department of education, he stated that the story of the great swordsman Musashi was not a proper subject for the admiration of the youth, because it is a story of vengeance. He was speaking from the standpoint of ideal education, and from that standpoint his criticism is not disputable. But ideal education, in the present state of humanity, he himself would acknowledge to be impossible. It is only something toward which we can all work a little, slowly and patiently. In the meantime, the same objection made to the story of Musashi might equally well be made to all the epic poems of the Western world, and to nearly all the great romances of the past. To begin with, the grand poems of Homer, both the Iliad and the Odyssey, are epics of vengeance. The great story of King Arthur is a narrative full of incidents of revenge and even of crime. We can scarcely mention any great composition which is not full of vengeance, and which is not also admired. But I wonder what could Mr. Spencer say of the Volsunga Saga or the Nibelungenlied. For all stories of vengeance ever told, whether in verse or prose, pale before the immense quarrel and cruelty of these. They are terrible stories, and the Volsunga version is even more terrible than the German.

The story takes its name from the great family of the Volsung. It opens with an account of the might and power of King Volsung, the heroism of his sons and the beauty of his only daughter Signy. These rule in the far North. After a time the King of the Goths in the South, hearing of the wonderful beauty of Signy, asks for her hand in marriage, and obtains it. He goes to the country of the Volsung to wed her, and during the wedding he becomes jealous of the splendour and strength of the Volsung family. When he takes his bride South with him there is an evil purpose in his heart—the purpose to destroy the family of his bride by treachery whenever opportunity offers. What follows does not belong to the German story at all; it is only to be found in the Norse.

Siggeir, the Gothic king, next year invites the King Volsung and his sons to come South and pay him a visit. The sons of King Volsung suspect treachery, and they advise their father not to go without a great army. But the old king wants to see his daughter, and he thinks that it would be showing fear to go with a great army, so he tells his sons that they must go as invited, with only a small following. They go. But the suspicion of the sons was justified by events. In the middle of the festival of welcome, King Volsung and his party are attacked by an immense force, and nearly all the followers of the king are killed. The sons are taken prisoners and left in a wood tied to trees for the wolves to devour. Only one escapes, Sigmund. He hides in the forest and becomes a hunter, and dreams of vengeance.

But the real avenger is Signy, the daughter of the dead King Volsung and the wife of the murderer. Signy knows that her brother Sigmund is alive. But that makes only two Volsungs; and two young people alone cannot hope to destroy a king and an army. But Signy believes that three can do it. Secretly she keeps her brother supplied with provisions and weapons, and she resolves to raise up sons to avenge the wrong. When her first son is born she begs to train him, and when he is old enough to begin to learn what war means, she sends him to her brother in the wood that he may teach the lad.

Sigmund does not much like the boy. He thinks that he talks too much to be really brave. He tests the lad's courage in different ways, telling him, among other things, to bake and knead cake in which a poisonous snake has been hidden. The boy is afraid of the snake. Sigmund sends him back to Signy, saying that he will not do.

Signy almost despairs. Must her sons be cowards because they have a coward father? Suddenly a strange idea comes to her. "I shall do as the Gods did in ancient times," she said; "only my brother can produce such a child as I wish for, and I shall have a child by him." She goes to a witch, who changes her body, transforms her so completely that her brother can have no suspicion of what has taken place. Then by him she has a son, Sinfiotli. When he is old enough she sends the boy to Sigmund.

Sigmund is astonished by the extraordinary fierceness and sullenness of the child. "Is it possible," he wonders, "that my sister can have such a child by her husband?" The boy scarcely speaks at all, but does whatever he is told, and is afraid of nothing. Sigmund gives him flour to knead and bake containing a poisonous snake. Instead of being afraid of the serpent, the child breaks and crushes the creature in his fingers and rolls the poisonous body in the flour, and makes the whole thing into cakes. Sigmund is delighted. He sends word to his sister, "This boy will do."

The rest of this part of the story you can imagine. The boy grows up a giant, and is trained in all arts by Sigmund. On a certain day these two unexpectedly force their way into the palace of the King Siggeir, slaughter his people and himself, and set fire to the palace. Thus King Volsung is avenged. But Signy, after having told her brother the story of Sinfiotli, goes back into the burning house of the king, and voluntarily dies. She has done her duty, but she does not care to live any longer. This ends the great episode of the Volsung Saga.

The next part contains the story of the dragon Fafnir. Here we have no more Sigmund. Sinfiotli has been poisoned, Sigmund has been killed in battle. But there is still one child of the Volsung blood alive in the world. This is Sigurd (the Siegfried of the German story). Sigurd is kindly brought up by a foster father, a Viking, who teaches him all the arts of seamanship and war. One of the teachers who helped the Viking in the work is a strange old man called Regin, who much resembles the Merlin of the story of King Arthur. Sigurd wants a sword, a magical sword, that will not break in his hand; for he is so strong that common swords are of no use to him. Regin alone knows the art. But he does not wish to give Sigurd such art. He makes in succession a number of swords. Sigurd takes each one of them and strikes the anvil with it, whereupon the blade flies into pieces. He threatens Regin so terribly that the latter at last is obliged to make the magical sword. When he finished, Sigurd strikes the anvil with the blade, and the anvil is cut in two pieces. In the musical presentation of the story by Wagner, the finest episode is this forging of the sword. If you ever see that performed in a great theatre, you will not easily forget it. But in the German story it is not Regin but the hero himself who

makes the blade. The anvil is placed upon the stage and
all the forging is really done there. When the anvil is
cut in two, a flash as of lightning follows the blade of the
sword; the spectacle is very grand.

But to return to the Volsung legend. Sigurd needs the
sword in order that he may perform great deeds in the
world, and the first great deed that he wishes to perform
is to secure a magical hoard of wealth, belonging to the
Dwarfs of the underworld and guarded by the terrible
dragon Fafnir. He goes with Regin to the place of the
hoard, and meets the dragon, and kills him. Regin then
says to him, "Give me his heart—cut it out and roast it."
Sigurd obeys, cuts out the heart of the dragon, and begins
to roast it over the fire. But while roasting it, some grease
gets upon his fingers, and he licks it off with his tongue.
Immediately a wonderful thing happens—he can understand the language of birds and animals. In the trees above
him he hears the birds speaking, and they give him warning
that Regin intends to kill him. Thereupon he kills Regin.
This story of the dragon's heart is very famous in European
literature, and you will find many references to it in the
poetry and prose of to-day.

The next part of the story is one of the finest—the meeting of Sigurd and Brynhild, the first love episode. Brynhild is half human, half divine. Though born among men,
she had been taken to heaven by Odin and made a Valkyria,
one of the celestial virgins called the "Choosers of the
Slain." But for a fault which she committed she had
been sent back to earth again, to suffer pain and sorrow.
In an enchanted sleep she was left upon the summit of a
mountain, and all about her sleepingplace towered a wall of
never-dying fire. "Only the man brave enough to ride
through the fire shall have this maiden"—so spake Odin.

Sigurd rides through the fire, and the fire, although roaring like the sea, does not hurt him, because he is brave.
Entering the enchanted circle, he there sees a human figure

lying, all in golden armour not made by any human smith. He tries to awake the sleeper, but cannot. He tries to take off the armour, but he cannot unfasten it. Then he takes his wonderful sword and cuts open the armour as easily as if it were silk. Then he finds that the sleeper is a woman, more beautiful than any woman of earth. She opens her eyes and looks at him. They fall in love with each other, and pledge themselves to become man and wife. Probably this part of the story is one of the sources from which the beautiful fairly tale of the Sleeping Beauty came into our child literature. But the idea is also found in very ancient Eastern literature.

The third part of the great story treats of the history of Brynhild especially. Being a Valkyria, she has power to see much of the future; she can foretell things in a dim way. She warns Sigurd that there is danger for him if he should ever be untrue to her. Sigurd accepts the warning in the noblest spirit. But the Fates are against him. He goes upon a warlike expedition to the kingdom of Niblung in the North. The Niblung family, after a great battle which Sigurd has helped them to win, wish to adopt him as a son, and the beautiful daughter of the King falls in love with him. Her father and her brothers wish Sigurd to marry the girl, whose name is Gudrun. But Sigurd remembers his promise to Brynhild. Then the wicked Queen Grimhild, the mother of Gudrun, gives Sigurd a poisonous drink that causes him to forget the past; and while he is under the influence of this magical drink he is persuaded to marry Gudrun.

But this is not the worst thing that he is obliged to do through the magical arts of Grimhild. He is obliged to go to Brynhild, and persuade her to become the wife of young Gunnar, the brother of Gudrun. He rides through the fire again, and persuades Brynhild to become the wife of Gunnar. She obeys his will, but the result is the destruction of Sigurd and all concerned. For the two women pres-

ently begin to quarrel. Brynhild loves Sigurd with a
supernatural love, and he knows that he has been deceived.
Gudrun also loves Sigurd fiercely, and her jealousy quickly
perceives the secret affection of Brynhild. In short, the result of the quarrel between the women is that the brothers
of Gudrun resolve to kill Sigurd while he sleeps. One of
them stabs him in the middle of night. Sigurd, awakening,
throws his sword after the escaping murderer with such
force that the man is cut in two. But Sigurd dies of his
wound, and Brynhild then kills herself, and the two are
burnt upon the same funeral pyre.

The last part of the story is the revenge of Gudrun, one
of the most terrible characters in all Northern stories. She
lives only to avenge Sigurd. On finding that her brothers
have caused his murder, she curses her house, her family,
her people, and vows that they shall all suffer for the wrong
done her. Her brothers, who know her character, are afraid,
but there is a hope that time will make her heart more
gentle. At all events she cannot remain always a widow.
Presently she is asked for in marriage by Atli, king of the
Goths. Her brothers wish for this marriage, all except
one, who is against it. Gudrun marries Atli. This gives
her power to plan her longed-for revenge. She persuades
her husband that the great treasures which Sigurd got by
killing the dragon are worth securing even at the cost of
the lives of her brothers and father. She does not lie to
the King; she frankly tells him that she hates her people,
and he believes her. By treachery, all the Niblungs are al-
lured to Atli's hall. In the middle of the day of their ar-
rival, they are suddenly attacked. They make a great fight,
but all their followers are killed, and they themselves are
taken prisoners—that is, the brothers, the father having
died before the occurrence. During the fight Gudrun is
present and the blood spurts upon her dress and hands, but
the expression of her face never changes. This is one of
the most awful scenes in the poem.

When all the brothers are dead but two, Hogni and Gunnar, the King says to Gunnar, "Give me the treasure of the Niblungs, and I will spare your life." Gunnar answers: "I must first see the heart of my brother Hogni cut out of his breast and laid upon a dish." The King's soldiers take among the prisoners a tall man whom they imagine to be Hogni, but who is really only a slave, and they cut out the man's heart and put it upon a dish and bring it to Gunnar. Gunnar looks at it and laughs and says, "That is not my brother's heart; see how it trembles —that is the heart of a slave!" Then the soldiers kill the real Hogni and cut out his heart and bring it upon a plate. This time Gunnar does not laugh. He says, "That is really my brother's heart. It does not tremble. Neither did it ever tremble in his breast when he was alive. There were only two men in the world yesterday who knew where the treasure of the Niblungs is hidden, my brother and myself. And now that my brother is dead, I am the only one in the world who knows. See if you can make me tell you. I shall never tell you." He is tortured and killed, but he never tells.

There is only one of the whole Niblung race still alive, Gudrun. She has avenged her husband upon her own brothers, but that does not satisfy her. By the strange and ferocious Northern code she must now avenge her kindred, though they be her enemies, upon the stranger. She has used Atli in order to destroy her brothers; but, after all, they were her brothers and Atli only her husband. She sets fire to the palace, kills Atli with her own hands, and then leaps into the sea. Thus all the characters of the story meet with a tragic end. There is no such story of vengeance in any other literature. Yet this epic, or romance, is the greatest of mediæval compositions, and every student ought to know something about it, either in its Scandinavian or its German form. In the German form the character of Gudrun—she is there called Kriemhild—is much less savage; and the German story is altogether a more civilised expression of feeling. But any form of the story (and there are several other forms besides those of which I have spoken) shows the moving passion to be vengeance; and to return to the subject of Mr. Spencer's criticism, we may say that there is no great tale, Western or Eastern, in which this passion has no play.

The values of the story are in the narration, in the descriptions of battles, weapons, banquets, weddings, in the heroic emotions often expressed in speeches or pledges, and in the few chapters of profound tenderness strangely mingled among chapters dealing only with atrocious and cruel passions; all these give perpetual literary worth to the composition, and we cannot be tired of them. The subject was a grand one for any English poet to take up, and Morris took it up in a very worthy way. He has put the whole legend into anapestic verse of sixteen syllables, a long swinging, irregular measure which has a peculiar exultant effect upon the reader. To give an example of this work is very difficult. Any part detached from the rest, loses by detachment—for Morris, although a good poet, and a correct poet, and a spiritual poet, is not an exquisite poet. He does not give to his verses that supreme finish which we find in the compositions of the greater Victorian poets. However, I shall attempt a few examples. I thought at first of reading to you some passages regarding the forging of the sword; but I gave up the idea on remembering how much better Wagner has treated the same incident where the hero chants as he strikes out the shape of the blade with his hammer, and at last, with a mighty shout lifts up the blade and cuts the anvil in two. Perhaps a better example of Morris's verse may be found in these lines:

By the Earth that groweth and giveth, and by all the Earth's increase
That is spent for Gods and man-folk, by the sun that shines on these;

By the Salt-Sea-Flood that beareth the life and death of men;
By the Heaven and Stars that change not, though Earth die out
    again;

.   .   .   .

I hallow me to Odin for a leader of his host,
To do the deeds of the Highest, and never count the cost;
And I swear, that whatso great-one shall show the day and the deed,
I shall ask not why nor wherefore, but the sword's desire shall
    speed:
And I swear to seek no quarrel, nor to swerve aside for aught
Though the right and the left be blooming, and the straight way
    wend to nought,
And I swear to abide and hearken the prayer of any thrall,
Though the war-torch be on the threshold and the foemen's feet
    in the hall:
And I swear to sit on my throne in the guise of the kings of the
    earth,
Though the anguish past amending, and the unheard woe have birth:
And I swear to wend in my sorrow that none shall curse mine eyes
For the scowl that quelleth beseeching, and the hate that scorneth
    the wise.
So help me Earth and Heavens, and the Under-sky and Seas,
And the Stars in their ordered houses, and the Norns that order
    these!
And he drank of the cup of Promise, and fair as a star he shone,
And all men rejoiced and wondered, and deemed Earth's glory won.

This will serve very well to show you the ringing spirit
of the measure. Here is an example of another kind taken
from the pages describing the first secret love of the maiden
Gudrun for Sigurd. It is true to human nature; the Northern woman is apt to be most cruel to the man whom she
loves most, and these few lines give us a dark suggestion of
the character of Gudrun long before the real woman re-
veals herself—immensely passionate and immensely strong
in self-control.

But men say that howsoever all other folk of earth
Loved Sigmund's son rejoicing, and were bettered of their mirth,
Yet ever the white-armed Gudrun, the dark haired Niblung Maid,
From the barren heart of sorrow her love upon him laid;

He rejoiceth, and she droopeth; he speaks and hushed is she;
He beholds the world's days coming, nought but Sigurd may she see.
He is wise and her wisdom falters; he is kind, and harsh and strange
Comes the voice from her bosom laden, and her woman's mercies
    change.
He longs, and she sees his longing, and her heart grows cold as a
    sword.
And her heart is the ravening fire, and the fretting sorrows' hoard.

A great deal is said in these lines by the use of sugges-
tive words and words of symbolism. Paraphrased these
verses mean much more. "No matter how much all other
people showed their love and admiration for Sigurd by
making festival and public rejoicing, feeling happier and
better for having seen him, all their affection was as nothing to the love that Gudrun secretly felt for him, out of
her lonesome heart; and great was her secret grief at the
thought that he might not love her. Then she acted with
him after the manner of the woman resolved to win. Whenever she saw him rejoice she became sad. Whenever he
spoke to her, she remained silent. Many things Sigurd
knew—so wise he was that he could see even the events
of the future; but she saw nothing and knew nothing thereafter except Sigurd, nor did she wish to see or to know
anything else. And when he showed himself wise, she
acted as a foolish child. And when he tried to be kind to
her she answered him with a strange and harsh voice, and
suddenly became without pity. And at last when he began to long for love, and she perceived it, then her heart
became cold as a sword. So was the soul of this woman
in the time of her passion—now like ravening fire, now
again desolate with all the sorrows that corrode and destroy."

Because she sees still that love is not for her, the whole
scene of the courting—this is one of the cases where the
maiden woos the man without ever losing her dignity as a
maiden—is of consummate skill, showing Gudrun at one

moment simple and sweet as a child, revealing suddenly, at
another time, the strange height and depth of her, many
things terrible in her, capable of the making or the ruin
of a kingdom.

I am not going to quote, but I hope that you will notice
particularly the fine scene of the death of Brynhild. There
is a grand thought in it. I did not tell you, in the brief
epitome of the plot which I gave you, about the second
wooing of Brynhild. When Sigurd wooed her for King
Gunnar, he lay down beside her at night; but he placed his
naked sword between them. This episode is famous in
Western literature. So he brought her chaste to her bridegroom. And when afterwards Brynhild kills herself, in
order that she may be able to join him in the spirit world,
she shows her admiration of Sigurd's action by saying,
"When you put my dead body on the funeral pyre beside
the dead body of Sigurd, put his naked sword again between us, as it was put between us when he wooed me long
ago, for the sake of King Gunnar." The suicide chapter
is very grand. And the ending of the long tragedy has
also a peculiar grandeur, when Gudrun leaps into the sea.

The sea-waves o'er her swept;
And their will is her will henceforward; and who knoweth the deeps
    of the sea
And the wealth of the bed of Gudrun, and the days that yet shall be?

A finer simile could not be imagined than this sudden
transformation of a passionate woman's will into the vast
motion and unimaginable depths of the sea. The idea is,
"Deep and wide was her soul like the sea; and the strength
of her and the depth of her are now the strength and depth
of the ocean; and who knows what her spirit may hereafter
accomplish?"

In concluding this little study of the romance, I may
say that some of its incidents are probably immortal because they contain perpetual truth. I am not now speak-

ing particularly of Morris's work, but only of the legend of
Sigurd. The studies in it of evil passions need not demand our praise, but the stories of heroism, like that of the
naked sword laid between the man and the maid, will
always seem to us grand. Symbolically we may say that
the wealth of the world is still guarded by dragons as truly
as in the story of Sigurd; formidable and difficult to overcome are the powers opposing success in the struggle of
life, and the acquisition of the prize can be only for the
hero, the strong man mentally or morally. Again that
strange fancy of Brynhild ringed about in her magical sleep
with a wall of living fire—I do not know how it may seem
to the far Eastern reader, but to the Western it is the
symbol of a real truth, that beauty, the object of human
desire, is still truly ringed about by fire, in the sense that
the winner of it must risk all possible dangers of body and
soul before he succeeds. Still in Northern countries the
finest woman is for the best man; only the hero can truly
ride through the fire of the gods.

I have said enough about the great poems of Morris; I
do not think that it will be necessary to say anything about
"The Life and Death of Jason." If you like his other
work, probably you will like that book also. But I think
that the story of Jason is more charmingly told by Charles
Kingsley in his Greek fairy tale, and that Morris was at
his best, so far as long narrative poems are concerned, in
Norse subjects. I have already told you about his strong
personal interest in Norse literature, and about his work
as a prose translator. In this connection I may mention a
queer fact. Morris, who claimed to have Norse blood in
his own veins, became so absorbed by the Norse subjects
that his character seems to have been changed in later life.
He became stark and grim like the old Vikings, even to his
friends. But if he offended in this wise, he certainly made
up for the fault by that tremendous energy which he ap-

peared to absorb from the same source. No man ever worked harder for romantic literature and romantic art, and few men have made so deep an impression upon the æsthetic sentiments of the English public.

CHAPTER VII

CHARLES KINGSLEY AS POET

You may remember my having told you that the best ex-amples of the hexameter in English were written by the admirable novelist Charles Kingsley. I may have also said something in a general way about Kingsley's place in the nineteenth century, but time did not permit of a spe-cial lecture in regard to his verse—which, nevertheless, is of very great importance, and is constantly obtaining wider recognition. No man of the century who figures in Eng-lish literature had more of the soul of the poet than Kings-ley; and a very great poet he might have become had he possessed sufficient means to devote all of his powers to poetry. He had very little time for poetry. But little as the time was that he could devote, it sufficed him to write the best hexameters of an English poet, and to compose songs which have been translated into almost every modern language. "The Three Fishers" has been translated into Japanese, so I need not repeat it to you. The "Sands of Dee" has been translated even into Arabic. Kingsley had the divine gift of exciting the deepest emotions with the simplest words, and it is to this faculty in particular that I will call your attention to-day. Later on we shall study some of his hexameters; but these do not show how great a poet he was nearly so well as do the things which read so simply that you might fancy a young boy had written them, until their magic begins to stir the emotions.

Let us first take the "Sands of Dee." It is only a little song about a peasant girl being drowned by a high tide, which rose unexpectedly off the coast where she was taking care of her father's cows; but the whole world has learned it.

"O Mary, go and call the cattle home,
    And call the cattle home,
    And call the cattle home
    Across the sands of Dee";
The western wind was wild and dank with foam,
    And all alone went she.

The western tide crept up along the sand,
    And o'er and o'er the sand,
    And round and round the sand,
    As far as eye could see.
The rolling mist came down and hid the land;
    And never home came she.

"Oh! is it weed, or fish, or floating hair—
    A tress of golden hair,
    A drownèd maiden's hair
    Above the nets at sea?
Was never salmon yet that shone so fair
    Among the stakes on Dee!"

They rowed her in across the rolling foam,
    The cruel crawling foam,
    The cruel hungry foam,
    To her grave beside the sea:
But still the boatmen hear her call the cattle home
    Across the sands of Dee.

But for the grazing cattle, this incident might happen
upon any coast in the world; everywhere you see the nets
and the stakes, and the "cruel crawling foam." It is
curious that John Ruskin found fault with this poem, declaring that sea-foam did not seem to crawl. He was con-
tradicted, indeed, by many observers; but his criticism must
be mentioned, as it is so well known. "Crawling" means
moving like a creeping worm or a slow winding serpent; and
it is true that you do not see this stealthy motion of the
foam upon all coasts. To see it, you must be upon a coast
where there is a wide beach of smooth sand; you may then
see it at the time of a rising tide. The great waves are

yet very far away, but over the smooth shallows you see
the water gradually rising and spreading, edged with foam
that really seems to crawl.   I have often seen this on parts
of the English and the Irish coasts; and I think that the
word crawling, so far from being wrong, is one of the very
happiest words in the song.   I suppose you know that the
salmon is a very beautiful large fish, and can be seen shining like silver, or rather like pale gold, at a very considerable distance.

Now observe the extraordinary brevity with which the
tale is told.   There are indeed four stanzas, but several
lines of each stanza are repeated, or partly repeated, so that
the telling of the story is really done within eight lines less
than the total number of the poem.   Yet within this little
space we have two very definite pictures created in the
reader's mind.   The first is of the darkening of the evening sky, the rising of the sea-fog over the sands, and the
scents and colours of the coming storm.   We are not told
about the girl's being drowned; it is implied much more
effectively by the statement that she never came home.
The second little picture, the appearance beyond the break-
ers of the gold hair, together with the reference to the stakes
of the fishermen, is a perfect water-colour made with a few
strokes.   Even this would be enough to make the poem
remarkable; but the supernatural touch at the end of the
recital, the reference to the fishermen's belief that the ghost
of the girl can still be heard at night calling to the cows,
completes the work in such a way as to leave it unmatched
among modern songs.   It is not scholarship (though Kingsley was a good scholar) that can enable a man to produce
such a gem as this; one must be born with the heart of a
poet.

You will remember that, during our lecture upon Keats
last year, I quoted for you the ballad of "La Belle Dame
Sans Merci," as one of the most weirdly beautiful things in
English literature.   Now there are not many poets who have

the ability to give the feeling of weird beauty, of ghostliness and æsthetic charm at the same time. But Kingsley had this gift, and his poems offer many examples of it. One of these I think to be very nearly if not quite equal to Keats's poem. You might say that Keats's poem probably inspired it; you would be partly right. But the treatment is so different and so many original elements have been introduced, that it is certainly a very original poem. Besides, we have in it a Christian element which is treated in a totally new and startling way. It is something like the story of Urashima, but the ending is unique of its kind.

THE WEIRD LADY

The swevens came up round Harold the Earl
　Like motes in the sunnés beam;
And over him stood the Weird Lady
In her charmèd castle over the sea,
　Sang, "Lie thou still and dream.

"Thy steed is dead in his stall, Earl Harold,
　Since thou hast been with me;
The rust has eaten thy harness bright,
And the rats have eaten thy greyhound light
　That was so fair and free."

Mary Mother she stooped from heaven,
And wakened Earl Harold out of his sweven,
　To don his harness on;
And over the land and over the sea
He wended abroad to his own countrie,
　A weary way to gon.

Oh but his beard was white with eld,
　Oh but his hair was grey;
He stumbled on by stock and stone,
And as he journeyed he made his moan
　Along that weary way.

Earl Harold came to his castle wall;
　The gate was burnt with fire;

Roof and rafter were fallen down,
The folk were strangers all in the town,
And strangers all in the shire.

Earl Harold came to a house of nuns,
And he heard the dead-bell toll;
He saw the sexton stand by a grave;
"Now Christ have mercy, who did us save,
Upon yon fair nun's soul!"

The nuns they came from the convent gate,
By one, by two, by three;
They sang for the soul of a lady bright
Who died for the love of a traitor knight:
It was his own lady!

He stayed the corpse beside the grave;
"A sign, a sign!" quod he.
"Mary Mother who rulest heaven,
Send me a sign if I be forgiven
By the woman who so loved me."

A white dove out of the coffin flew;
Earl Harold's mouth it kist;
He fell on his face, wherever he stood;
And the white dove carried his soul to God
Or ever the bearers wist.

We have here a story which has been told in a hundred different ways by hundreds of different poets, both foreign and English, yet perhaps no one ever told it more touchingly. The legend is found in Danish, Swedish, German, and old French literature. Some knight, betrothed to a fair lady, is tempted to break his vow by a strange woman, a fairy or enchantress. He yields to the temptation, and thereafter falls into a magical sleep. Returning home after his waking, he finds that many years have passed, that everything is changed, and that all his people are dead. In this case the Virgin Mary interferes to wake the sleeper; but this is quite a new idea. In most of the old Northern ballads the knight who meets a fairy lady meets misfortune. If he loves her, she enchants him, and he never returns home until centuries had passed.   But on the other hand, if he refuses to love her, he dies the same night.   The singers of the Middle Ages would have made a very long romance out of such a version as that which Kingsley adopted; yet he has condensed all the possibilities of the romance into nine little six line stanzas.

A peculiarity of Kingsley's work is the extraordinary novelty of its method, even when the subject happens to be of the most commonplace kind.   A good example of this original part is presented in his famous "Ode to the Northeast Wind," a piece which it is said no Englishman can read without feeling his heart beat faster.   The East wind in England, particularly the Northeast wind, is the bitterest and coldest of all winds, bringing death to the weak, and suffering even to domestic animals, so that there is an old English proverb which every child learns by heart in the nursery:

> When the wind is in the East
> 'Tis neither good for man nor beast.

The West wind, you know, is tempered by the warm gulf-stream.   But Kingsley remembered that it was by the Northeast wind that the Norsemen and the ancient English first sailed to Britain, and perhaps he was thinking also of the evolutional fact that Northern strength has been developed by cold and hardship.   Perhaps you know that Northern plants when taken to Southern countries multiply at the expense of Southern plants.   The strength of the Western world is from the North; that is the philosophy of Kingsley's ode.

> Welcome, wild North-easter!
>   Shame it is to see
> Odes to every zephyr,
>   Ne'er a verse to thee.

Welcome, black North-easter!
  O'er the German foam;
O'er the Danish moorlands,
  From thy frozen home.
Tired we are of summer,
  Tired of gaudy glare,
Showers soft and steaming,
  Hot and breathless air.
Tired of listless dreaming,
  Through the lazy day.
Jovial wind of winter,
  Turns us out to play!
Sweep the golden reed-beds;
  Crisp the lazy dyke;
Hunger into madness
  Every plunging pike.
Fill the lake with wild-fowl;
  Fill the marsh with snipe.

.   .   .   .   .

Let the luscious South-wind
  Breathe in lovers' sighs,
While the lazy gallants
  Bask in ladies' eyes.
What does he but soften
  Heart alike and pen?
'Tis the hard grey weather
  Breeds hard English men.
What's the soft South-wester?
  'Tis the ladies' breeze
Bringing home their true loves
  Out of all the seas.
But the black North-easter,
  Through the snowstorm hurled,
Drives our English hearts of oak
  Seaward round the world.
Come, as came our fathers,
  Heralded by thee
Conquering from the eastward,
  Lords by land and sea.
Come; and strong within us
  Stir the Vikings' blood;
Bracing brain and sinew;
  Blow, thou wind of God!

Of course the whole force of the poem is in the last seven or eight lines, but these are grand. There is an allusion here to the old Viking custom of going to sea in a storm. They did not attack a coast in fine weather; they came only in the time of terrible storms, when nobody was expecting them, and when the watchmen were driven away from the coasts by the wild weather. Somewhere or other Prof. Saintsbury criticised the last line of the poem as very strange, probably because it was written by a Christian clergyman; for here destroying force is called divine—a creed much more of the old Norse than of Christianity. But Kingsley's Christianity was very Norse in many respects; he would have said that might is right, when the might has been acquired by self-control and power to bear pain. And, after all, we find a very similar thought even in the poems of the gentle Quaker Whittier:

> The vigour of the Northern brain
> Shall nerve the world outworn.

At all events, Kingsley's influence in making Englishmen proud of their Norse ancestry has been a healthy one, however it might be judged from a severely orthodox standpoint. As a clergyman and a teacher he was never afraid to take up any subject that he thought beautiful, whether very religious people approved of it or not. A fair example is the story of the search for King Harold's body on the field of battle. The body was so disfigured by wounds that even his own mother could not recognise him. There was only one person in the world who could identify Harold's corpse—that was his mistress. She was sent for. The story is very beautifully told in Kingsley's verse:

> Evil sped the battle play
> On the Pope Calixtus' day:
> Mighty war-smiths, thanes and lords,

In Senlac slept the sleep of swords.
Harold Earl, shot over shield,
Lay along the autumn weald,
Slaughter such was never none,
Since the Ethelings England won.
Thither Lady Githa came,
Weeping sore for grief and shame;
How may she her first-born tell?
Frenchmen stript him where he fell,
Gashed and marred his comely face;
Who can know him in his place?
    Up and spake two brethren wise,
"Youngest hearts have keenest eyes;
Bird which leaves its mother's nest
Moults its pinions, moults its crest;
Let us call the Swan-Neck here,
She that was his leman dear;
She shall know him in this stound;
Foot of wolf, and scent of hound,
Eye of hawk, and wing of dove,
Carry woman to her love."
    Up and spake the Swan-Neck high,
"Go! to all your thanes let cry
How I loved him best of all,
I whom men his leman call;
Better knew his body fair
Than the mother which him bare.
When ye lived in wealth and glee,
Then ye scorned to look on me;
God hath brought the proud ones low,
After me afoot to go."
    Rousing erne and sallow glede,
Over franklin, earl, and thane,
Heaps of mother-naked slain,
Round the red field tracing slow,
Stooped that Swan-Neck white as snow,
Never blushed nor turned away,
Till she found him where he lay;
Clipt him in her armés fair,
Wrapped him in her yellow hair,
Bore him from the battle-stead
Saw him laid in pall of lead,

Took her to a minster high,
For Earl Harold's soul to cry.

Thus fell Harold, bracelet-giver;
Jesu rest his soul forever;
Angels all from thrall deliver;
Miserere Domine!

This is of course an imitation of the old ballad forms, so far as language goes, hence the few curious Middle English words. But without any appearance of effort, and without any attempt at decorative expression, the result is very pathetic and powerful, all the more powerful, perhaps, because we know that the incident is true. "Swan-Neck" was a pet name only, given because she had a very beautiful long neck. The poet has not mentioned one cruel fact, that William the Conqueror would not allow Harold to be buried in a churchyard. So he was buried on the seashore.

By this time I think you will see how very clever Kingsley is in the art of touching emotions with simple words. Had he had the time to devote himself to the ballad form, which he loved, I think he would have done much greater things than Whittier, in the same direction of emotional and religious song. As it is, a few of the things which he did in this form are puzzlingly beautiful; it is hard to find out how the effect has been produced. It is not art of words so much as pure feeling, always expressed in the briefest possible way. I do not know any simple ballad, in modern poetry, more touching than the little composition called "The Mango Tree." But how the emotion is produced, how the art is inspired, you must feel for yourselves. The subject is the commonest possible, the story of a soldier's wife in India. She followed the army in its wanderings about the world, and she lost her husband and all her children by fever at some Indian station. I suppose you know that common English soldiers are allowed to marry under

certain conditions, and the government pays for the travelling expenses of the woman and the children.   We have
here only the thoughts of a very simple mind, remembering the past, but how touching the remembrance is:

> He wiled me through the furzy croft;
>   He wiled me down the sandy lane,
> He told his boy's love, soft and oft,
>   Until I told him mine again.

Probably a village on the Scotch coast is here intended; it
is certainly suggested by the use of the adjective furzy;
and the term "sandy lane" suggests the proximity of the sea.
Observe there is a very little in this first stanza as it stands;
but at the end of the poem you will see what use it really
has.

> We married, and we sailed the main;
>   A soldier, and a soldier's wife.
> We marched through many a burning plain;
>   We sighed for many a gallant life.
>
> But his—God kept it safe from harm.
>   He toiled and dared, and earned command;
> And those three stripes upon his arm
>   Were more to me than gold or land.
>
> Sure he would win some great renown;
>   Our lives were strong, our hearts were high;
> One night the fever struck him down,
>   I sat, and stared, and saw him die.
>
> I had his children—one, two, three.
>   One week I had them, blithe and sound,
> The next—beneath this mango-tree,
>   By him in barrack burying-ground.
>
> I sit beneath the mango-shade;
>   I live my five years' life all o'er—
> Round yonder stems his children played;
>   He mounted guard at yonder door.

'Tis I, not they, am gone and dead.
   They live; they know; they feel; they see.
Their spirits light the golden shade
   Beneath the giant mango-tree.

All things, save I, are full of life;
   The minas, pluming velvet breasts,
The monkeys, in their foolish strife,
   The swooping hawks, the swinging nests;

The lizards basking on the soil,
   The butterflies who sun their wings;
The bees about their household toil,
   They live, they love, the blissful things.

Each tender purple mango-shoot,
   That folds and droops so bashful down;
It lives; it sucks some hidden root;
   It rears at last a broad green crown.

It blossoms; and the children cry—
   "Watch when the mango-apples fall."
It lives: but, rootless, fruitless, I—
   I breathe and dream;—and that is all.

Thus am I dead; yet cannot die:
   But still within my foolish brain
There hangs a pale blue evening sky;
   A furzy croft, a sandy lane.

The pathos here is not so much in the natural thoughts,
touching as these are; it is in the sudden return to the Scotch
memory described in the very first stanza, the sudden contrast between the burning colours and the fantastic splendour of that tropical scenery beheld with the eyes, and that
pale Scotch scenery of five years before beheld in the
mind. This is a bit of great poetical skill; and I do not
know whether Wordsworth was ever equally successful in
the use of the same art of contrast. I suppose that you
remember his study of the servant girl in London hearing
a caged bird sing, and seeing at once through the gloom

of the ugly streets the bright fields where she used to play as a child. Nevertheless, that little poem about the servant girl and the thrush does not reach the heart like the last stanza of Kingsley's "Mango-tree."

I shall make only one more quotation before turning to the subject of Kingsley's classical verse. Both in his novels and in his poems he appears to us as a constant observer of small things having philosophical meanings. Nature spoke to him with the lisping of leaves, the murmuring of streams, the humming of bees; even the sunlight upon the rocks had a message for him. But sights and sound which are beautiful in themselves influence every poet. The surprise is when we find Kingsley extracting poetry from the vulgar or the commonplace. What is less poetical than a field of potatoes or turnips or cabbages? Yet there is poetry even here for a thinker, as Kingsley teaches us.

THE POETRY OF A ROOT-CROP

Underneath their eider-robe
Russet swede and golden globe,
Feathered carrot, burrowing deep,
Steadfast wait in charméd sleep;
Treasure-houses wherein lie,
Locked by angels' alchemy,
Milk, and hair, and blood, and bone.
Children of the barren stone.

How many of you must have sometimes had a thought like this, without perhaps developing it, while walking about the field of a farmer, either in winter or in summer. The vegetables below there mean many great strange things to the modern dreamer. The substance of them is indeed to become milk and hair and blood and bone, but it is to become even more than that—human feeling, human thought. Kingsley calls vegetables children of the stones, because only vegetables can extract the substance of life, protoplasm, from the soil. But even in the dead clay and

stones there is life hidden, the same life that beats in our
hearts and thinks in our minds.   All is life; there is no
grander discovery of modern science than the knowledge
that the sentient issues from the non-sentient, the conscious from the unconscious.   But there is even more than
this thought in the sight of a vegetable field.   Not only will
all that substance be changed into future human life; but
it has been life before, thousands of times, millions of times.
Nor are the elements of life within those vegetables derived
only from the earth in which thy grow; they are not only
children of the barren stone; they are also:

> Children of the flaming Air,
> With his blue eye keen and bare,
> Spirit-peopled smiling down
> On frozen field and toiling town—
> Toiling town that will not heed.

The vegetable grows, you know, not only by taking into itself material from the earth, but also by absorbing material
from the great blue air, which the poet describes for
us as a blue-eyed spirit gazing down upon the world.
Such, too, is our own growth, from air and clay.   Dying,
all life-shapes melt back again, partly into the ground, partly
into gasses that mingle with the atmosphere.   Thus not
only the ground on which we walk is old life, but the air
all about us and above us is life also that once was and
that will again be.   There is really very much to think
about in these little verses, not at all so simple in meaning as they might at first appear.

Now let us turn to Kingsley's classical poems.   As a
dramatist, his long play called "The Saint's Tragedy" is
a failure; perhaps it is a failure because it was written for
a particular argumentative purpose.   Poetry written for any
didactic or special purpose is likely to prove a failure.
Quite otherwise was it when Kingsley attempted to write
great poetry only for the joy of writing and for the beauty

of the thought in itself.   He is, as I told you before, the
writer of the best hexameters in the English language, and
that is a very great glory.   I suppose you know that the
hexameter is not considered altogether possible in English;
it is a Greek measure, and most of the poets who have tried
to write English hexameters have failed.   Longfellow's
"Evangeline," a beautiful poem emotionally, is a proof of
the difficulty of the hexameter, for it is somewhat a failure
in its verse form.   Tennyson wisely left the hexameter almost alone.   Swinburne succeeded with it upon a small
scale; Kingsley succeeded with it upon a very considerable
scale.   But in both cases this success will be found due,
in great part, to the use of Greek words and words of Greek
derivation.   Even so, the feat is very remarkable in Kingsley's case.   He chose for his subject the story of Perseus
and Andromeda, a subject which he has also treated with
wonderful beauty in prose; I refer to the story of Perseus
in his Greek fairy tales, "The Heroes," one of the most
exquisite books ever written.   You ought to know something of this story before we make quotations from the
verses.   The whole of it is too long to tell now, nor is it
necessary to tell all, because Kingsley in the poem treats
of one episode only, the delivery of Andromeda.

Andromeda was the most beautiful of maidens in the
old Greek story, the daughter of Queen Cassiopeia.   One
day the Queen rashly said that her daughter was more beautiful than the gods, more beautiful than the divinity of
the sea.   Thereupon the divinity of the sea became angry,
and sent a great sea-monster to ravage the coast, as a punishment for the Queen's words.   When the cause of this
visitation was discovered, the priests decided that Andromeda should be given to the sea-monster in expiation of
the mother's words.   Accordingly the girl was chained naked
to a rock by the sea-shore.   But when the sea-monster came
to devour her, she was delivered by the hero Perseus, who
came flying over the sea to save her, moving through the

air on winged sandals of gold, the gift of the gods. The poem treats of the discovery of the Queen's words, the sentence of the priests, the chaining of the maiden to the rock, her despair, the passing of the sea-gods, refusing to save her, the coming of Perseus, and the promise of marriage. You know that the Greeks named constellations after their heroes and divinities; and it may interest you to remember that the characters of this beautiful old story appear in the figures of the celestial globe even in these days of modern astronomy.

Perhaps the best idea of Kingsley's excellence in this verse can be obtained by quoting the passage describing the sea-gods. It is rather long; but I shall only quote a few lines of the best:

. . . Far off, in the heart of the darkness,
Bright white mists rose slowly; beneath them the wandering ocean
Glimmered and glowed to the deepest abyss; and the knees of the
    maiden
Trembled and sank in her fear, as afar, like a dawn in the mid-
    night,
Rose from their seaweed chamber the choir of the mystical sea-maids.
Onward toward her they came, and her heart beat loud at their
    coming,
Watching the bliss of the gods, as they wakened the cliffs with
    their laughter.
Onward they came in their joy, and before them the roll of the
    surges
Sank, as the breeze sank dead, into smooth green foam-flecked
    marble,
Awed; and the crags of the cliff, and the pines of the mountain
    were silent.
Onward they came in their joy, and around them the lamps of the
    sea-nymphs,
Myriad fiery globes, swam panting and heaving; and rainbows
Crimson and azure and emerald, were broken in star-showers,
    lighting
Far through the wine-dark depths of the crystal, the gardens of
    Nereus,
Coral and sea-fan and tangle, the blooms and the palms of the
    ocean.

Onward they came in their joy, more white than the foam which
    they scattered,
Laughing and singing, and tossing and twining, while eager, the
    Tritons
Blinded with kisses their eyes, unreproved, and above them in
    worship
Hovered the terns, and the seagulls swept past them on silvery
    pinions,
Echoing softly their laughter; around them the wantoning dolphins
Sighed as they plunged, full of love; and the great sea-horses which
    bore them
Curved up their crests in their pride to the delicate arms of the
    maidens,
Pawing the spray into gems, till a fiery rainfall, unharming,
Sparkled and gleamed on the limbs of the nymphs, and the coils of
    the mermen.

This is a fair example, not so much to be admired because it is like a picture by Titian or Giorgione, but because it represents a triumph over a supremely difficult form
of verse. I have chosen the extract also because it contains fewer Greek words than other parts of the poem, which
are otherwise more beautiful—such as the description of the
maiden's first sight of Perseus, at the very moment when
she is reproaching the gods for their cruelty:

Sudden she ceased, with a shriek: in the spray, like a hovering
    foam-bow,
Hung, more fair than the foam-bow, a boy in the bloom of his
    manhood,
Golden-haired, ivory-limbed, ambrosial; over his shoulder
Hung for a veil of his beauty the gold-fringed folds of the goat-
    skin.

The most beautiful word in the above lines is the Greek
"ambrosial"; it is the value of this word that makes the
line in which it occurs so much more perfect than the
other four. Of course, without the use of many Greek
words the poem could not have been written at all; but
the longer extract which I gave you contains remarkably
few.

My object was to show you by extracts the really important place that Kingsley occupied in nineteenth century literature. It is not a small thing to have written the best songs of the period, songs which have been translated into so many languages; and it is not a small thing to have written the best English hexameters. Nor is it common that a man capable of writing an immortal song should also be capable of severe verse. Altogether Kingsley must be considered as a very extraordinary phenomenon, a true genius whose powers were unfortunately prevented by the difficulties of life from fully developing themselves. He was like a bird whose wings were clipped. To study him will reward you richly, if you will remember his limitations. Do not read his dramatic poem; and do not be shocked by discovering in the rest of his work some short poems of no importance. It has happened to very few poets in this world to produce work uniformly good. Tennyson did this; Rossetti did this, or very nearly did it; but scarcely any other has done it. You do not read the whole of Wordsworth, nor of Coleridge, nor of Byron, nor even of Shelley. And for the same reason I should not advise you to read every bit of verse that Kingsley wrote. There is some rubbish. But the jewels among that rubbish have a peculiar colour and splendour that distinguish them from everything else written during the same period.

CHAPTER VIII

MATTHEW ARNOLD AS POET

For a number of years the prose work of Matthew Arnold has been considered to some degree as affording excellent models of English composition, and his essays have been studied as class texts all over the English-speaking world. I venture to say that this has been a mistake, and that the value of Matthew Arnold's essays has been greatly exaggerated in regard to the matter of style. Matthew Arnold's essays are very valuable indeed, in thought and instruction, but they are not great models of perfect English; they do not represent a vigorous nor a clear nor a concentrated style. It is quite different in regard to his poetry, which is not so well known, but which is steadily growing in the estimation of the literary world.

Now there are two ways of judging poetry. It is either great or not great by reason of its form or by reason of its thought. And I must tell you that the very greatest masters of form are not likely to be the very greatest masters of thought. Shakespeare, our greatest genius, is often very deficient in regard to form. The greatest of French poets, Victor Hugo, is a perfect master of form, and a very poor thinker; he is a magician, he is not a philosopher. The greatest of German poets and thinkers of his time, Goethe, a man who excelled in form and thought, said in his old age that if he could begin his literary life again he would give all his attention to the thought, and waste very little time upon the form. Among modern English poets we may take the cases of Browning and George Meredith as opposed to Rossetti and Swinburne. Swinburne is the greatest master of English verse that ever lived, but he is very unimportant as a thinker; there are only two or three of his poems in which we find a grand flash of thought. Rossetti was perhaps the very greatest of our emotional poets during the nineteenth century, and he was nearly as great a master of form as Swinburne; but Rossetti did not teach men to think new thoughts about the great problems of life. He hated science, and he was not, in the modern sense of the word, a philosopher. But Browning and Meredith are philosophers, deep thinkers, great teachers—more especially Meredith. Neither of them was a master of form in the highest meaning of the term. They are both great sinners in the matter of obscurity and imperfect construction. They have followed the suggestion of Goethe to sacrifice the form to the thinking. I should like to be able to speak to you of some poet of our own day who is equally great as a thinker and as a verse-maker, but I cannot cite a single name. The nearest approach to such a person is Tennyson, but as a thinker Tennyson is much below Meredith. We have to take our choice in this world between two kinds of perfection in poetry which are seldom united in any one individual. In considering Matthew Arnold as a poet we must bear this in mind.

For Arnold cannot be placed among the great masters of form. He is very uninteresting in regard to form. It is chiefly as a thinker that we must study him, as a thinker of a very peculiar kind. Not for a moment could we place him upon the same level as George Meredith. His value is not the value of an expositor of new ideas, but the value of the man himself, a personal value, a value of character. Again, this character is not important because it is extremely original; quite the contrary. It is because Matthew Arnold's character and way of thinking faithfully represent hundreds of thousands of similar characters and similar ways of thinking during the middle of the present century, the thought of cultivated minds. In this class there was a great deal of solid thinking done, thinking based upon the whole experience of the past—the moral experience of the English race. Macaulay's essays take much of their value from this kind of thinking. It is not new, but it is very good, very true in a certain sense, and likely to remain so for thousands of years to come. So we find the poetry of Matthew Arnold to be valuable as a crystallisation of the best thinking of the time.

But now we must say a word about the time. It was the time of Darwin and Spencer, when evolutional philosophy first began to upset old doctrines and to shake the faith of the educated classes. It was the time also of the Oxford movement toward a new religious spirit—I might say toward a religious revival. For the sudden introduction of new and startling ideas must always produce two effects. One effect is to destroy old ways of feeling and thinking. The other effect is to create a violent reaction in favour of them. And the middle of the century witnessed both of these effects. Among the university men of Arnold's time there were three attitudes of mind. The strong men, like Clifford, went over to the new philosophy altogether. Less strong minds became frightened and fled for refuge into religious circles. Between these two there was a very remarkable class of young students, who were profoundly religious in feeling but much too intelligent to refuse to understand the new methods of science. They could not continue to believe in the old way, and yet the new way caused them terrible sorrow and pain. Intellectually they were sceptics; emotionally and by inheritance they were intensely religious.

Persons of this kind suffered much from the conflict between their natural character and their fresh convictions. Most noteworthy among them were Arthur Hugh Clough and Matthew Arnold. Both became poets, both expressed their feelings and thoughts in very good verse, but Matthew Arnold was altogether the greater man, and left the deeper mark upon the literature of his time. He was born in 1822 and died in 1888, so that he enjoyed a fairly long life. It was not, however, a happy life. He was a son of Dr. Arnold, perhaps the greatest English educator in modern times. Dr. Arnold laid down a plan for teaching which is still followed, which will probably continue to be followed for all time in the best English schools. He taught that education itself, in the sense of learning from books or lectures, was a very secondary matter, and that the first and most important matter was the formation of character. He was a Christian, of course, but he was not a sectarian in the narrow sense of the term, and his plan of education was not religious at all. It was based upon the simplest rules of social morality. But as a matter of fact, to be good in this world is an extremely difficult thing; and it was to cultivate a knowledge of this difficulty and a knowledge of how to meet it that Dr. Arnold changed the system of education in those institutions which he controlled. It was very important that a young man should study well and obey the rules, but Dr. Arnold taught that it was more important for the student to learn how to master himself and how to be a great man and a gentleman outside of the class room and outside of the college. Matthew Arnold was severely trained by his father in this way, and he went to Oxford a model of everything that his father could have desired. There, after having distinguished himself, having won several prizes in various literary studies, he graduated, and soon afterwards obtained the position of Inspector of Schools. He kept this position until the time of his death, but after middle life he was also Professor of Poetry at Oxford. All his literary work of importance was done somewhat later than one might suppose; it would indeed seem as if he had never wished to become a poet until after he had ceased to be a young man. These simple facts will help us to explain the very remarkable merits and shortcoming of his verse.

You will see that Matthew Arnold's intellectual and religious training must have been rather of the eighteenth than of the nineteenth century.   His great father, with all his greatness, was essentially a man of the old traditions, a man who belonged in principles and in feelings rather to the time of Dr. Johnson than to the time of the Lake poets. The principles and the feelings were right and true, but in form they were old-fashioned.   To understand the position of Matthew Arnold in a period of transition, you must imagine the son of an old-fashioned *samurai*, educated strictly according to the ancient system, and then suddenly introduced to the new condition of *meiji*.   Such a one would necessarily suffer not a little in this new order of things. So it was with Matthew Arnold.   He had been made a perfect gentleman, a true man, a good scholar, but he had not been prepared for the times of Darwin and Spencer and Huxley.   Neither had he been prepared for the new feeling in poetry and in other branches of literature.   By heredity and sentiment he was essentially religious; yet his religious ideas were necessarily changed by the new learning.   By heredity and education he was essentially classic; yet he found himself suddenly placed in the middle of the romantic movement in literature.   And what is more worth while for you to know than anything else, his duties were of the most monotonous and unsympathetic kind.   There is no position more tiresome, more uninviting, more hopeless for a man of original power than the position of Inspector of Schools.   But Matthew Arnold remained in that position during the rest of his life.   Thus he was out of sympathy with the thought of his age in philosophy, with the literature of his age in poetry, and with the very conditions upon which his living depended.

If I have kept you thus upon the subject of the man's life, it is only because you should understand very clearly Matthew Arnold's curious position in English poetry.   Our nineteenth century has been especially the century of the romantic movement in poetry.   Even Wordsworth, with all his seriousness, was romantic. Byron, Shelley, Keats, Coleridge, Southey, all were romantics. And the great Victorian poets brought the romantic feeling to its highest possible degree of perfected expression. It would be hard to mention any great poet of the century who escaped the new influences. Even Matthew Arnold could not altogether escape them, but he had no sympathy with them—he disliked even Tennyson; and the all-important fact about Matthew Arnold for you to remember is that he remains a classical spirit in the middle of the romantic movement.

A good deal of his poetry reflects, as you might expect, his dissatisfaction with the new order of things, and with the tendency to new ways of thinking and feeling. One of his earliest poems bears witness to his sentiment in this regard. He had heard a clergyman of liberal tendencies utter some advice to his congregation about life in harmony with nature; and this advice, probably inspired by the same kind of feeling which characterises the teaching of Rousseau, at once aroused his indignation, as the following verses testify.

IN HARMONY WITH NATURE

(TO A PREACHER)

"In harmony with Nature?" Restless fool,
Who with such heat dost preach what were to thee,
When true, the last impossibility—
To be like Nature strong, like Nature cool!

Know, man hath all which Nature hath, but more,
And in that *more* lie all his hopes of good.
Nature is cruel, man is sick of blood;
Nature is stubborn, man would fain adore;

Nature is fickle, man hath need of rest;
Nature forgives no debt, and fears no grave;
Man would be mild, and with safe conscience blest.

Man must begin, know this, where Nature ends;
Nature and man can never be fast friends.
Fool, if thou canst not pass her, rest her slave!

This is fine, and, in a particular sense, it is very true.   If we understand by Nature merely the creating and destroying forces of the universe, we can understand the poet's indignation.   The great thinker Huxley well said, that if humanity were simply to follow the laws of Nature in this sense, the successful man in the world would be the man with the strongest muscles and the hardest heart—in other words, one would have to become a cruel brute to succeed in life.   The same teacher has also boldly said that everything good in human nature has been made not by acting according to the laws of the universe, but by opposing them, by fighting against them, by resisting them even in the face of death.   When Matthew Arnold tells us, however, that man has something more than Nature has, we see there something of religious feeling expressing itself.   A much greater man than Matthew Arnold, Shakespeare, better said that the highest excellencies of man, however supernatural they may seem, have been made by Nature.   The whole meaning of poetry like this, the whole value of it, depends upon how one understands the word Nature.   Huxley could make the observation which I have quoted, only after he had clearly defined what he meant by Nature.   Nature can seem to the popular imagination something distinct from intelligent life and moral feeling.   But Huxley reminds us at the same time that the opinion of Shakespeare is a correct one.   All life throughout the universe is one, and Nature, in the modern scientific sense, would mean the universe itself.   A pupil of the new philosophy would solve the riddle in this way: "It is true that man has become moral by resisting certain natural impulses, but even his resistance was compelled by other eternal and natural laws."   What Nature really says to man is this: "It is not enough to obey me when you find an inclination to do it; it is much more important to disobey me—to make yourself strong with constant wrestling with me.   I love only those who can fight me well."   Nor is this all.   Nature helps us to do this fighting against her own impulses. Consider the most powerful of human passions, the sexual instinct; this is natural, most certainly, and the natural tendency is to indulge it. But without talking about reason at all, we have other natural impulses given us to oppose selfish indulgence even in this direction. For example, there is the love of children—maternal and paternal affection. These forms of affection are equally natural, and yet they more than anything else prevent either men or animals from committing certain forms of sexual excess. The love of offspring acts as a check upon the very impulse that produces the offspring, it makes the family, and the family depends upon the observance of certain moral obligations. Again, we have all of us the instinct of revenge, which is natural, and which has its uses even in the formation of society. It is natural that a man should strike back when he is struck. But he must not gratify even his natural instinct beyond a certain extent. For there is in all men the instinct also of self-preservation, and when a man indulges revenge beyond a certain limit, all men become afraid of him, and kill him in order to protect themselves. Their action is quite as natural as the action of the man to strike. There is no form of virtue which would not, upon close examination, be found quite as natural as the vice which is opposed to it. Nature gives both, like the God of the Hebrews, who says, "I am the Lord thy God, creating both good and evil." And, therefore, I should certainly think that the preacher thus criticised by Matthew Arnold was nearer to the truth than his critic. But mediæval religion regarded Nature as a kind of demon, inspiring the evil passions only, and the poet argues only from the mediæval standpoint. If the preacher meant, with Shakespeare, that "Nature is made better by no means, but Nature makes that means," then, I should say, his position was beyond criticism. It is not a case of human choice at all; we must live in harmony with Nature, or else disappear from the face of the earth. But when we recognise this, we must recognise also that Nature makes morality, and Matthew Arnold could not recognise that. His thoughts were in the eighteenth century.

He was much happier in his philosophy when he wrote from the results of personal experience, not from the results of theory. At an early time he thought, for example, of what the pains of life mean—of the difficulty of being good, of the impossibility of obtaining more than one is really fitted for. He recognised a certain terrible Justice in the very Nature that he had spoken ill of. A man's chances in this world really depend very much upon his personal power, more so in Western countries even than in Japan. But one of the last things which a man can learn is the extent of his weakness. A young man scarcely ever discovers this. If young men really knew their weaknesses, their deficiencies, their ignorance, they never could succeed in life; such knowledge would make them afraid. But after the great struggle is over, then they learn why many things happened to them which they formerly thought unjust and cruel and wicked. They begin to understand that their own deficiencies were in great part the reason of their sorrows and of their failures. Oriental philosophy meets the puzzle of life better than Western religion in this regard. It teaches that the misfortunes of this life are consequent upon faults committed in former lives; modern science, in other language, teaches exactly the same thing. The best things are for the strong man; if the man is not strong, that is the fault of the race from which he springs, the consequence of something that happened perhaps hundreds of years before he was born. In a little poem called "Human Life" Matthew Arnold expresses a dim perception of the truth.

> What mortal, when he saw
> Life's voyage done, his heavenly Friend,
> Could ever yet dare tell him fearlessly:
> "I have kept uninfringed my nature's law;

The dimly-written chart thou gavest me,
To guide me, I have steer'd by to the end?"

Ah! let us make no claim,
On life's incognisable sea,
To too exact a steering of our way;
Let us not fret and fear to miss our aim,
If some fair coast have lured us to make stay,
Or some friend hail'd us to keep company.

Ay! we would each fain drive
At random, and not steer by rule.
Weakness! and worse, weakness bestow'd in vain.
Winds from our side the unsuiting consort rive,
We rush by coasts where we had lief remain;
Man cannot, though he would, live chance's fool.

No! as the foaming swath
Of torn-up water, on the main,
Falls heavily away with long-drawn roar,
On either side the black deep-furrowed path
Cut by an onward-labouring vessel's prore,
And never touches the ship-side again;

Even so we leave behind,
As, charter'd by some unknown Powers,
We stem across the sea of life by night,
The joys which were not for our use design'd;—
The friends to whom we had no natural right,
The homes that were not destined to be ours.

This grave poetry is not attractive at first sight, neither
is it easy to understand. But when we examine it patiently, we shall find that it repays study. Let us paraphrase it: What man after his death could dare to say to
God, "I have never done anything wrong, I have always
obeyed my conscience"? We must not pretend to be too
good, we do not know anything about the secrets of this
great sea of life upon which we sail, and we must not be
afraid of our mistakes in youth. If we have sometimes

yielded to temptation caused by beauty or friendship, we need not on that account despair.

Why? Simply because we cannot do as we would altogether, either in the direction of right or wrong. Of course we should like to do as we please, instead of following rules. But that is useless and foolish. Whatever we, wish, good or bad, our wishes are not likely to be gratified. If we love a woman who is not suited to us—either because she is too good or because we are too bad, the result is separation. If we want to live in some beautiful place where our lives would not be useful, we find that we cannot stop there. There is a law that governs everything which we do, and it is quite impossible for men to escape that law.

Just as the water that is cut by a ship closes again after the ship passes, and never again touches that ship, so each man, as he passes over the great sea of life, has to leave behind him everything that according to the eternal law of fitness he ought not to have. He would like to have certain men as friends, but he is not naturally fitted to become intimate with them, therefore he cannot have their friendship. He wishes for certain pleasures, but if his natural capacities have not entitled him to such pleasures, he will never obtain them. He would like to have a beautiful home; that also is a wish only to be gratified in the case of men of larger powers. He must remember, to console himself, that he is only indeed a ship chartered to cross the sea of life and death, and to follow a fixed course. That is his destiny—not a blind destiny, but a destiny evolved by his own past history, by his own inheritance of greater or of less ability than his fellow man.

This is sad in tone, but it is also wise and true. Equally true is a piece upon the folly of prayer. Did you ever think what could happen if the gods were to answer all the prayers that are made to them every day? The world would be very soon destroyed. For example, in Western countries all Christian people every day pray for food, that they may have enough to eat. If they did have all the food which they desired, the result would be an enormous increase of population that could only end in misery, war, or destruction of some horrible kind. Again, who does not pray for long life? But many of the miseries of this world are caused by excess of population, and if all men could live as long as they wish, the world would eventually become unendurable. People do not often think about these things, and Matthew Arnold is one of the very few who make us think about them. In a poem called "Consolation" he makes a series of little pictures of life in different parts of the world, and shows us how in each of these places people are praying to the gods, and how all the prayers contradict each other. The poem is a little too long to quote complete, but we may cite the verses about young lovers which conclude the composition.

> Two young, fair lovers,
> Where the warm June-wind,
> Fresh from the summer fields
> Plays fondly round them,
> Stand, tranced in joy.
>
> With sweet, join'd voices,
> And with eyes brimming;
> "Ah," they cry, "Destiny,"
> Prolong the present!
> Time! stand still here!"
>
> The prompt stern Goddess
> Shakes her head, frowning;
> Time gives his hour-glass
> Its due reversal;
> Their hour is gone.
>
> With weak indulgence
> Did the just Goddess
> Lengthen their happiness,
> She lengthen'd also
> Distress elsewhere.

The hour, whose happy
Unalloy'd moments
I would eternalise,
Ten thousand mourners
Well pleased see end.

The bleak, stern hour,
Whose severe moments
I would annihilate,
Is pass'd by others
In warmth, light, joy.

Time, so complain'd of,
Who to no one man
Shows partiality,
Brings round to all men
Some undimm'd hours.

This has the value of suggestion more than of poetical art, as we generally understand the term, but even considered only as form it is admirably and severely correct. Cold Matthew Arnold's poetry certainly is, but it makes us think. As I said before, he is especially successful in telling the result of his own mental experience, and this is an instance. Evidently he has thought a great deal about the world in relation to human will, and has recognised that none of us could have our desires fulfilled, except at the expense of some other person's happiness. We recognise this truth in more familiar ways every day. For example, when we regret that the weather is rainy instead of fine, we do not reflect that this rain which spoils our pleasure is bringing fertility to the crops, benefit to farmers. Also we soon learn that a man sometimes cannot become rich, unless somebody else becomes poor. But we are not apt to remember, as we ought to do, that many of our wishes fall under the same universal law. What we wish for can often be obtained only at somebody else's cost. After all, the world is not so very bad, for even the most unfortunate among us have some bright, or, as the poet calls them, undimmed hours.

The preceding verses are, I must tell you, rather cheerful,

considering how very gloomy much of Matthew Arnold's poetry is.   But it is in his glooms and shadows that his best work is, the work which affords food for thought because it has grown out of the memories and personal sufferings of the man.   As an example of warmer feeling in the same melancholy direction, there is nothing more touching than the little poem which he calls "The Voice."   Have you ever noted that a voice is one of those things that longest remain in memory?   Sometimes even after we have forgotten the face of some dead friend, forgotten even his name, kind words which he spoke to us continue to resound in our remembrance, with the very same tone in which they were uttered.   The poet here is speaking, however, about the voice of a dead woman, remembered in his old age. This woman very often appears in his poems, a girl—a French girl, probably—whom he met when he was very young, and whom he was only prevented from marrying by reason of some social obstacle, we know not what, perhaps duty, perhaps want of money.   I shall quote only two stanzas.   The last is more than beautiful.

> Like bright waves that fall
> With a lifelike motion
> On the lifeless margin of the sparkling Ocean;
> A wild rose climbing up a mouldering wall—
> A gush of sunbeams through a ruin'd hall—
> Strains of glad music at a funeral—
> So sad, and with so wild a start
> To this deep-sober'd heart,
> So anxiously and painfully,
> So drearily and doubtfully,
> And oh, with such intolerable change
> Of thought, such contrast strange,
> O unforgotten voice, thy accents come,
> Like wanderers from the world's extremity,
> Unto their ancient home!
>
> In vain, all, all in vain,
> They beat upon mine ear again,

> Those melancholy tones so sweet and still.
> Those lute-like tones which in the bygone year
> Did steal into mine ear—
> Blew such a thrilling summons to my will,
> Yet could not shake it,
> Made my tost heart its very life-blood spill,
> Yet could not break it.

Why these comparisons about the breaking waves on a dreadful shore, about roses blooming on broken walls, sunlight in a ruined chamber, music at a funeral? Because the time of youth and hope and love is utterly dead, and the memory of the voice recalling it also recalls years of pain, but not of joy. The contrast between what is and what might have been is itself, as Dante teaches in a certain immortal verse, the greatest of all sorrows. The voice referred to might have said, "Take me! I can make your life beautiful—I am youth, love, and happiness." But duty would have said, "Impossible." The poem suggests the desperate character of the struggle between inclination and reason. Reason proved the stronger, duty was obeyed, but at how terrible a cost. The reference to the breaking of the heart becomes very pathetic if you understand that the English phrase "to break one's heart" signifies to die of grief. The line "yet could not break it" implies a wish to die of the struggle instead of living to endure all its consequences.

The meditative character in Matthew Arnold's poetry, in its most personal form, is also beautifully shown in a composition recording his thoughts while listening to the roar of the sea at night. This piece is called "Dover Beach," but the incident might be anywhere, on any coast in the world, in Japan as well as in England. There is only the presentation of thoughts awakened by the sound of the sea in the mind of a scholar and a doubter.

> The sea is calm to-night.
> The tide is full, the moon lies fair

Upon the straits;—on the French coast the light
Gleams and is gone; the cliffs of England stand,
Glimmering and vast, out in the tranquil bay.
Come to the window, sweet is the night-air!
Only from the long line of spray
Where the sea meets the moon-blanch'd land,
Listen! you hear the grating roar
Of pebbles which the waves draw back, and fling,
At their return, up the high strand,
Begin, and cease, and then again begin,
With tremulous cadence slow, and bring
The eternal note of sadness in.

Sophocles long ago
Heard it on the Ægæan, and it brought
Into his mind the turbid ebb and flow
Of human misery; we
Find also in the sound a thought,
Hearing it by this distant northern sea.

The Sea of Faith
Was once, too, at the full, and round earth's shore
Lay like the folds of a bright girdle furl'd.
But now I only hear
Its melancholy, long, withdrawing roar,
Retreating to the breath
Of the night-wind, down the vast edges drear
And naked shingles of the world.

Ah, love, let us be true
To one another! for the world, which seems
To lie before us like a land of dreams,
So various, so beautiful, so new,
Hath really neither joy, nor love, nor light,
Nor certitude, nor peace, nor help for pain;
And we are here as on a darkling plain
Swept with confused alarms of struggle and flight,
Where ignorant armies clash by night.

We may paraphrase a part of this, the better to show its
beauty and its relation to the writer's own experience.
Telling us to listen to the sound of the waves, he thus pro-

ceeds: "Thousands of years ago, by the shores of the Greek sea, the great poet and dramatist Sophocles listened to that sound as we are doing now and it made him think of the great sea of life, with all its confused sounds of joy and pain. We also in this nineteenth century can find in that sound something to think about, just as Sophocles did, although the world has greatly changed since his time, and although this is not the warm coast of Greece, but the cold Northern shore of England.

"I hear the roar of the retreating tide, fainter and fainter as the moments pass. Then it seems to me that I am listening, not to the sounds of the sea on the English coast, but to the sound of the ebbing of the great sea of religion. Once men believed in God and a future life; once Christianity covered the whole world like the water of a sea. But to-day in the age of new philosophy, in this age of scientific doubt, the tide of religious faith is beginning to ebb away, leaving only naked barren sands and stones behind it.

"Then let us who love each other, draw close to each other. There is nothing left in this world but friendship and love. For all that the world promises of pleasure, proves to be empty and worthless, and there is really no beauty nor glory, nor rest nor happiness, no certainty and no God to pray to. We are like people alone in darkness in the middle of a great plain, where armies are fighting without light."

To an Oriental thinker, I fancy, the sound of the sea by night would bring suggestions of the great sea of birth and death, in which suggestion there is much consolation of a certain kind. Feeling that we are a part of the sea that has no shore, no beginning, and no end, we cannot feel very anxious or very unhappy about the future. The fact that we now exist is proof positive that we have always existed; it is equal proof that we never can cease to exist. To-day this would be the position of the most advanced Western philosopher. But Matthew Arnold's time was the interval between the death of old ideas and the birth of new convictions. And men of such a time are likely to be very unhappy. A man who trusts entirely to religion, to belief in God and Heaven and the reward of good conduct, becomes utterly miserable if he suddenly discovers that he cannot longer believe the doctrines which once gave him so much consolation. This poem expresses faithfully and painfully the thoughts of many men of that time.

But it also expresses something more—the melancholy of old age. You may have read of what are called the "disillusions of a man of fifty." I do not think that any of you could exactly understand what the phrase means, for the simple reason that none of you is fifty. But you can imagine a good deal about it. When a man has lived for fifty years in this world, he has learned a great many things that never could be learned from books, some things which are not pleasant to learn and which make him serious. He cannot trust his fellow men as he did in other times, because he has learned a great deal about human motives and human weaknesses. He cannot believe in a great many things which it is happiness to believe in, because these have been proved impossible by his personal experience. He has learned that scarcely any honest ambition can be gratified except at such a cost that the result is not worth struggling for. And then his capacity for pleasure has become very much lessened. I do not mean only that his bodily strength has been diminished and his passions impaired, but I mean especially that his mind has become less sensitive either to pleasure or to pain. The sweet fresh air that delights the boy, the beauty of a summer sunset or an autumn afternoon, the singing of birds, the blossoming of flowers—all these make very little impression upon the man who is beginning to grow old. And Matthew Arnold is, I think, almost the only Englishman who has written a poem upon the subject. Of course he is expressing only his own feeling, but this is the feeling of thousands and thousands who have attempted to do what he tried to do, and who have failed even more than he failed.

GROWING OLD

What is it to grow old?
Is it to lose the glory of the form,
The lustre of the eye?
Is it for beauty to forego her wreath?
—Yes, but not this alone.

Is it to feel our strength—
Not our bloom only, but our strength—decay?
Is it to feel each limb
Grow stiffer, every function less exact,
Each nerve more loosely strung?

Yes, this, and more; but not
Ah, 'tis not what in youth we dream'd 'twould be!
'Tis not to have our life
Mellow'd and soften'd as with sunset-glow,
A golden day's decline.

'Tis not to see the world
As from a height, with rapt prophetic eyes,
And heart profoundly stirr'd;
And weep, and feel the fulness of the past,
The years that are no more.

It is to spend long days
And not once feel that we were ever young;
It is to add, immured
In the hot prison of the present, month
To month with weary pain.

It is to suffer this,
And feel but half, and feebly, what we feel.
Deep in our hidden heart
Festers the dull remembrance of a change,
But no emotion—none.

It is—last stage of all—
When we are frozen up within, and quite

The phantom of ourselves,
To hear the world applaud the hollow ghost
Which blamed the living man.

I suppose that this is one of the most horrible pictures of
old age ever written, but it is true of the old age of many
a good and great man in the history of civilisation. It was
certainly the history of Matthew Arnold's old age. Only
at a very late day did success come to him, when he could
no longer enjoy it. But you must not think that his poetical complaint signifies weakness. He was too well trained
by his father to show weakness. The despair of the pessimist never took hold upon him. He only thought of himself as a soldier in a losing battle, certain of defeat, but
resolved to die bravely. The brave note, mixed with a
little bitterness, we find in another poem of much simpler
form called "The Last Word."

> Creep into thy narrow bed,
> Creep, and let no more be said!
> Vain thy onset! all stands fast.
> Thou thyself must break at last.
>
> Let the long contention cease!
> Geese are swans, and swans are geese.
> Let them have it how they will!
> Thou art tired; best be still.

In other words, "Go to your grave in silence, and stop
talking truth. It is no use. You have been fighting with
a society too powerful for you, prejudices too strong for
you, superstitions impregnable. Society, prejudice, superstition, are not only stronger than you, they are longer
lived; you must die before they die. Stop your hopeless
fighting. Of course you know that geese are not swans, but
since people persist in saying that they are swans, it is no
use for you to be angry with them. Why be angry with
stupidity?"

But the reformer states that he has other reasons to be angry, in the injustice and cruelty and malice of men.

> They out-talk'd thee, hiss'd thee, tore thee?
> Better men fared thus before thee;
> Fired their ringing shot and pass'd,
> Hotly charged—and sank at last.
>
> Charge once more, then, and be dumb!
> Let the victors, when they come,
> When the forts of folly fall,
> Find thy body by the wall!

This is excellent advice to any reformer who despairs or feels like despairing. It is good to remember that no matter what injustice the world may do to you, it has done injustice to greater men in past times, and will doubtless continue to do greater injustice to still greater men in the future. If you want to benefit the world, you must make up your mind about two things; you must be content to sacrifice your life or your happiness or both, and whatever you do, you must not expect to be told or to hear of your own success. The new truth which you wish to teach will certainly be some day accepted, if it is truth, but you must not hope to have even the reward of seeing it accepted. Great reforms demand the absolute sacrifice of self.

Now, the thinker who observes the tendencies of modern civilisation often finds reason to doubt not only the possibilities of ethical reform, but the possibilities even of mental or moral development in the highest sense. It seems to him that the necessities of this civilisation are turning men's minds away from noble ideas to selfish and material ambitions. It seems to him that even the feeling which makes poetry must die. It seems to him that the spiritual and moral ideals of the past must be forgotten in the great hurried hungry struggle for money and position. The world is becoming material in the ugliest meaning of the term. The great cities are drawing away from nature the millions who used to feel and know the poetry of country life. The fields are no longer cultivated by men, but by machinery, and vast parts of America and of other countries which are tilled by steam, remain practically uninhabited except in the season of the harvests. Everywhere the population increases, and always the struggle for existence becomes fiercer, and always the duties of life become heavier and harder. Will there be in the future any time to think, any time to feel, any time to be happy, any time to cherish noble motives and sublime thoughts? Certainly things look dark. Herbert Spencer told us that the period of the greatest possible human suffering has yet to come. Scientific civilisation cannot save us from that; on the contrary it will bring it about, by increasing the population of the world to a degree never before known. The struggle for life in Europe will become like the struggle for life in China.

All these thoughts are suggested in a little poem by Matthew Arnold called "The Future." In this poem the course of human progress is compared to the flowing of a river, down which the soul of man is floating. The idea of the River of Life is very old, and has been used by many thousands of poets, but Matthew Arnold has treated the subject in a new way. In the first part of the poem there is not much which is new, only a comparison of humanity's first joy in the life of the world to the joy of a child in a boat upon a little country stream. Somewhat further on, as it recedes from its source, the stream broadens, and great shapes of mountains and forests appear on the horizon. "As is the world on the banks, so is the mind of man." Human knowledge of the world itself has always been, and still is, limited to impressions of the senses, and these are illusions. But while these illusions were beautiful in the past, men were comparatively happy. They were close to nature in ancient times; they did not live in great gloomy cities, full of dust and smoke, but they delighted in their

life in forests and fields, on mountains and by rivers. The
course of progress was then like the course of a river winding through sunlit valleys and plains, under a bright blue
sky. But with the development of material civilisation the
landscape darkens. Great cities appear on the banks of a
winding stream, blackening the sky with the smoke of their
innumerable fires, and the water itself is no longer clear and
pure. Still the spirit of man floats on with the stream, and
this spirit feels the sadness of the great change. Does this
sadness signify wisdom? Perhaps so, but as yet only in a
relative sense—that is, in relation to the world of which
man forms a part. But of the origin of the world itself,
of the source of the stream of Being, or of the destiny of
the stream, we know nothing at all. We float on, watching the banks, but we do not know where we came from nor
whither we are going. This only we know, that always as
we float with the stream the cities on either bank become
larger and more tumultuous and the sky darker and the
river stormier, and the horizon is black before us, so black
that we cannot see.

> And we say that repose has fled
> Forever the course of the river of Time.
> That cities will crowd to its edge
> In a blacker, incessanter line;
> That the din will be more on its banks,
> Denser the trade on its stream,
> Flatter the plain where it flows,
> Fiercer the sun overhead.
> That never will those on its breast
> See an ennobling sight,
> Drink of the feeling of quiet again.

That is, we feel as if the joy of calm had forever been destroyed by this new industrial civilisation, and the future,
as we behold it, looks so gloomy that we doubt whether
mankind can ever again be happy.

Still, who can predict what changes will come? A hun-

dred years ago, who could have believed in the power which
science has given us to-day? There may be a hope that
some new and totally unimaginable faculties will yet restore to us something of the happiness of those conditions of
peace which we have left behind. In the suggestion of this
hope, the poet gives us one beautiful touch of mysticism:

> But what was before us we know not,
> And we know not what shall succeed.
>
> Haply, the river of Time—
> As it grows, as the towns on its marge
> Fling their wavering lights
> On a wider, statelier stream—
> May acquire, if not the calm
> Of its early mountainous shore,
> Yet a solemn peace of its own.
>
> And the width of the waters, the hush
> Of the grey expanse where he floats,
> Freshening its currents and spotted with foam
> As it draws to the Ocean, may strike
> Peace to the soul of the man on its breast—
> As the pale waste widens around him,
> As the banks fade dimmer away,
> As the stars come out, and the night-wind
> Brings up the stream
> Murmurs and scents of the infinite sea.

You remember the previous description of the mountain
stream descending to the plain, and widening, and always
flowing over flatter ground. Observe that the word "flat"
means not only level, but also commonplace, dull, uninteresting, vulgar. What gives poetry life is our sense of the
beautiful, our sense of duty, our idea of conditions better
than any which we have. Now, the tendency of industrial
civilisation is to compel men to think more about money
than ever before, and less about truth and beauty and divine things. This is what the poet means when he expresses the fear that the River of Life will be flowing in

the future through a flatter world than now, more selfish, more vulgar. It does indeed seem as if mankind were going to lose all spiritual ambitions, and to think only about commonplace and vulgar things. We imagine greater cities, greater wealth, more people, more material power in the future, but we cannot at the same time imagine great nobility of mind, greater beauty of thought, or finer qualities of emotion. However, says the poet, we do not know the future; we do not even know the past. Being ignorant as to where we came from, how can we tell whither we are going? One thing only is certain—that we issued originally out of the Infinite Mystery and that we must return to the Mystery. Outside of us, outside this world, all about us the Infinite lies like a sea without shore, and the drifting of all life is to that fathomless deep. Thither flows this River of Time, with the spirit of man floating upon it through countless different kinds of illusions, like the scenery of landscapes. When and how and where the stream will enter the sea, we cannot tell. But it is possible that at some time, before we all pass back into that Unknown out of which we came, some sudden revelation will come to us. Mankind will continue to learn, and continue to hope, and continue to pray for rest through all the centuries, while the world grows older and approaches the end. If you have ever descended a river to the sea in a boat, you will remember the pleasure of the moment when you first began to smell the salt air of the sea, and to feel the pure, fresh sea wind in your face. At once you feel stronger and happier, and all your senses seem to become sharper and finer. So it may be with humanity, as it descends the River of Time toward the Sea of Eternity. Perhaps it will be only in the moment when we first perceive the odour of that Infinite Sea, and hear far away the muttering of its waves— that is to say, perhaps it will only be when the life of the world is nearly done—that we shall suddenly discover some great truth that will make us happy.

In his power of suggestiveness, Matthew Arnold is certainly very remarkable, and not only when he treats of large subjects. We notice this characteristic still more when he touches upon slighter things than the destiny of man or the meaning of the universe. For example, he has written a little poem about the great French actress Rachel, which is, I think, a very wonderful thing, because the whole story and meaning of her life is put into fourteen lines. You know Rachel was the greatest actress of modern times. She was a Jewess, and always remained true to her religion and race, but she found pleasure sometimes in reading Christian and other religious books. She was the child of very poor people, and belonged to an oppressed race, yet she rose to the very highest rank in her profession, and obtained from kings and emperors the highest marks of honour and esteem. She never married, and she died, before her time, of consumption. What Matthew Arnold writes about her might be called a little study in the great problem of heredity.

> Sprung from the blood of Israel's scattered race,
> At a mean inn in German Aarau born,
> To forms from antique Greece and Rome uptorn,
> Trick'd out with a Parisian speech and face,
>
> Imparting life renew'd, old classic grace;
> Then, soothing with thy Christian strain forlorn,
> A-Kempis! her departing soul outworn,
> While by her bedside Hebrew rites have place—
>
> Ah, not the radiant spirit of Greece alone
> She had—one power, which made her breast its home!
> In her, like us, there clash'd, contending powers,
>
> Germany, France, Christ, Moses, Athens, Rome.
> The strife, the mixture in her soul, are ours;
> Her genius and her glory are her own.

Here was a curious mingling of emotional elements, artistic elements, and race elements—a Jewess acting as a

Greek woman of the past in the Paris of the present. But there was yet another curious fact, the interest that this Jewess took in Christian mysticism. When she was dying the prayers repeated at her bedside were Hebrew prayers, but she read in those moments "The Imitation of Christ" by Thomas à Kempis. So we have in her history mingled religious sentiments also. What does such a life as this signify?

That is the question which Matthew Arnold asks and answers in his own way. He says: Rachel had genius and fame born of genius; these were peculiar to her; nobody else had such a genius or such a fame. But Rachel had nothing else which other people have not. Just as in her soul there were mingled the spirit of Greece and the spirit of Rome, of Judaism and Christianity, of modern Germany and modern France, so with every one who inherits the fruits of the ancient and the modern civilisation. It is not only a mental inheritance which many of us have, there is a physical inheritance also—sometimes the blood of many races in one person. I suppose you know the curious fact that most of the great Englishmen of the present century, even of the men of science, are men who have descended from unions between different races. Even Tennyson had some French blood. The English race itself has been made by a mingling of many peoples. Scientifically, there is no unmixed race. Is it, the poet asks, for this reason that the minds of many of us are constantly in a state of struggle, as though between impulses and emotions originally belonging to different civilisations, different religions, different nations? Very possibly, but every man who passes through the whole range of modern university education must have the like experience and like struggle, for he mentally inherits not only the wisdom but the conflicting emotions and sentiments of many vanished civilisations.

The sonnet is the form generally chosen by Matthew Arnold for short philosophical studies of this kind. It is

the sonnet in its simplest and oldest form—at least, the oldest English form, for the early foreign form was more elaborate.   We have sonnets treating about bits of life seen in
the street, about the meaning of religion, about the nature
of God, about the difficulty of being good in this world,
about pictures seen in ancient houses, and about many other
things.   These are not the least interesting of Arnold's compositions, and I want to quote several of them.   Let us first
take one which has a bit of street life for its subject.   I remember that a student of the literature class, last year,
wrote for me a little story or sketch of exactly the same
experience, though I am tolerably sure that he never read
Matthew Arnold's "West London."   As a matter of fact,
you will observe the same thing in Tokyo or in any part
of the civilised world, exactly as the poet saw it in London.

> Crouched on the pavement, close by Belgrave Square,
> A tramp I saw, ill, moody, and tongue-tied.
> A babe was in her arms, and at her side
> A girl; their clothes were rags, their feet were bare.
>
> Some labouring men, whose work lay somewhere there,
> Passed opposite; she touch'd her girl, who hied
> Across, and begg'd, and came back satisfied.
> The rich she had let pass with frozen stare.
>
> Thought I: "Above her state this spirit towers;
> She will not ask of aliens, but of friends,
> Of sharers in a common human fate.
>
> "She turns from that cold succour, which attends
> The unknown little from the unknowing great,
> And points us to a better time than ours."

By "cold succour" the poet means public charity, for in
London there are hundreds of places where poor people can
go and ask for food, and get it upon certain unpleasant conditions.   Thousands of rich people subscribe for such public charities, and a rich person usually answer's a beggar's

request by saying, "Why do you not go to the proper place for help?" Poor people hate public charities, for many reasons. But the main truth of the poem is the fact that suffering makes sympathy. Rich people who do not understand the pain of hunger and cold or the difficulty of living, do not pity the poor in most cases; they refuse to give. On the other hand the workingman, the poor labourer, knows what pain is, and little as he has, he will give when his heart is touched. In the essay written for me last year the writer said that he had seen exactly the same thing on the way to Ueno. A woman with a little boy was begging on that street, and she asked many persons to help her, but the only one who gave her any money was a poor carpenter on his way home after a hard day's work. Why does Matthew Arnold say that this instinct of the poor to ask help from the poor "points us to a better time than ours"? Because the fact in itself suggests that when all classes of men have learned what suffering is, there will be much more sympathy and much less suffering. If the rich are not kind, it is often because they do not know.

Another sonnet on the difficulty of life is of equal interest. It is inspired by a reading of Marcus Aurelius. Marcus Aurelius was the most virtuous of all the Roman Emperors, although living at an age when the people were very corrupt. The important thing to know about him in this connection is that he wrote a beautiful little book which has been translated into all Western languages, and which is still studied by everybody who loves modern philosophy. The book begins with a history of the Emperor's own life, from boyhood; then follow a number of chapters containing his thoughts about many things, but especially about morality, the gods, and the future life. This book is called "The Thoughts of Marcus Aurelius."

Now, this emperor found it very difficult to be as good as he wished to be; he frankly tells us that in a very high position it is much harder to be good than in a very humble position. It is very curious to read what he says about the little miseries of his every day life, about the pain of having to meet disagreeable people and vicious people and ungrateful people, and of knowing how to act justly with them. But he adds, "Even in a palace a man can live a good life." This is the sentence that Matthew Arnold writes a poem about, under the title of "Worldly Place."

> *Even in a palace life may be led well!*
> So spake the imperial sage, purest of men,
> Marcus Aurelius. But the stifling den
> Of common life, where, crowded up pell-mell,
>
> Our freedom for a little bread we sell,
> And drudge under some foolish master's ken
> Who rates us if we peer outside our pen—
> Match'd with a palace, is not this a hell?
>
> *Even in a palace!* On his truth sincere,
> Who spake these words, no shadow ever came;
> And when my ill-school'd spirit is aflame
>
> Some nobler, ampler stage of life to win,
> I'll stop, and say: "There were no succour here!
> The aids to noble life are all within."

The compact language may be paraphrased as follows: "What a strange thing to say, that even in a palace a man can be virtuous! Yet the man who said it was himself an emperor, a philosopher, and the purest of men in his own life. Yet, when we think of our own pain and trouble, how difficult it is for us to believe that the state of an emperor is not happier than the state of a common man. Think of the trouble that we have to earn a living—obliged to work every day in some uncomfortable position, watched by some man not wiser than ourselves, but often even more foolish, who is only watching our work in order to find fault with us. Surely the Emperor, who is the master of all men, and who is not obliged to obey anybody, or even

obliged to do anything he does not wish to do, ought to be
happier than we.   But these are the words of the wisest
and noblest of the Roman emperors—'Even in a palace!'
Therefore we must understand that it is still harder for an
emperor to be good and happy than it is for a common
man.   To believe this may be difficult, but Marcus Aurelius said it, and in his whole life he never told even the
shadow of a lie.   I believe him.   When I feel myself dis-
satisfied, when I wish to leave the work that I now do, in
order to obtain a higher or a better position, I remember
the words of Marcus Aurelius.   The secret of happiness
and the power of virtue are in our hearts.   That is the
meaning of life as it was understood by that great teacher
and great emperor."

So excellently does this poem represent the moral teaching of Matthew Arnold, that no other example of the same
kind is necessary.   You will see the same idea repeated in
hundreds of passages, and really there is no better teaching.
The all-important fact to know in the first place is the
nature of duty; when we know this, the rules of conduct
can be tolerably well understood without any teaching of
creed or dogma.   On this subject of dogma, Matthew
Arnold is liberal enough.   Nowhere does he plainly declare
himself a Christian, and we cannot always be sure of the
meaning which he attaches to the word "God."   He uses
the word frequently (so does Mr. Swinburne, who does not
believe in what is usually understood by God); but he may
use it in a signification which is not by any means Christian,
nor even religious in the sectarian sense.   Sometimes God
means not the poet's idea of the Supreme Unknown, but
the idea of goodness and justice, personified.   In one place
we have a plain statement of sympathy with a Christian
definition, but you must not suppose this sympathy to mean
that the poet accepts the definition in the original meaning.
He sympathises with it only because it symbolises for him

a truth independent of any religion.   The statement to
which I refer is in a sonnet entitled "The Divinity."

"Yes, write it in the rock," Saint Bernard said,
Grave it on brass with adamantine pen!
'Tis God himself becomes apparent, when
God's wisdom and God's goodness are display'd,

"For God of these his attributes is made."—
Well spake the impetuous Saint, and bore of men
The suffrage captive; now, not one in ten
Recalls the obscure opposer he outweigh'd.

God's wisdom and God's goodness!—Ay, but fools
Mis-define these till God knows them no more.
Wisdom and goodness, they are God!—what schools

Have yet so much as heard this simple lore?
This no Saint preaches, and this no Church rules;
'Tis in the desert, now and heretofore.

Saint Bernard was a great church reformer, who lived in
the twelfth century; I think that the best account of him
is that which we find in Froude's Essays.   The incident
which Matthew Arnold mentions happened in the year
1148, when Bernard was accused of heresy for saying that
wisdom and goodness were God.   But he was not ashamed
or afraid of what he had said, and he argued so well that
he silenced his accusers.   You must know the Church of
Rome at no time would acknowledge that goodness could
exist outside faith; in other words a person could not be
good who was not a Christian, according to mediæval opinion.   No matter how kind or how generous or how noble
a man might be, unless he were a Christian his good deeds
could not save him.   Therefore it seemed to many people
shocking to say that wisdom and goodness were identical
with divinity.   Matthew Arnold's thought about this declaration is that it is really true from a modern philosophical

point of view. Wisdom is divine, goodness is divine. From the oldest time the great value of belief in God has been the value of recognising the divine nature of wisdom and of goodness. I think Saint Bernard was right, says Matthew Arnold, when he called these God. But according to sectarian and dogmatic declarations, what are wisdom and goodness? Do they mean the highest knowledge and the highest morality? No, they do not. Religious prejudice calls wisdom what is not wisdom, and goodness what is not goodness. If we should take the highest conception of goodness and of wisdom, we should certainly find these to be divinity in the deepest and grandest meaning. But to-day there is nobody in the churches to teach such a truth; very few men would have the courage to utter it. Therefore the voice of Saint Bernard is still a voice in the desert, a voice speaking alone in the great ignorant silence of the past and of the present. If mankind ever generally recognise that wisdom and goodness are divine, they will have learned the best that any religion could teach them. There is something in this little poem that reminds us also of Renan, who said, in one of his philosophical dialogues, that perhaps there is no God existing at present, but that men are gradually working to make a God, and that out of all the sorrow and the labour of mankind, a God will be created at last. Well, this God of the French philosopher, not yet made but in process of being made, would certainly be the same God suggested by Matthew Arnold's verses— infinite goodness and infinite knowledge.

I do not wish to keep you too long at the study of this grey, colourless, but very curious poetry. Still, I may cite to you another sonnet, about a picture which Matthew Arnold once saw. You must know that this picture really exists. Long ago an English nobleman, a great warrior and great statesman, very brave but also very proud and positive in his character, became angry one day with his little son, a boy of six or seven years old, and thoughtlessly struck him.   Perhaps a man would scarcely have been pained by the blow, but a child's brain and body are very delicate things, and the shock of the blow destroyed the little brain.   The child never again knew anything; he was without any remembrance even of what had happened; he could not even understand why his father asked for pardon.   In order to punish himself, the father had a great picture painted of the cruel act which he had committed, so that all the world might know his own shame and sorrow. This picture still hangs in the Abbey at Newstead.

I presume you remember that Newstead Abbey was the residence and property of Lord Byron.   Because of his great memory, Newstead Abbey has long been a place of literary pilgrimage, strangers from all parts of the world making visits there in order to see the relics of the great poet.   It was while upon such a visit that Matthew Arnold saw this picture, and wrote the following sonnet about it:

> What made my heart, at Newstead, fullest swell?—
> 'Twas not the thought of Byron, of his cry
> Stormily sweet, his Titan-agony;
> It was the sight of that Lord Arundel
>
> Who struck, in heat, his child he loved so well,
> And his child's reason flicker'd, and did die.
> Painted (he will'd it) in the gallery
> They hang; the picture doth the story tell.
>
> Behold the stern, mail'd father, staff in hand!
> The little fair-hair'd son, with vacant gaze,
> Where no more lights of sense or knowledge are!
>
> Methinks the woe, which made that father stand
> Baring his dumb remorse to future days,
> Was woe than Byron's woe more tragic far.

I do not know any poem more painful than this in modern literature, and scarcely any equally touching—perhaps

Coventry Patmore's poem "The Toys" comes nearest to it in the latter quality. And yet how very simply the thing is told!

My purpose in this lecture has been to make you interested in those parts of Matthew Arnold's work which are least known to the general reader. School text books and anthologies contain plenty of extracts from Arnold, but no extracts which really give you any idea of the thought and the feelings of the man. Such extracts are usually chosen because of the beauty of the verse, and they are therefore chosen usually from those longer poems in which Arnold shows himself a student of Milton, as in "Thyrsis," or a student of the Greek tragedians, as in "Merope." You will also find quotations made from "Sohrab and Rustum," one of which is so famous that it is quoted in hundreds of books—I mean the passage about the Chinese porcelain maker. But these would not at all serve the object which I had in view—namely, to make you see the great, sad, tender mind of the man. This you will learn only by reading and liking those shorter pieces, such as I have quoted, which are a little difficult to study, but which repay study much better than the most of the poet's more ambitious work. In writing these he probably did not intend or expect to appear as a great poet, yet it is here indeed that the great poet is, rather than in even such beautiful lines as the following:

> Then, with weak hasty fingers, Sohrab loosed
> His belt, and near the shoulder bared his arm,
> And showed a sign in faint vermilion points
> Prick'd; as a cunning workman, in Pekin,
> Pricks with vermilion some clear porcelain vase,
> An emperor's gift—at early morn he paints,
> And all day long, and when night comes, the lamp
> Lights up his studious forehead and thin hands.

Milton might have written that, it is so truly beautiful.

But it is not characteristic of Matthew Arnold otherwise than by being in the style of Milton. The imitation of a great poet may be admirable, but original thought always proves in the end to be the supreme test of poetical value.

CHAPTER IX

A NOTE ON JEAN INGELOW

As the term is drawing to a close, so that we shall have only two or three more days together, I have thought it better, having completed the last lecture, not to begin a new lecture upon the same scale, but to give a short lecture about some single famous poem. And I have chosen for this purpose Jean Ingelow's famous poem, "The High Tide on the Coast of Lincolnshire." Sometimes a poet becomes celebrated by the writing of one poem only. This happens to be the case with Miss Ingelow. She wrote several volumes of poems which were very popular in England and even in America. But popularity, during the lifetime of a writer, is no proof of literary merit; and it was not so in Miss Ingelow's case. She really wrote only one great poem; and by that one poem her name will always be preserved in the history of English literature.

The subject of this poem ought to interest you. The subject is only too familiar in Japan—a tidal wave (*tsunami*). There are few more terrible things possible for man to endure, in the form of what are called "natural visitations," than earthquakes and tidal waves. These two dreadful forms of calamity have been more common in this country than in Europe; but Europe has not been entirely exempt from them. There is only one other kind of natural calamity which can be at all compared with them—a volcanic eruption. But it is seldom indeed that a volcanic eruption, in any civilised country, produces such destruction of life as may be caused by an earthquake or a tidal wave.

It is about three hundred years since England had a great cataclysm of this sort; and it has never been forgotten by the people of the coast where it happened. That coast happens to be quite low. At one time, indeed, it was little better than a great salt-marsh. But several miles inland there was very good farm-land, and plenty of farms and towns and villages. Miss Ingelow herself lived very near the scene of her poem. You must imagine a river flowing through the low country, widening very much toward the mouth—the river Lindis; Boston town stands near the bank. When the tidal wave came, the immediate effect was to force the river back, so that even distant parts of the country which the sea could not reach were flooded by the river. There is only one more thing to tell you about the poem— that it is written in English of the sixteenth century, yet there are only two or three queer words in it; everything is easy to understand. The verses are of different form and the stanzas of irregular length.

> The old mayor climbed the belfry-tower,
> The ringers ran by two, by three;
> "Pull, if ye never pulled before;
> Good ringers, pull your best," quoth he.
> "Play uppe, play uppe, O Boston bells!
> Ply all your changes, all your swells,
>   Play uppe 'The Brides of Enderby.' "

The church tower of St. Botolph's, which still stands, is the belfry-tower here referred to. That was long before the time of telegraphs and railroads, and the only way of quickly sending news of danger through the country used to be to ring the great bells of the churches. It was therefore very important to have good bells; and every great church had a number of them, all of different sizes, so arranged that different tunes could be played upon them. You can still hear this kind of ringing in many parts of Europe. The tunes are usually very simple tunes known to all the people, and commonly hymn tunes, but not always. In time of danger it was agreed that particular tunes should be played. In the district of Lincolnshire, the tune that meant danger was the tune of an old ballad, called "The Brides of Enderby," and when people heard the church bells play it they knew that something terrible was going to happen. I believe you know it requires a number of men to ring the bells in this way; and it used to be a regular calling. The word "changes" in the sixth line means variation in the modern musical sense; the word "swells" refers to a particular way of ringing two or more bells together, so that the sounds of all would blend into one great wave of tone.

You must understand that the whole story is being told by an old grandmother; she relates everything as she saw it and felt it, in a simple and touching way.

> Men say it was a stolen tyde—
> The Lord that sent it, He knows all;
> But in myne ears doth still abide
> The message that the bells let fall:
> And there was naught of strange, beside
> The flights of mews and peewits pied
> By millions crouched on the old sea wall.
>
> I sat and spun within the doore,
> My thread brake off, I raised myne eyes;
> The level sun, like ruddy ore,
> Lay sinking in the barren skies;
> And dark against day's golden death
> She moved where Lindis wandereth,
> My sonne's faire wife, Elizabeth.
>
> "Cusha! Cusha! Cusha," calling,
> Ere the early dews were falling,
> Farre away I heard her song.
> "Cusha! Cusha!" all along;
> Where the reedy Lindis floweth,
>   Floweth, floweth,
> From the meads where melick groweth
> Faintly came her milking song—
>
> "Cusha! Cusha! Cusha!" calling,
> "For the dews will soone be falling;

> Leave your meadow grasses mellow,
> Mellow, mellow,
> Quit your cow-slips, cow-slips yellow;
> Come uppe Whitefoot, come uppe Lightfoot;
> Quit the stalks of parsely hollow,
> Hollow, hollow,
> Come uppe Jetty, rise and follow,
> From the clovers lift your head;
> Come uppe Whitefoot, come uppe Lightfoot
> Come uppe Jetty, rise and follow,
> Jetty, to the milking shed."

The expression "stolen tide" in the first stanza is strange to you, I think; it is strange even to English readers who are not aware that country-folk often use the word "stolen" in the sense of contrary to nature, monstrous, magical. Now you have the old grandmother talking to you, recalling her memories. She tells you that upon the evening of the great tidal wave, the first thing that startled her was the sound of the church bells signalling danger. It startled her so that she broke the thread which she was spinning at the door; then she looked up to see if there was anything unusual in sky or field. Nothing in the sky; it was what she called "a barren sky"—that is, a sky without a single cloud; and the sun was sinking beautifully, making all the West full of gold light. Nothing in the field—no, but what was that upon the sea-wall? Of course you know what a sea-wall is; they are very common in Japan, built to protect fishing villages or low coasts against the surf of heavy storms. Yes; there was something strange on the sea-wall; millions of sea-birds were crowded there—white gulls, and parti-coloured gulls, called peewits from their melancholy cry. The danger was probably from the sea—but what was it? While wondering what it could be, the old woman heard her son's wife singing to the cows. I am not sure whether you know about this custom. Milk-cows, in England, are left all day to graze in the meadows, when the weather is fine; and at evening they are called home,

milked, and put in their stables.   The men or boys who
take care of them, or the girls—dairymaids as they are
termed—often sing a kind of song to call the animals home;
they come at once when they hear the song.   Names are
given to them, usually names indicating the appearance of
the cow, or something peculiar about it.   In this song, the
name Whitefoot probably means a red or a black cow with
pure white feet.   The name Lightfoot might mean a thor-
oughbred cow—that is, a cow of very fine race—with a
particularly light quick walk.   The name Jetty probably
refers to a perfectly black cow, black as jet.   There is
nothing else to explain, except the queer old word "melick,"
the name of a particular kind of grass.   "Cow-slips" are,
you know, long yellow flowers, very common in European
fields.

> If it be long, ay, long ago,
> When I beginne to think howe long,
> Againe I hear the Lindis flow,
> Swift as an arrowe, sharpe and strong;
> And all the aire, it seemeth me,
> Bin full of floating bells (sayth shee),
> That ring the tune of Enderby.
>
> Alle fresh the level pasture lay,
> And not a shadowe mote be seene,
> Save where full fyve good miles away
> The steeple towered from out the greene.
> And lo! the great bell farre and wide
> Was heard in all the country side
> That Saturday at eventide.
>
> The swanherds where their sedges are
> Moved on in sunset's golden breath,
> The shepherde lads I heard afarre,
> And my sonne's wife, Elizabeth;
> Till floating o'er the grassy sea
> Came downe that kyndly message free,
> The "Brides of Mavis Enderby."
>
> Then some looked uppe into the sky,
> And all along where Lindis flow:

To where the goodly vessels lie,
And where the lordly steeple shows.
They sayde, "And why should this thing be?
What danger lowers by land or sea?
They ring the tune of Enderby!

"For evil news from Mablethorpe,
Of pyrate galleys warping downe;
For shippes ashore beyond the scorpe,
They have not spared to wake the towne:
But while the west bin red to see,
And storms be none, and pyrates flee,
Why ring 'The Brides of Enderby'?"

The conditional mood at the beginning of the first of the stanzas just quoted, is only suggested; there is no sequence, no main clause. You must understand the meaning to be something like this: "You ask me if it was long ago. If it was long ago! Ah, perhaps, it was long ago—yet when I try to think how long ago it was, I see and hear everything so plainly that it seems to me even now." In the fourth line, the adjectives "sharp and strong" refer, of course, to the arrow—a heavy war-arrow would fly much faster and with a louder sound than the sporting arrow. Archery was still kept up in the sixteenth century. But the old woman is not thinking only of the arrow; she is thinking of the sound made by the strong current of the river. It had a sharp sound, she tells us, like the sound of a heavy arrow. Notice in the sixth line the use of "bin" for "is." In the following stanza, you need only observe the curious old perfect "mote" used where we would now say "might" or "could." In the third line, you will find the term "good miles." Why should people speak of a good mile or a good distance? In such places the word "good" has the sense of "at least," "fully," "not less than."

The description goes on very vividly; after speaking of the beautiful clear weather, with nothing in all the level of the flat country to break the skyline, except the far-away shape of the church steeple, the old woman speaks of the swans in the high river grass, the shouting of the shepherd boys, calling home their sheep, and the sweet song of the young wife waiting to milk the cows as they return from pasture.   There was nothing at all of danger visible; and the peasants wondered why the bells sounded danger.   Observe in the fourth of this group of stanzas the use of the word "lowers" in the sixth line.   To-day we more commonly spell it "lour"—though originally the meaning was very much the same.   When clouds hang down very low, it is a sign of storm; when brows are lowered in a frown it is a sign of anger.   So when we speak of a lowering sky we mean a threatening sky; but however we spell the word, we pronounce it with a very full sound of "ow" in the sense of "to threaten."   "What danger is threatening us from the land or from the sea?"   That is what the people ask each other.   Why do they ring the bells in that way? If pirates had attacked the neighbouring port of Mablethorpe, or if there were any ships wrecked beyond the rockline (scorpe), then there would be some reason for calling up all the people.   The expression "wake" the town, does not mean to awaken, but to summon, to call.   This is a quaint idiom.

Very suddenly, though, the old grandmother learns what the danger is:

> I looked without, and lo! my sonne
> Came riding downe with might and main!
> He raised a shout as he drew on,
> Till all the welkin rang again,
> "Elizabeth!   Elizabeth!"
> (A sweeter woman ne'er drew breath
> Than my sonne's wife, Elizabeth.)
>
> "The olde sea-wall (he cried) is downe,
> The rising tide comes on apace,
> And boats adrift in yonder towne
> Go sailing uppe the market-place."

He shook as one that looks on death:
"God save you, mother!" straight he saith;
"Where is my wife, Elizabeth?"

"Good sonne, where Lindis winds away,
With her two bairns I marked her long;
And ere yon bells beganne to play
Afar I heard her milking song."
He looked across the grassy lea,
To right, to left, "Ho Enderby!"
They rang "The Brides of Enderby!"

With that he cried and beat his breast;
For, lo! along the river's bed
A mighty eygre reared his crest,
And uppe the Lindis raging sped.
It swept with thunderous noises loud;
Shaped like a curling snow-white cloud,
Or like a demon in a shroud.

In the fourth line of the first of the above stanzas occurs the word "welkin," much less often used now than formerly. It most commonly signifies the sky, the vault of heaven. But we may often understand the word merely in the sense of atmosphere, the whole expanse of blue air. Indeed the word chiefly lingers in modern use in this meaning, as is illustrated by the common idiom "to make the welkin ring." This simply means to make all the air shake, and resound with a noise or a shout. It is thus that the word is used in the present poem.

In the following stanza observe the word "apace"—it is now very old-fashioned. The meaning is "very quickly" or "suddenly"—so that it does not at all appear to be what it means. We are apt to think of the verb "to pace," meaning to walk slowly with full strides; but apace is exactly the contrary of slowly. In the next stanza the word "bairns," meaning young children, is familiar to anybody acquainted with Scotch dialect; and we have got accustomed to think of the word as purely Scotch. But it is not: it is very old English, and is much used in the provinces outside of Scotland.   In the next stanza we find an especially curious and very ancient word, "eygre." This word can be found in the most ancient Anglo-Saxon poems, and it still lingers in various English provincial dialects.   But it is not often spelt in this way; the common spelling is "eagre."   It means an immense wave or billow; and it has a very weird effect in this stanza.   For it is the real tidal wave that the old woman describes by that terrible word.   All the flood that had come before was only the precursor of the great sea rising to follow.   Now it comes roaring up the river, with a sound of thunder— all black below, all white above with foam, so that it suggests to the old grandmother's terrified fancy the idea of a great black demon moving with a funeral shroud thrown over his head.   You must understand that she sees the wave at an angle, not in front.   Now comes an excellent description of the immediate result of the wave.

> And rearing Lindis backward pressed,
> Shook all her trembling bankes amaine;
> Then madly at the eygre's breast
> Flung uppe her weltering walls again,
> Then bankes came downe with ruin and rout—
> Then beaten foam flew round about—
> Then all the mighty floods were out.
>
> So far, so fast, the eygre drave,
> The heart had hardly time to beat,
> Before a shallow seething wave
> Sobbed in the grasses at oure feet:
> The feet had hardly time to flee
> Before it brake against the knee,
> And all the world was in the sea.

You must understand that the Lindis River flowing through a very low country, constantly liable to inundation, has to be confined between artificial banks to provide against accidents.   In England there are but very few rivers to which it has been found necessary to furnish artificial banks; but in America many great rivers have to be thus banked for immense distances. For instance, the great Mississippi River flows between artificial banks for a distance of many hundreds of miles; and when you read of terrible floods in the Southern States, it generally means that the banks have been somewhere broken. These banks rise much above the surrounding country, like great walls. So it was in the landscape of the present poem—the river was flowing between high banks like walls. When the great wave came from the sea, moving at a tremendous speed, the first effect was to check and throw back the river current; and this made a great counter wave. But the counter wave could not resist the pressure of a sea wave; and the consequence was that the whole force of the river was diverted sidewards, with the result that the banks were at once broken to pieces. That caused an immediate inundation of fresh water; but the fresh water inundation was almost instantly followed by the rush of the sea, a much more dangerous and terrible affair.

In the fourth line of the stanza about the rising of the river, you must understand the word "weltering" to have the meaning of the word "liquid"; and the term "weltering walls" to signify only high waves rising like walls in vain opposition to the mighty tidal wave. In the stanza following, the term "shallow seething wave" refers to the first burst of the fresh water over the country; but the last three lines of the same stanza refer to the rush of the sea following after. Before a person had time even to move, the water was up to his knees; the next minute it was high enough to cover the greater part of the houses.

> Upon the roofe we sate that night,
> The noise of bells went sweeping by;
> I marked the lofty beacon light
> Stream from the church tower, red and high—
> A lurid mark and dread to see;

And awsome bells they were to me,
That in the dark rang "Enderby."

They rang the sailor lads to guide
From roofe to roofe who fearless rowed;
And I—my sonne was at my side,
And yet the ruddy beacon glowed;
And yet he moaned beneath his breath,
"O come in life, or come in death!
O lost! my love, Elizabeth!"

Some of the houses, of two or three stories and strongly built, withstood the flood for a time, and people took refuge upon the roofs. Then from the neighbouring port sailors came with boats, and went from roof to roof, to take the people away. The phrase "sailor-lads" does not necessarily mean sailor boys or young sailors, though the English "lad" strictly means a person between the ages of boyhood and of manhood—let us say from sixteen to twenty-one. That is the strict meaning; but for a very long time this word had a caressing meaning, when it is attached to another word so as to make such compounds, as for example, soldier-lads, sailor-lads. In these instances the word "lad" has a meaning something like "dear" or "good." The beacon fire, lighted upon the top of a church tower, is described as "lurid." This word "lurid" has somewhat changed its meaning in modern times. It is from the Latin, and the Latin meaning was a dim green or a very dim yellow. The idea suggested by the Latin word was the gloomy light in a deep forest, or the indistinct light in a time of eclipse. But modern writers have used it a great deal, and somewhat incorrectly, in the signification of red light —light having an awful colour; for the ancient word always conveyed some idea of fear, and this idea has never been lost in English. Whenever you see in literature something described as lurid, you may be sure that the meaning is a terrible and unnatural light. Of course the church tower, used for a beacon light, had a square flat roof. As a matter of fact, when we see the word "church tower" used in English, a flat-topped tower is meant; the pointed form being more correctly indicated by the word "spire."

So much for the scene described—the tragedy continues with the lamentation of the sorrowing husband for his lost wife and children. He asks her to come to him alive or dead, so that he may at least know what has become of her in that awful night. If you think a moment about the matter, you will see that the expression is quite natural; people usually almost expect that those whom they loved will give them some signs in case of sudden death—such as a visit in dreams, or an apparitional visit. In this case the wife comes to her husband dead, but not as a ghost:

> And didst thou visit him no more?
> Thou didst, thou didst, my daughter deare;
> The waters laid thee at his doore,
> Ere yet the early dawn was clear.
> Thy pretty bairns in fast embrace,
> The lifted sun shone on thy face,
> Downe drifted to thy dwelling-place.

Many poets have used this fancy, in poetry about death by drowning, and perhaps the idea first came into superior poetry with the study of the popular ballads. In many English ballads we read about the corpse of a mother and a child being carried by some flood or storm to the door of the husband; sometimes the floating body which thus returns is that of a betrayed girl. The idea is artistically excellent, because it is so natural that no amount of use can wear it out. It was a favourite incident with Rossetti. The narrative continues, with certain reflections:

> That flow strewed wrecks about the grass,
> That ebbe swept out the flocks to sea;
> A fatal ebbe and flow, alas!
> To manye more than myne and me;
> But each will mourn his own (she saith).

> And sweeter woman ne'er drew breath
> Than my sonne's wife, Elizabeth.

In this stanza you must understand that the word "flow" means the incoming tide, as ebb means the outgoing tide, though the use of the word "flow," all by itself, in the first line is a little unusual. The fifth line is the line to which I particularly wish to call your attention:

> But each will mourn his own.

This line, simple as any commonplace, simple as the most trite of household phrases, is nevertheless, by reason of its opportune use in this place, a very fine bit of human poetry. The old grandmother remembers and relates the great destruction of life, both of animals and human beings; and in the recollection of that immense calamity, with the vision of a thousand past sorrows before her, she suddenly feels like reproaching herself for talking so much about her own particular grief. She apologises for this involuntary selfishness by citing the old saying that each person feels his or her own sorrow most; "each will mourn his own"; perhaps it is bad, yet who can help it, and who can fail to find a kindly excuse for it?

Really that is almost the best line in the poem; and I want to talk about it, because it suggests so many things. It is quite true that each person best understands sorrow or joy by his or her sorrow and joy; and in a certain way, a person is not wrong in imagining his joy or pain to be the greatest joy or the greatest pain in the whole world. There are many proverbial sayings, quoted in opposition to the indulgence of personal feeling; I suppose that they really serve a good purpose by checking a tendency to over-effusiveness. For example, you have heard many sayings about the admiration of a mother for her child, to the effect that every mother thinks her own child to be the very best child alive. So a son invariably thinks that his own mother is the best of all mothers; he may not say so, but he is very likely to think so. And there are household phrases relating to a corresponding feeling on the part of brother and sister, husband and wife, father and son. The tendency to laugh at or to repress expressions of such innocent feeling certainly have their special use: we must so think of them. But most people utter the mockery, and there stop —without asking themselves anything about the reason and about the truth of such feeling. After all, there is a great deal of truth in it. The value of an affection, the value of a personality, to each of us is quite special. The son who thinks of his mother as the best of all mothers thinks quite truly so far as the relation of that mother to himself is concerned. She is the best of all mothers for him; and no human being could ever take her place. So with the relation of the child to the parent. It is a question of relativity. Everybody feels this—though it is not easily expressed by simple minds, which can only think as the old grandmother thinks in the story, that each one cannot help "mourning his own," and faintly justify by an appeal to universal experience, the declaration that no one could be sweeter or better than the one who has been lost.

The poem concludes with the memories of the song and the singer:

> I shall never hear her more
> By the reedy Lindis shore,
> "Cusha! Cusha! Cusha!" calling,
> Ere the early dews be falling;
> I shall never hear her song
> "Cusha! Cusha!" all along,
> Where the sunny Lindis floweth,
> Goeth, floweth;
> From the meads where melick groweth,
> When the water winding down,
> Onward floweth to the town.

I shall never see her more
Where the reeds and rushes quiver,
        Shiver, quiver;
Stand beside the sobbing river,
Sobbing, throbbing, in its falling
To the sandy lonesome shore;
I shall never hear her calling,
"Leave your meadow grasses mellow,
        Mellow, mellow;
Quit your cow-slips, cow-slips yellow;
Come uppe Whitefoot, come uppe Lightfoot;
Quit your pipes of parsley hollow,
        Hollow, hollow;
Come up Lightfoot, rise and follow;
        Lightfoot, Whitefoot,
From your clovers lift the head;
Come uppe Jetty, follow, follow,
Jetty, to the milking shed."

CHAPTER X

"THREE SILENCES"

I HAVE said in another lecture that Swinburne and Rossetti had no imitators of any worth to literature. Nevertheless it sometimes happens that a new poet, although not imitating his predecessors, may so represent in his verse a blending of the best qualities of some of them, that we must say, this man's work was developed by the study of such and such singers. We say that Tennyson is the poetical descendant of Keats, but we never could say that Tennyson imitated Keats. You will now understand exactly what I mean when I say that Arthur O'Shaughnessy, the author of the poem entitled "Three Silences," is the descendant both of Swinburne and of Rossetti. He has united some of the best qualities of both—of Swinburne as to form and as to colour, of Rossetti as to feeling. This poem shows his relation to Swinburne and Rossetti, more especially to Rossetti. The feeling borders upon mystical tenderness, but you will discern in it the melancholy doubt of the nineteenth century. Perhaps this only adds to its sweetness.

We may suppose that the poet is referring to the three great sorrows of human existence. The first great sorrow might be, for example, the death of one's mother—a shock of pain which the child cannot even fully understand as a fact. If he asks the meaning of it, really no one can tell him; and the tender things that are told him in order to console him, do not in the least illuminate for him the awful mystery of the fact.

The next great sorrow might be the death of the woman he loved. As Huxley says, the man who stands with his dead before the abyss of the eternal, has questions to ask. Some of them he asks his own heart, some of them he asks the dead—but there is no answer. The second shock of death finds him very much wiser and stronger than he was when a child, yet the mystery is not any nearer to solution for him; it is even further away.

Later come other surprises of pain—doubts of humanity, doubts of the worth of life, doubts of everything; and, in the moment of some great sorrow, one turns back to the habit of childhood, to the resource of prayer. And there is no answer.

We can suppose these to be the Three Silences. Nevertheless this is not a philosophical poem but a love poem. It is in a moment of disappointed affection, in the moment of a fourth silence, that the poet remembers the other three periods of pain. This is what gives the poem its extraordinary qualities of melancholy and tenderness.

'Tis a world of silences. I gave a cry
    In the first sorrow my heart could not withstand;
I saw men pause, and listen, and look sad,
As though no answer in their hearts they had;
    Some turned away, some came and took my hand,
        For all reply.

I stood beside a grave. Years had pass'd by;
    Sick with unanswer'd life I turn'd to death,
And whisper'd all my questions to the grave,
And watch'd the flowers desolately wave,
    And the grass stir on it with a fitful breath,
        For all reply.

I rais'd my eyes to heaven; my prayer went high
    Into the luminous mystery of the blue;
My thought of God was purer than a flame,
And God it seem'd a little nearer came,
    Then pass'd, and greater still the silence grew,
        For all reply.

But you! If I can speak before I die,
    I spoke to you with all my soul, and when

I look at you 't is still my soul you see,
Oh, in your heart was there no word for me?
  All would have answer'd had you answer'd then
    With even a sigh.

The last line but one is the most beautiful in the whole poem. Love casts out sorrow and fear and doubt in the first moment of its ecstasy; the lover says that had she answered, the grave and the heaven and God himself would have answered at the same time, because in perfect happiness there is no doubt and no fear and no regret. You will observe that this approaches to the tone of Rossetti, and that there is nevertheless within it a something which is not of Rossetti, something sweeter and simpler, and in spite of this simplicity, equally artistic.

CHAPTER XI

A NOTE ON WATSON'S POEMS

AMONG the minor poets of to-day, there is one figure deserving special attention—William Watson. As a minor poet his rank has been a high one from the first, and he is constantly rising to a higher place. His appearance also has some significance in relation to the general poetical movement of the century. He represents, not the romantic feeling of Rossetti and his school, nor the splendid warmth and colour and finish of Tennyson's school; rather he represents the reaction. I told you that after the romantics had exhausted their art, and the art of the English language as well, further advance became impossible, and whoever attempted to create poetry would either have to be an imitator, or would have to go back to simpler forms. Mr. Watson took the latter course, and he has won success in it. Spiritually he is a descendant of Wordsworth; the best feeling of Wordsworth glows all through him in a new form and with the colours of another time. In form he is not exactly classic, but he goes back to the models of the early nineteenth century, rarely attempting any of those more elaborate forms of verse which the Victorian period brought to the highest pitch of excellence. One of his favourite forms is the sonnet; this is perhaps the most complicated which he uses. A great deal of his work is in simpler forms. He loves quatrains—complete poems in four lines. He has attempted, not unsuccessfully, to use the very early English forms of rhymeless alliteration, the old Runic measure, in which very few moderns have excelled. Here are a few examples of this form; you will remember, from the lecture on Anglo-Saxon poetry, the rule of values in this metre:

England, my mother,
Wardress of waters,
Builder of peoples,
    Maker of men,—

Hast thou yet leisure
Left for the muses?
Heed'st thou the songsmith
    Forging the rhyme?
    .   .   .   .

Song is no bauble—
Slight not the songsmith,
England my mother
    Maker of men!

There are some fine stanzas in the composition from which
these extracts are made, but you will see that the Runic form
is not strictly preserved, and the thing, as a whole, lacks
force.   Tennyson and Charles Kingsley are the only two
nineteenth century poets that I know of who used the Northern measure with real success.   The best example in Tennyson is the translation of the "Battle of Brunanburh"; the
best example in Kingsley is to be found among the songs
scattered through the novels of "Hypatia" and "Hereward."
    But if Watson has not always been successful with the
simpler forms of verse as verse, he has sometimes been remarkably successful in the direction of imagination and
force.   He has given us a very remarkable composition entitled, "The Dream of Man," which deserves attention especially because it was inspired by the new evolutional philosophy.   In this poem the poet considers the great problem of Pain in the universe—why it exists, what would happen if it could be entirely suppressed.   Accepting the existence of a God as creator, he imagines the future of man
in a new way.   The figure of God is necessary for the
dramatic conception which follows.   Man conquers all the
obstacles which Nature and his own weaknesses oppose to
progress.   He learns how to vanquish disease, how to con-

quer tempests, and how to render danger no longer possible.
He even conquers pain—that is, he learns how to relieve
all physical pain. But moral pain remains, and the dread
of death. Death is a power which he cannot oppose. He
can do almost everything else that he pleases, except make
himself immortal. He discovers even means of communi-
cation with other solar systems, and extends his influence into
other planets; but death is always with him. He determines to make one last tremendous battle against death.
In the meantime he has forgotten the existence of God,
who has been watching all his progress, but in whom he has
almost ceased to believe. When God observes that the
man is about to fight against death, he thinks it is time
to warn him. He shows himself to the spirit of man and
speaks:

"O great in thine own conceit,
I will show thee thy source, how humble, thy goal, for a god how
    unmeet."

Thereat, by the word of the Maker, the Spirit of Man was led
To a mighty peak of vision, where God to His creature said,
"Look Eastward toward Time's sunrise, and age upon age untold."
The Spirit of Man saw clearly the past as a chart out-rolled—
Beheld his base beginnings in the depths of time, and his strife,
With beasts and crawling horrors for leave to live, when life
Meant but to slay and to procreate, to feed and to sleep, among
Mere mouths, voracities boundless, blind lusts, desires without
    tongue,
And ferocities vast, fulfilling their being's malignant law,
While nature was one hunger, and one hate, all fangs and maw.

This, of course, is the vision of the evolutionist looking
back to the past, and holding that man, evolved from a
speck of protoplasm, passed gradually upward from the
very lowest forms of life, through innumerable transforma-
tions, before reaching the state of intelligence. But the
period especially referred to in these lines is the period
before maternal love showed itself, the period preceding the

appearance of the mammalia or milk-giving animals.   Then indeed Nature was, as the poet says, only hunger and lust. Reason had not yet gleamed.   For the moment that he first perceives this vision of his own past, man feels a little humble, and his pride is abased.   But very soon he turns to God with a reproach upon his lips, saying, "Is not this fact the proof of my divinity?   If I have been able to rise up from such depths, shall I not be able in the future to rise far beyond them?   I am not ashamed."   God answers, "Look now to the future that you talk about; I will give you the power to see."   Then man looks, and he perceives the great periods of disintegration and of dissolution which philosophers tell us about, the periods when worlds become old and suns burn dim, and are finally extinguished forever in the infinite night.   For evolution does not mean only a development; it likewise means a decline.   Here, however, there is a slight criticism to be made upon the poet's idea.   There are two great phases of evolution correctly suggested by him; but there is a vaster phase of the subject which, unlike George Meredith, he does not appear to have perceived.

Indeed, the digression which I now venture to make embodies the principal object of this lecture.   It is quite as important that you should understand the philosophical weaknesses of a poet, as that you should understand his strong points.   Otherwise he might be able to set up in your minds a totally wrong train of thinking.   Those who have a superficial knowledge only of evolutional philosophy are apt to imagine that it teaches a definite end and a definite beginning of universes.   As for a beginning, the philosophy confesses itself to be sublimely ignorant.   Here it can only theorise.   It is not impossible, nor even improbable, that there may have been a beginning of what we call matter, because the latest chemical science gives some evidence of the extraordinary possibility that all compound forms of matter have been evolved in a totally un-

known way, from simpler forms. On the other hand, we
have tolerably good evidence as to how universes begin
and end as systems. But this beginning or ending is only
a beginning or ending of particular forms. Really an ending is utterly inconceivable. The end of one evolution is
only the beginning of another. When the suns burn out
and worlds crumble to dust, new suns and worlds arise from
the wreck. That is the real teaching of evolutional philosophy, and it is in accord with Oriental thought. But
there is more than this. It is almost certain that the history of one universe will affect the history of a succeeding
universe, just as the actions and habits of our own genera-
tion must certainly have some effect upon the habits and
manners of our descendants. The experience not only of
mind, but even of what we call matter, have tendencies
that will influence future forms of mind and matter; and
thus an enormous ethical system is suggested by the real
evolutional philosophy. Meredith is the only English poet
who has fully expressed this truth. Watson has not even
perceived it. But this fact does not prevent his poem
from being very interesting in itself, because of the way it
treats a problem that no philosophy can perfectly explain.

To return to the story. Man is not distressed by perceiving the future which God shows him—the end of the
human race and the crumbling of the world in darkness.
On the contrary, with desperate courage he proclaims, "I
shall conquer death and make myself the equal of God."
A tremendous time of struggle follows; but human intelligence at last wins the battle. Death is conquered; and even
God is surprised.

So to each star in the heavens the exultant word was blown,
The annunciation tremendous, *Death is overthrown!*
And Space, in her ultimate borders, prolonging the jubilant tone,
With hollow ingeminations, sighed, *Death is overthrown!*
And God, in His house of silence, where he dwelleth aloof, alone,
Paused in His tasks to hearken: *Death is overthrown!*

But what is the consequence? For a short time man is very happy indeed, but only for a time. All things have become possible to him—and he has nothing more to do. He has no pleasure of hope, because there is nothing to hope for which he has not already got. He has no pleasure of effort, because there is nothing for which to make an effort. Pleasures soon become uninviting to the idle; man's intelligence has at last condemned him to eternal agonies. Then for the first time he recognises that pleasure is impossible without pain, that they are connected inseparably as light and shadow. In a little while man becomes frightfully unhappy, cursed with eternal life and unable to use that life to any purpose. So he humbles himself at last before God, praying for only one thing, the blessed gift of death. God hears the prayer. Death is loosened and returns among men; and they welcome him as their best friend. And God says to the spirit of man in conclusion, as an explanation of all that man could not understand:

"O Man, my creature, thy lot was more blest than mine.
I taste not delight of seeking, nor the boon of longing know,
There is but one joy transcendent, and I hoard it not but bestow.
I hoard it not, nor have tasted, but freely I gave it thee—
The joy of most glorious striving, which dieth in victory."

Thus the poem proclaims that there is really no happiness worth having except the happiness of effort. This is not a commonplace saying at all. It is a very deep saying, and contains what seems to me the nearest possible approach to the truth of life. Perhaps there may occur to you, in contrast to it, the Eastern religious saying that the highest happiness is rest. But the two declarations do not really contradict each other. Rest would be the highest happiness, perhaps, for unconditioned being; but for being having form, having body, capable of joy and sorrow, pain and pleasure, rest could be of no possible value. In the last part of the poem the poet really brings us face to face with an apparent solution of the problem of pain.   The verse is sometimes rough and uneven; the poem is great only as a fancy; but as a fancy it is one of the most remarkable composed during the Victorian age; and I should therefore recommend you to read it carefully and to think about it. I also venture to say that it is the most remarkable thing which Watson has done, though by no means the most perfect.   Much more perfect is a little piece, somewhat in the manner of Blake, called "World-Strangeness."

> Strange the world about me lies,
>   Never yet familiar grown—
> Still disturbs me with surprise,
>   Haunts me like a face half known.
>
> In this house with starry dome,
>   Floored with gem-like plains and seas,
> Shall I never feel at home,
>   Never wholly be at ease?
>
> On from room to room I stray;
>   Yet my Host can ne'er espy,
> And I know not to this day,
>   Whether guest or captive I.
>
> So, between the starry dome
>   And the floor of plains and seas,
> I have never felt at home,
>   Never wholly been at ease.

CHAPTER XII

A NOTE ON ROBERT BUCHANAN

AMONG the minor poets of the Victorian period, Robert Buchanan cannot be passed over unnoticed. A contemporary of all the great singers, he seems to have been always a little isolated; I mean that he formed no strong literary friendships within the great circle. Most great poets must live to a certain extent in solitude; the man who can at once mix freely in society and find time for the production of masterpieces is a rare phenomenon. George Meredith is said to be such a person. But Tennyson, Rossetti, Swinburne, Browning, Fitzgerald, were all very reserved and retired men, though they had little circles of their own, and a certain common sympathy. The case of Buchanan is different. His aloofness from the rest has been, not the result of any literary desire for quiet, but the result, on the contrary, of a strong spirit of opposition. Not only did he have no real sympathy with the great poets, but he represented in himself the very prejudices against which they had to contend. Hard headed Scotchman as he was, he manifested in his attitude to his brother poets a good deal of the peculiar, harsh conservatism of which Scotchmen seemed to be particularly capable. And he did himself immense injury in his younger days by an anonymous attack upon the morals, or rather upon the moral tone, of such poets as Rossetti and Swinburne. Swinburne's reply to this attack was terrible and withering. That of Rossetti was very mild and gentle, but so effective that English literary circles almost unanimously condemned Buchanan, and attributed his attack to mere jealousy. I think the attack was less due to jealousy than to character, to prejudice, to the harshness of a mind insensible to particular forms of beauty.   And for more than twenty years Buchanan has suffered extremely from the results of his own action. Thousands of people have ignored him and his books simply because it was remembered that he gave wanton pain to Rossetti, a poet much too sensitive to endure unjust criticism.   I suppose that for many years to come Buchanan will still be remembered in this light, notwithstanding that he tried at a later day to make honourable amends to the memory of Rossetti, by dedicating to him, with a beautiful sonnet of apology, the definitive edition of his own works.

But the time has now passed when Buchanan can be treated as an indifferent figure in English literature.   In spite of all disadvantages he has been a successful poet, a successful novelist, and a very considerable influence in the literature of criticism.   Besides, he has written at least one poem that will probably live as long as the English language, and he has an originality quite apart and quite extraordinary, though weaker than the originality of the greater singers of his time.   As to his personal history, little need to be said.   He was educated at Glasgow University, and his literary efforts have always been somewhat coloured by Scotch sentiment, in spite of his long life in literary London.

Three volumes represent his poetical production.   In these are contained a remarkable variety of poems—narrative, mystical, fantastic, classical, romantic, ranging from the simplest form of ballad to the complex form of the sonnet and the ode.   The narrative poems would, I think, interest you least; they are gloomy studies of human suffering, physical and moral, among the poor, and are not so good as the work of Crabbe in the same direction.   The mystical poems, on the contrary, are of a very curious kind; for Buchanan actually made a religious philosophy of his own, and put it into the form of verse.   It is a Christian mysticism, an extremely liberal Unitarianism forming the basis of it; but the author's notions about the perpetual order of things are all his own. He has, moreover, put these queer fancies into a form of verse imitating the ancient Celtic poetry. We shall afterward briefly consider the mystical poetry. But the great production of Buchanan is a simple ballad, which you find very properly placed at the beginning of his collected poems. This is a beautiful and extraordinary thing, quite in accordance with the poet's peculiar views of Christianity. It is called "The Ballad of Judas Iscariot." If you know only this composition, you will know all that it is absolutely necessary to know of Robert Buchanan. It is by this poem that his place is marked in nineteenth century literature.

Before we turn to the poem itself, I must explain to you something of the legend of Judas Iscariot. You know, of course, that Judas was the disciple of Christ who betrayed his master. He betrayed him for thirty pieces of silver, according to the tradition; and he betrayed him with a kiss, for he said to the soldiers whom he was guiding, "The man whom I shall kiss is the man you want." So Judas went up to Christ, and kissed his face; and then the soldiers seized Christ. From this has come the proverbial phrase common to so many Western languages, a "Judas-kiss." Afterwards Judas, being seized with remorse, is said to have hanged himself; and there the Scriptural story ends. But in Church legends the fate of Judas continues to be discussed in the Middle Ages. As he was the betrayer of a person whom the Church considered to be God, it was deemed that he was necessarily the greatest of all traitors; and as he had indirectly helped to bring about the death of God, he was condemned as the greatest of all murderers. It was said that in hell the very lowest place was given to Judas, and that his tortures exceeded all other tortures. But once every year, it was said, Judas could leave hell, and go out to cool himself upon the ice of the Northern seas. That is the legend of the Middle Ages.

Now Robert Buchanan perceived that the Church legends

of the punishment of Judas might be strongly questioned from a moral point of view. Revenge is indeed in the spirit of the Old Testament; but revenge is not exactly in the spirit of the teaching of Christ. The true question as to the fate of Judas ought to be answered by supposing what Christ himself would have wished in the matter. Would Christ have wished to see his betrayer burning for ever in the fires of hell? Or would he have shown to him some of that spirit manifested in his teachings, "Do good unto them that hate you; forgive your enemies"? As a result of thinking about the matter, Buchanan produced his ballad. All that could be said against it from a religious point of view is that the spirit of it is even more Christian than Christianity itself. From the poetical point of view we must acknowledge it to be one of the grandest ballads produced in the whole period of Victorian literature. You will not find so exquisite a finish here as in some of the ballads of Rossetti; but you will find a weirdness and a beauty and an emotional power that make up for slenderness in workmanship.

In order to understand the beginning of the ballad clearly, you should know the particulars about another superstition concerning Judas. It is said that all the elements refused to suffer the body to be committed to them; fire would not burn it; water would not let it sink to rest; every time it was buried, the earth would spew it out again. Man could not bury that body, so the ghosts endeavoured to get rid of it. The Field of Blood referred to in the ballad is the Aceldama of Scriptural legend, the place where Judas hanged himself.

> 'Twas the body of Judas Iscariot
>   Lay in the Field of Blood;
> 'Twas the soul of Judas Iscariot
>   Beside the body stood.
>
> Black was the earth by night,
>   And black was the sky.

Black, black were the broken clouds,
   Though the red Moon went by.

.   .   .   .   .   .

Then the soul of Judas Iscariot
   Did make a gentle moan—
"I will bury underneath the ground
   My flesh and blood and bone.

.   .   .   .   .   .

"The stones of the field are sharp as steel
   And hard and cold, God wot;
And I must bear my body hence
   Until I find a spot!"

'Twas the soul of Judas Iscariot,
   So grim, and gaunt, and grey,
Raised the body of Judas Iscariot
   And carried it away.

And as he bare it from the field
   Its touch was cold as ice,
And the ivory teeth within the jaw
   Rattled aloud, like dice.

The use of the word "ivory" here has a double function;
dice are usually made of ivory; and the suggestion of white-
ness heightens the weird effect.

As the soul of Judas Iscariot
   Carried its load with pain,
The Eye of Heaven, like a lanthorn's eye,
   Opened and shut again.

Half he walk'd, and half he seemed
   Lifted on the cold wind;
He did not turn, for chilly hands
   Were pushing from behind.

The first place that he came unto
   It was the open wold
And underneath were pricky whins,
   And a wind that blew so cold.

The next place that he came unto
   It was a stagnant pool,
And when he threw the body in
   It floated light as wool.

He drew the body on his back,
   And it was dripping chill,
And the next place he came unto
   Was a Cross upon a hill.

A Cross upon the windy hill,
   And a cross on either side,
Three skeletons that swing thereon,
   Who had been crucified.

And on the middle cross-bar sat
   A white Dove slumbering;
Dim it sat in the dim light,
   With its head beneath its wing.

And underneath the middle Cross
   A grave yawned wide and vast,
But the soul of Judas Iscariot
   Shiver'd, and glided past.

We are not told what this hill was, but every reader knows that Calvary is meant, and the skeletons upon the crosses are those of Christ and the two thieves crucified with him. The ghostly hand had pushed Judas to the place of all places where he would have wished not to go. We need not mind the traditional discrepancy suggested by the three skeletons; as a matter of fact, the bodies of malefactors were not commonly left upon the crosses long enough to become skeletons, and of course the legend is that Christ's body was on the cross only for a short time. But we may suppose that the whole description is of a phantasm, purposely shaped to stir the remorse of Judas. The white dove sleeping upon the middle cross suggests the soul of Christ, and the great grave made below might have been prepared out of mercy for the body of Judas. If the dove had awoke and spoken to him, would it not have said, "You can put your body here, in my grave; nobody will torment you." But the soul of Judas cannot even think of daring to approach the place of the crucifixion.

> The fourth place that he came unto,
>   It was the Brig of Dread,
> And the great torrents rushing down
>   Were deep, and swift, and red.
>
> He dared not fling the body in
>   For fear of faces dim,
> And arms were waved in the wild water
>   To thrust it back to him.

There is here a poetical effect borrowed from sources having nothing to do with the Judas tradition. In old Northern folklore there is the legend of a River of Blood, in which all the blood ever shed in this world continues to flow; and there is a reference to this river in the old Scotch ballad of "Thomas the Rhymer."

> It was mirk, mirk night, and there was nae light,
> And they waded in red blude up to the knee,
> For a' the blude that's shed on earth,
> Rins through the springs o' that countrie.

Judas leaves the dreadful bridge and continues his wanderings over the mountain, through woods and through great desolate plains:

> For months and years, in grief and tears,
>   He walked the silent night;
> Then the soul of Judas Iscariot
>   Perceived a far-off light.
>
> A far-off light across the waste,
>   As dim as dim might be,
> That came and went like a lighthouse gleam
>   On a black night at sea.

'Twas the soul of Judas Iscariot
  Crawled to the distant gleam;
And the rain came down, and the rain was blown
  Against him with a scream.

'Twas the soul of Judas Iscariot,
  Strange, and sad, and tall,
Stood all alone at dead of night
  Before a lighted hall.

And the wold was white with snow,
  And his foot-marks black and damp,
And the ghost of the silver Moon arose,
  Holding her yellow lamp.

And the icicles were on the eaves,
  And the walls were deep with white,
And the shadows of the guests within
  Passed on the window light.

The shadows of the wedding guests
  Did strangely come and go,
And the body of Judas Iscariot
  Lay stretch'd along the snow.

But only the body. The soul which has carried it does
not lie down, but runs round and round the lighted hall,
where the wedding guests are assembled. What wedding?
What guests? This is the mystical banquet told of in the
parable of the New Testament; the bridegroom is Christ
himself; the guests are the twelve disciples, or rather, the
eleven, Judas himself having been once the twelfth. And
the guests see the soul of Judas looking in at the window.

'Twas the Bridegroom sat at the table-head,
  And the lights burnt bright and clear—
"Oh, who is that," the Bridegroom said,
  "Whose weary feet I hear?"

'Twas one look'd from the lighted hall,
  And answered soft and slow,

"It is a wolf runs up and down
   With a black track in the snow."

The Bridegroom in his robe of white
   Sat at the table-head—
"Oh, who is that who moans without?"
   The blessed Bridegroom said.

'Twas one looked from the lighted hall,
   And answered fierce and low,
" 'Tis the soul of Judas Iscariot
   Gliding to and fro."

'Twas the soul of Judas Iscariot
   Did hush itself and stand,
And saw the Bridegroom at the door
   With a light in his hand.

The Bridegroom stood in the open door
   And he was clad in white,
And far within the Lord's Supper
   Was spread so broad and bright.

The Bridegroom shaded his eyes and looked,
   And his face was bright to see—
"What dost thou here at the Lord's Supper
   With thy body's sins?" said he.

'Twas the soul of Judas Iscariot,
   Stood black, and sad, and bare—
"I have wandered many nights and days;
   There is no light elsewhere."

'Twas the wedding guests cried out within,
   And their eyes were fierce and bright—
"Scourge the soul of Judas Iscariot,
   Away into the night!"

The Bridegroom stood in the open door
   And he waved hands still and slow,
And the third time that he waved his hands
   The air was thick with snow.

And of every flake of falling snow,
    Before it touched the ground,
There came a dove, and a thousand doves
    Made sweet sound.

'Twas the body of Judas Iscariot
    Floated away full fleet,
And the wings of the doves that bare it off
    Were like its winding-sheet.

'Twas the Bridegroom stood at the open door,
    And beckon'd, smiling sweet;
'Twas the soul of Judas Iscariot
    Stole in, and fell at his feet.

"The Holy Supper is spread within,
    And the many candles shine,
And I have waited long for thee
    Before I poured the wine!"

It would have been better, I think, to finish the ballad at this stanza; there is one more, but it does not add at all to the effect of what goes before. When the doves, emblems of divine love, have carried away the sinful body, and the Master comes to the soul, smiling and saying: "I have been waiting for you a long time, waiting for your coming before I poured the wine"—there is nothing more to be said. We do not want to hear any more; we know that the Eleven had again become Twelve; we do not require to be told that the wine is poured out, or that Judas repents his fault. The startling and beautiful thing is the loving call and the welcome to the Divine Supper. You will find the whole of this poem in the "Victorian Anthology," but I should advise any person who might think of making a Japanese translation to drop the final stanza and to leave out a few of the others, if his judgment agrees with mine.

Read this again to yourselves, and see how beautiful it is.

The beauty is chiefly in the central idea of forgiveness; but the workmanship of this composition has also a very remarkable beauty, a Celtic beauty of weirdness, such as we seldom find in a modern composition touching religious tradition. It were interesting to know how the poet was able to imagine such a piece of work. I think I can tell a little of the secret. Only a man with a great knowledge and love of old ballads could have written it. Having once decided upon the skeleton of the story, he must have gone to his old Celtic literature and to old Northern ballads for further inspiration. I have already suggested that the ballad of "Thomas the Rhymer" was one source of his inspiration, with its strange story of the River of Blood. Thomas was sitting under a tree, the legend goes, when he saw a woman approaching so beautiful that he thought she was an angel or the Virgin Mary, and he addressed her on his knees. But she sat down beside him, and said, "I am no angel nor saint; I am only a fairy. But if you think that I am so beautiful, take care that you do not kiss me, for if you do, then I shall have power over you." Thomas immediately did much more than kiss her, and he therefore became her slave. She took him at once to fairy land, and on their way they passed through strange wild countries, much like those described in Robert Buchanan's ballad; they passed the River of Blood; they passed dark trees laden with magical food; and they saw the road that reaches Heaven and the road that reaches Hell. But Buchanan could take only a few ideas from this poem. Other ideas I think were inspired by a ballad of Goethe's, or at least by Sir Walter Scott's version of it, "Frederick and Alice." Frederick is a handsome young soldier who seduces a girl called Alice under promise of marriage, and then leaves her. He rides to join the army in France. The girl becomes insane with grief and shame; and the second day later she dies at four o'clock in the morning. Meantime Frederick unexpectedly loses his way; the rest I may best

tell in the original weird form.   The horse has been frightened by the sound of a church bell striking the hour of four.

> Heard ye not the boding sound,
>   As the tongue of yonder tower,
> Slowly, to the hills around,
>   Told the fourth, the fated hour?
>
> Starts the steed, and snuffs the air,
>   Yet no cause of dread appears;
> Bristles high the rider's hair,
>   Struck with strange mysterious fears.
>
> Desperate as his terrors rise,
>   In the steed the spur he hides;
> From himself in vain he flies;
>   Anxious, restless, on he rides.
>
> Seven long days, and seven long nights,
>   Wild he wandered, woe the while!
> Ceaseless care, and causeless fright,
>   Urge his footsteps many a mile.
>
> Dark the seventh sad night descends;
>   Rivers swell, and rain-streams pour
> While the deafening thunder lends
>   All the terrors of its roar.

At the worst part of his dreary wandering over an unknown and gloomy country, Frederick suddenly sees a light
far away.   This seems to him, as it seemed in Buchanan's
ballad to the soul of Judas, a light of hope.   He goes to
the light, and finds himself in front of a vast and ruinous
looking church.   Inside there is a light; he leaps down from
his horse, descends some steps, and enters the building.
Suddenly all is darkness again; he has to feel his way.

> Long drear vaults before him lie!
>   Glimmering lights are seen to glide!—
> "Blessed Mary, hear my cry!
>   Deign a sinner's steps to guide!"

> Often lost their quivering beam,
>   Still the lights move slow before,
> Till they rest their ghastly gleam
>   Right against an iron door.

He is really in the underground burial place of a church, in the vaults of the dead, but he does not know it. He hears voices.

> Thundering voices from within,
>   Mixed with peals of laughter, rose;
> As they fell, a solemn strain
>   Lent its wild and wondrous close!

> 'Midst the din, he seem'd to hear
>   Voice of friends, by death removed;—
> Well he knew that solemn air,
>   'Twas the lay that Alice loved.

Suddenly a great bell booms four times, and the iron door opens. He sees within a strange banquet; the seats are coffins, the tables are draped with black, and the dead are the guests.

> Alice, in her grave-clothes bound,
>   Ghastly smiling, points a seat,
> All arose with thundering sound;
>   All the expected stranger greet.

> High their meagre arms they wave,
>   Wild their notes of welcome swell;
> "Welcome, traitor, to the grave!
>   Perjured, bid the light farewell!"

I have given the greater part of this strange ballad because of its intrinsic value and the celebrity of its German author. But the part that may have inspired Buchanan is only the part concerning the wandering over the black moor, the light seen in the distance, the ghostly banquet of the dead, and the ruined vaults. A great poet would have easily found in these details the suggestion which Buchanan

found for the wandering of Judas to the light and the unexpected vision of the dead assembling to a banquet with
him—but only this. The complete transformation of the
fancy, the transmutation of the purely horrible into a
ghostly beauty and tenderness, is the wonderful thing.
After all, this is the chief duty of the poet in this world,
to discover beauty even in the ugly, suggestions of beauty
even in the cruel and terrible. This Buchanan did once
so very well that his work will never be forgotten, but
he received thereafter no equal inspiration, and the "Ballad of Judas" remains, alone of its kind, his only real claim
to high distinction.

The poetry of Robert Buchanan is not great enough as
poetry to justify many quotations, but as thinking it demands some attention. His third volume is especially of
interest in this respect, because it contains a curious ex-
position of his religious idealism. Buchanan is a mystic;
there is no doubt that he has been very much influenced by
the mysticism of Blake. The whole of the poems collec-
tively entitled "The Devil's Mystics," must have been suggested by Blake's nomenclature. This collection belongs
to "the Book of Orm," which might have been well called
"The Book of Robert Buchanan." Orm ought to be a
familiar name to students of English literature, one of the
old English books also being called "The Ormulum," because it was written by a man named Orm. Buchanan's Orm is represented to be an ancient Celt, who has
visions and dreams about the mystery of the universe, and
who puts these visions and dreams, which are Buchanan's,
into old-fashioned verse.

The great Ernest Renan said in his "Dialogues Phi-
losophiques" that if everybody in the world who had thought
much about the mystery of things were to write down his
ideas regarding the Infinite, some great truth might be
discovered or deduced from the result. Buchanan has tried
to follow this suggestion; for he has very boldly put down

all his thoughts about the world and man and God. As to results, however, I can find nothing particularly original except two or three queer fancies, none of which relates to the deeper riddles of being. In a preface in verse, the author further tells us that when he speaks of God he does not mean the Christian God or the God of India nor any particular God, but only the all-including Spirit of Life. Be that as it may, we find his imagery to be certainly borrowed from old Hebrew and old Christian thinkers; here he has not fulfilled expectations. But the imagery is used to express some ideas which I think you will find rather new—not exactly philosophical ideas, but moral parables.

One of these is a parable about the possible consequences of seeing or knowing the divine power which is behind the shadows of things. Suppose that there were an omnipotent God whom we could see; what would be the consequences of seeing him? Orm discovered that the blue of the sky was a blue veil drawn across Immensity to hide the face of God. One day, in answer to prayer, God drew aside the blue veil. Then all mankind were terrified because they saw, by day and by night, an awful face looking down upon them out of the sky, the sleepless eyes of the face seeming to watch each person constantly wherever he was. Did this make men happy? Not at all. They became tired of life, finding themselves perpetually watched; they covered their cities with roofs, and lived by lamp light only, in order to avoid being looked at by the face, God. This queer parable, recounted in the form of a dream, has a meaning worth thinking about. The ultimate suggestion, of course, is that we do not know and see many things because it would make us very unhappy to know them.

An equally curious parable, also related in the form of a dream, treats of the consolations of death. What would become of mankind if there were no death? I think you will remember that I told you how the young poet William Watson took up the same subject a few years ago, in his remarkable poem "A Dream of Man." Watson's supposition is that men became so wise, so scientific, that they were able to make themselves immortal and to conquer death. But at last they became frightfully unhappy, unutterably tired of life, and were obliged to beg God to give them back death again. And God said to them, "You are happier than I am. You can die; I cannot. The only happiness of existence is effort. Now you can have your friend death back again." Buchanan's idea was quite different from this. His poem is called "The Dream of the World without Death." Men prayed to God that there might be no more death or decay of the body; and the prayer was granted. People continued to disappear from the world, but they did not die. They simply vanished, when their time came, as ghosts. A child goes out to play in the field, for example, and never comes back again; the mother finds only the empty clothes of her darling. Or a peasant goes to the fields to work, and his body is never seen again. People found that this was a much worse condition of things than had been before. For the consolation of knowledge, of certainty, was not given them. The dead body is a certificate of death; nature uses corruption as a seal, an official exhibit and proof of the certainty of death. But when there is no body, no corpse, no possible sign, how horrible is the disappearance of the persons we love. The mystery of it is a much worse pain than the certain knowledge of death. Doubt is the worst form of torture. Well, when mankind had this experience, they began to think that, after all, death was a beautiful and good thing, and they prayed most fervently that they might again have the privilege of dying in the old way, of putting the bodies of their dead into beautiful tombs, of being able to visit the graves of their beloved from time to time. So God took pity on them and gave them back death, and the poet sings his gratitude thus:

And I cried, "O unseen Sender of Corruption,
I bless thee for the wonder of Thy mercy,
Which softeneth the mystery and the parting.

"I bless Thee for the change and for the comfort,
The bloomless face, shut eyes, and waxen fingers,—
For Sleeping, and for Silence, and Corruption."

This idea is worth something, if only as a vivid teaching of the necessity of things as they are. The two fantasies thus commented upon are the most original things in the range of this mystical book. I could not recommend any further reading or study of the poet, except perhaps of his "Vision of the Man Accurst." But even this has not the true stamp of originality; and only the "Ballad of Judas Iscariot" is certain not to be soon forgotten.

CHAPTER XIII

A NOTE ON MUNBY'S "DOROTHY"

THERE are several reasons why the poem entitled "Dorothy" should be made well known to you.   First of all it represents in a very striking manner a new spirit of pastoral poetry in the latter part of the Victorian period.   In the second place it is a poem which has been very widely read and admired both in England and America—in fact, wherever the English language is read.   And in the third place it can give you some notions about the life of the peasant classes in England and about their relation to the upper classes, almost better than any other book can do.   Finally I may add that it touches strongly and sensibly upon certain economic facts of life, opposing the sentimental laws forbidding women to do the work of men.   You know that there are several sides to this question; it is not to be lightly decided, and I am not a teacher of ethics or economics, or of the relation between ethics and economics, so I shall not attempt to express any opinion on the subject at present.   But you should certainly be interested in the view of the matter taken by the author of this book, who ought to be able to judge of such matters well, since he is an eminent lawyer, a good scholar, an official representing government interests in the country districts, and a farmer and a poet.   Such a combination of knowledge and experience should entitle a man to express an opinion about the conditions of the peasantry.

When this book first appeared it was published anonymously.   But now it is well known as the work of Arthur Joseph Munby, an English lawyer who occasionally visits London, but who has lived for the greater part of his life in the country, especially in Surrey.   Munby was born in

Yorkshire, which district, by the way, possesses the finest peasantry in England. His birth was in 1828, so that he must now be quite an old man; but he published a volume of new poems only this year. It is rather a curious combination which he presents—farmer, country squire, and lawyer all in one, yet finding time to be a poet. University training developed his power to write poetry almost as easily as other men write prose; this partly may account for the phenomenon. I do not mean to say that it is great poetry; no man can be a great poet and exercise three other professions at the same time. But it is not bad poetry, it is actually better than the work of Arthur Hugh Clough, the friend of Matthew Arnold, who wrote very much the same kind of verse, and there is a merit in it besides that of poetry proper. As a romance in verse, the measure and construction of "Dorothy" do not greatly impress the reader; in fact you are sometimes surprised, and almost made angry, by the apparent indifference to poetical rules. But after you have read the work, the impression left upon the mind is very strong and very pleasing, and you will not forget it. The book has the power to charm; it has charmed tens of thousands of readers. The secret of the charm is not, as I have suggested, in the literary art, but in the feeling of the book, in the author's grasp of the subject, in his knowledge of and sympathy with country life. From boyhood this man liked the peasants, saw their good qualities and admired them, learned their dialects and liked to talk to them. I may mention here also that he has written a good deal of poetry in peasant dialect, although a university scholar. And one day he conceived the idea of trying to interest the English upper classes in the humble life of these country folk whom they pretended to despise. But he had many prejudices to face in order to be able to do this well. He had to be prepared to meet every possible kind of sneer and jeer on the part of snobs and cads. He had to expect to be told that his peasants were dirty, smelled bad, had ugly hands, ugly faces, ugly feet, ugly manners, and detestable stupidity into the bargain. And then he met these prejudices and affectations simply by drawing peasant life as he saw it. He described all the dirt and the smell and the vulgarity and the ignorance in his poems —even exaggerating them; and nevertheless he made people like them, admire them, almost love them when he had done. The fact is, nearly all class prejudices, based upon social conditions, are utter humbug; and they would scarcely exist if the upper classes were less ignorant than they are of what is noble and good and human in the lowest classes. Munby did not attempt to fight prejudices by denying their cause or denying their assertions, but by bringing the real human facts into the light, and making people look at them fairly and squarely. I think this is all I need say about the social side of the poem.

But I must tell you something about English peasant life, country life, labouring life, before I quote to you anything from "Dorothy." I do not think that much is known in Japan about English country life, though a good deal is now known about the life of the cities and of their industrial classes. Japanese travellers do not have either the time or the opportunity to go out into the country and study the peasant. And yet, not to study the peasantry of a country must be to remain with a very imperfect knowledge of the nation. For the body, the strength, the whole power of the race is there. In England, perhaps, the difficulty of studying the agricultural classes is especially great, for the extraordinary reason that the agricultural classes are gradually disappearing. The entire country is owned by a few thousand people; there is no future in store for the common worker, and the advent of the complicated machinery into field work dispenses with a great deal of human labour. Therefore the English peasantry emigrates whenever it can, and in the future its place will perhaps be taken by an inferior foreign class.   But, as I have said, to know the English race one should know something about its peasants.   The excellent French thinker Taine, who made an admirable book of English travels, understood this perfectly well, and he based his studies of English character largely upon his observation of the agricultural and the working classes.

At the time when Munby wrote his poem, women in the English country district used to do extraordinary work, perhaps more than they do now.   There were plenty of women blacksmiths, women colliers, women farmers—in fact, almost every department of heavy labour had places for women as well as for men.   I believe that legislation subsequently changed a good many of these conditions, forbidding women, for example, to work in the coal mines dressed in men's clothes.   But as a boy I remember seeing much heavy work done by women, and I do not know that the legislation was altogether wise.   Only a very particular class of women could do the work against which the laws were passed, and that class of women were particularly well fitted by nature to do it.   You could not have told, by the eye alone, whether those working women were men or women; their voices might betray them, but not their walk or their bulk.   Among them were figures six feet high, with shoulders broad as a wrestler's, arms muscled like those of a man, and walking with the long swinging step of a man in great heavy shoes.   The impression you received on seeing them work was that there was nothing womanly about them, for their roughness of appearance was equal to the roughness of men.

Among the peasant class proper—I mean among those who remain all their lives at farm work—this masculinity does not appear to the same degree in manners.   The labouring woman in the country is often huge and strong but seldom unwomanly.   Her manner remains gentle and

kind. It is the contact with the life of the mines, with mechanical industries and manufactories, that seems to make
the woman rough. They lose the moral tone of their sex—
I do not mean by this that they become bad, but they cease
to act and talk like women. It is not so in the country; it
is so only in the manufacturing and mining towns. Now
it is of the country girl that Mr. Munby writes, and he takes
for his type one of the lowest class of workers, a female farm
servant.

I must tell you something about these female servants.
A woman must be very strong indeed to be a servant in the
country, not only in England but even in America. A
woman employed as servant on a farm must do what would
be considered in this country hard work for at least six persons. She must cook three times a day for the entire household, she must bake bread in addition to cooking, she must
do all the washing of the family, and keep the house clean,
and she must help with the work on the farm—milking and
feeding the cow, taking care of the poultry, doing, in short,
the work of both a man and a woman. One must be very
strong indeed for such labour; and it is no wonder that
women are gradually passing from the sphere of domestic
employment, to be replaced by men.

Can we imagine any romance in so hard a life? Our
English poet has proved to us that romance may be found
in it quite as well as in any other walk of life—though of a
different kind.

Let us take the plan of the story as he tells it to us,
giving extracts here and there to show the attraction of his
verse. It is good verse, all hexameters and pentameters
alternating; and although this kind of verse cannot be made
quite perfect in English by anybody, Mr. Munby's hexameters will certainly compare very well with either Longfellow's or Clough's. He first tells us about the birth of
the girl on the farm—an illegitimate child, and therefore·
destined to hard work without any parental affection to

soften the way for her, but honest, good, kind, and beautiful.   Here is a little description, which includes the description of a farm girl in general:

Weakly her mistress was, and weakly the two little daughters;
But by her master's side Dorothy wrought like a son;
Wrought out of doors on the farm, and labour'd in dairy and kitchen
Doing the work of two; help and support of them all.
Rough were her broad brown hands, and within, ah me! they were
    horny;
Rough were her thick ruddy arms, shapely and round as they were;
Rough too her glowing cheeks; and her sunburnt face and forehead
Browner than cairngorm seem'd, set in her amber-bright hair.
Yet 'twas a handsome face; the beautiful regular features
Labour could never spoil, ignorance could not degrade:
And in her clear blue eyes bright gleams of intelligence linger'd;
And on her warm red mouth, Love might have 'lighted and lain.
Never an unkind word nor a rude unseemly expression
Came from that soft red mouth; nor in those sunny blue eyes
Lived there a look that belied the frankness of innocent girlhood—
Fearless, because it is pure; gracious, and gentle, and calm.
Have you not seen such a face, among rural hard-working maidens
Born but of peasant stock, free from our Dorothy's shame?
Just such faces as hers—a countenance open and artless,
Where no knowledge appears, culture, nor vision of grace;
Yet which an open-air life and simple and strenuous labour
Fills with a charm of its own—precious, and warm from the heart?

I think the author insists too much in his poem upon the
roughness and hardness of Dorothy's hands.   As a matter
of fact, no soft-handed woman could be a good worker, and
it is the custom to look at a woman's hands before giving
her work to do on a farm.   If they are soft and white, they
belong to a lazy woman.   It is good to recognise the hon-
esty of a hard working hand, to recognise that there is a
certain nobility in labour, but I think that Munby insists
too much on the ugliness of hard hands.   Really hard hands
are not any uglier than any other hands, except to fastidious
persons; perhaps Mr. Munby was only desiring to antici-
pate fastidious criticism.   He goes on to give a description

of the girl on the farm in winter, spring, summer, and autumn.   The description of the spring work is fine; the subject is ploughing.   It is very hard to plough perfectly, unless you have been brought up to the work from a child. Prizes for straight ploughing used to be given in different parts of the country; perhaps they are still given, but the introduction of steam ploughing machinery from America is very likely to do away with hand ploughing in the course of time.   If that day comes, a description of ploughing like this will be remembered and read with a pleasure somewhat like that which we feel when we read in Virgil accounts of the work done upon old Roman farms:

Well can our Dorothy plough—as a girl she learnt it and loved it;
Leading the teams at first, followed by master himself;
Then when she grew to the height and the strength of a muscular
    woman,
Grasping the stilts in her pride, driving the mighty machine.
Ah, what a joy for her, at early morn in the springtime
Driving from hedge to hedge furrows as straight as a line!
Seeing the crisp brown earth, like waves in the bow of a vessel
Rise, curl over, and fall, under the thrust of the share;
Orderly falling and still, its edges all creamy and crumbling,
But on the sloping side, polished and purple as steel;
Till all the fields she thought looked bright as the bars of that gridiron
In the great window at church, over the gentle folks' pew:
And ever more as she strode she had cheerful companions behind her;
Rooks and smaller birds, following after her plough:
And ere the ridges were done, there was gossamer woven above them,
Gossamer dewy and white, shining like foam on the sea.

Of descriptions like these there are not many, for the subject of the poem is the description of character rather than of hills and fields, and descriptions of character are better given through the words and actions of a person than in any other way.   So a large proportion of the poem is simply a narrative of acts, mingled with a record of colloquial speech.   Still I may quote you a few lines about a sunset:

Well, there was something to see; for the sun was setting in glory,
Glowing through marvellous clouds, molten suffused with his light;
Clouds all rosy above, like the snows of an Alpine sunset,
But in the heart of their snow thrilled with a cavernous fire;
Clouds that were couched superb in a blaze of opal and emerald,
Haunting the clear, cool sky lucid and lovely and blue.

The quotations will show the very considerable power of art which the poet possesses and can use at will. But the art of showing the beauty and charm of a simple character is much more difficult than the painting of clouds, and this also the poet has done. He traces for us the life of the girl up to the time of her wedding, and the object of the whole work is certainly, in no small degree, the praise of honest labour that strengthens the body and keeps the mind pure. Why discourage women from labour in the fields, he asks, since such work is good both for the body and for the mind; and the women capable of such work become the mothers of the strong and steady men that make up the force of a country. It is not, he reminds us, the sickly and delicate girls working in factories or in shops, who are likely to be the mothers of the best men.

Probably this poem of Mr. Munby's had very little effect in checking the course of things, and probably the agricultural population of England must disappear. The whole country is becoming divided into nothing but manufacturing districts or ornamental estates. It does not pay to grow corn or wheat nor even to raise cattle and sheep in England. It is cheaper to buy such things from abroad. So the farming population is disappearing. The best men and women go to other countries—Canada, America, Australia; the weaker part of the peasant population drift into factory life. These things cannot be helped. But the poet has preserved for us a fine picture of this fine peasant life, which will be read when the peasant life itself has passed from England. The book suggests or ought to suggest a good deal to lovers of literature in other countries than England, especially the fact that peasant life is a subject for poetry; and that the poet able to perceive its relation to the moral and physical well-being of a nation has a great opportunity before him.

CHAPTER XIV

ROBERT BRIDGES

This poet, one of the greatest of the English minor poets of our time, and represented in literature by a very considerable bulk of work, happens to be one of the least known. He was never popular; and even to-day, when recognition is coming to him slowly, almost as slowly as it came to George Meredith, he is chiefly read by the cultivated classes. There are several reasons for this. One is that he is altogether an old-fashioned poet, writing with the feeling of the eighteenth rather than of the nineteenth century, so that persons in search of novelty are not likely to look at him. Then again he is not a thinker, except at the rarest moments, not touched at all by the scientific ideas of the nineteenth century. For that reason a great many people, accustomed to look for philosophy in poetry, do not care about his verse. I must confess that I myself should not have read him, had it not been for a beautiful criticism of his work published some five years ago. That tempted me to study him, with pleasant results. But I then found a third reason for his unpopularity—want of passion. When everything else is missing that attracts intellectual attention to a poet, everything strange, novel, and philosophical, he may still become popular if he has strong emotion, deep feeling. But Robert Bridges has neither. He is somewhat cool, even when he is not cold; his colours are never strong, though they are always natural; and there is something faint about his music that makes you think of the music of insects, of night crickets or locusts. You may therefore begin to wonder that I should speak about him at all. If a poet has no philosophy, no originality, and no passion, what can there be in him? Well, a great deal. It is not necessary to be original in order to be a poet; it is only necessary to say old things somewhat better than they have been said before. Such a non-original poet of excellence may be a great lover of nature; for nature has been described in a million ways, and we are not tired of the descriptions. Again, the feeling need not be very strong; it is not strong in Wordsworth, except at moments. I think that the charm of Robert Bridges, who is especially a nature-poet, lies in his love of quiet effects, pale colours, small soft sounds, all the dreaminess and all the gentleness of still and beautiful days. Some of us like strong sounds, blazing colours, heavy scents of flowers and fruits; but some of us do not— we prefer rest and coolness and quiet tones. And I think that to Japanese feeling Robert Bridges ought to make an appeal. Much of his work makes me think of the old Japanese colour prints of spring, summer, autumn, and winter landscapes. He is particularly fond of painting these; perhaps half of his poetry, certainly a third of it, deals with descriptions of the seasons. There is nothing tropical in these descriptions, because they are true to English landscape, the only landscape that he knows well. Now there is a good deal in English landscape, in the colours of the English seasons, that resembles what is familiar to us in the aspects of Japanese nature.

I cannot tell you very much about the poet himself; he has left his personality out of the reach of public curiosity. I can only tell you that he was born in 1844 and that he is a country doctor, which is very interesting, for it is not often that a man can follow the busy duties of a country physician and find time to make poetry. But Dr. Bridges has been able to make two volumes of poetry which take very high rank; and a whole school of minor poets has been classed under the head of "Robert Bridges and his followers" in the new Encyclopedia of English poets.

I do not intend at once to tire you by quoting this poet's descriptions of the seasons; I only want to interest you in him, and if I can do that, you will be apt to read these descriptions for yourselves. I am going to pick out bits, here and there, which seem to me beautiful in themselves, independently of their subjects. Indeed, I think this is the way that Robert Bridges wants us to read him. At the beginning of Book IV, of the shorter poems (you will be interested to know that most of his poems have no titles), he himself tells us what his whole purpose is, in these pretty stanzas:

> I love all beauteous things,
>   I seek and adore them;
> God hath no better praise,
> And man in his hasty days
>   Is honoured for them.

> I too will something make,
>   And joy in the making;
> Although to-morrow it seem
> Like the empty words of a dream
>   Remembered on waking.

With this hint I have no hesitation in beginning this lecture on Robert Bridges by picking out what seems to me almost the only philosophical poem in the whole of his work. The philosophy is not very deep, but the poem is haunting.

EROS

> Why hast thou nothing in thy face?
> Thou idol of the human race,
> Thou tyrant of the human heart,
> The flower of lovely youth that art;
> Yea, and that standest in thy youth
> An image of eternal Truth,
> With thy exuberant flesh so fair,
> That only Pheidias might compare,
> Ere from his chaste marmoreal form
> Time had decayed the colours warm;
> Like to his gods in thy proud dress,
> Thy starry sheen of nakedness.

> Surely thy body is thy mind,
> For in thy face is nought to find,
> Only thy soft unchristen'd smile
> That shadows neither love nor guile,
> But shameless will and power immense,
> In secret sensuous innocence.
>
> O king of joy, what is thy thought?
> I dream thou knowest it is nought,
> And wouldst in darkness come, but thou
> Makest the light where'er thou go.
> Ah yet no victim of thy grace,
> None who e'er longed for thy embrace,
> Hath cared to look upon thy face.

The divinity here described is not the infant but the more mature form of the god of Love, Eros (from whose name is derived the adjective "erotic," used in such terms as "erotic poetry"). This Eros was represented as a beautiful naked boy about twelve or thirteen years old. Several statues of him are among the most beautiful works of Greek art. It is one of these statues that the poet refers to. And you must understand his poem, first of all, as treating of physical love, physical passion, as distinguished from love which belongs rather to the mind and heart and which is alone real and enduring. There is always a certain amount of delusion in physical attraction, in mere bodily beauty; but about the deeper love, which is perfect friendship between the sexes, there is no delusion, and it only grows with time. Now the god Eros represented only the power of physical passion, the charm of youth. Looking at the face of the beautiful statue, the poet is startled by something which has been from ancient times noticed by all critics of Greek art, but which appears to him strange in another way—there is no expression in that face. It is beautiful, but it is also impersonal. So the faces of all the Greek gods were impersonal; they represented ideals, not realities. They were moved neither by deep love nor by deep hate—not at least in the conception of the artist and sculptor. They were above humanity, above affection, therefore above pity. Here it is worth while to remark the contrast between the highest Eastern ideals in sculpture and the highest Western ideals. In the art of the Far East the Buddha is also impersonal; he smiles, but the smile is of infinite pity, compassion, tenderness. He represents a supreme ideal of virtue. Nevertheless he is, though impersonal, warmly human for this very reason. The more beautiful Greek divinity smiles deliciously, but there is no tenderness, no compassion, no affection in that smile. It is not human; it is superhuman. Looking at the features of a Greek Aphrodite, an Eros, a Dionysius, you feel that they could smile with the same beautiful smile at the destruction of the world. What does the smile mean? You are charmed by it, yet it is mysterious, almost awful. It represents nothing but supreme content, supreme happiness —not happiness in the spiritual sense of rest, but happiness of perfect youth and innocence of pain. That is why there is something terrible about it to the modern thinker. It is without sympathy; it is only joy.

Now you will see the poem in its inner meaning. Let us paraphrase it:

"Why is there no expression in that divinely beautiful face of thine, O fair god, who art forever worshipped by the race of men, forever ruling the hearts of its youth without pity, without compassion! Thou who art the perfect image of the loveliness of youth, and the symbol of some eternal and universal law, so fair, so lovely that only the great Greek sculptor Pheidias could represent thee in pure marble, thou white as that marble itself, before time had faded the fresh colour with which thy statue had been painted! Truly thou art as one of his gods in the pride of thy nakedness—which becomes thee more than any robe, being itself luminous, a light of stars. But why is there no expression in thy face?

"It must be that thy body represents thy mind. Yet thy mind is not reflected in thy face like the mind of man. There I see only the beautiful old pagan smile, the smile of the years before the Religion of Sorrow came into this world. And that smile of thine shows neither love nor hate nor shame, but power incalculable and the innocence of sensuous pleasure.

"Thou king of Joy, of what dost thou think? For thy face no-wise betrays thy thought. Truly I believe thou dost not think of anything which troubles the minds of sorrowing men; thou thinkest of nothing. Thou art Joy, not thought. And I imagine that thou wouldst prefer not to be seen by men, to come to them in darkness only, or invisibly, as thou didst to Psyche in other years. But thou canst not remain invisible, since thy body is made of light, and forever makes a great shining about thee. For uncounted time thou hast moved the hearts of millions of men and of women; all have known thy presence, felt thy power. But none, even of those who most longed for thee, has ever desired to look into thy beautiful face, because it is not the face of humanity but of divinity, and because there is in it nothing of human love."

There is a good deal to think about in this poem, but to feel the beauty of it you ought to have before your eyes, when studying it, a good engraving of the statue. However, even without any illustration you will easily perceive the moral of the thought in it, that beauty and youth alone do not signify affection, nor even anything dear to the inner nature of man.

Now I shall turn to another part of the poet's work. Here is a little verse about a grown man looking at the picture of himself when he was a little child. I think that it is a very charming sonnet, and it will give you something to think about.

A man that sees by chance his picture, made
As once a child he was, handling some toy,

Will gaze to find his spirit within the boy,
Yet hath no secret with the soul portrayed:
He cannot think the simple thought which played
Upon those features then so frank and coy;
'Tis his, yet oh! not his: and o'er the joy
His fatherly pity bends in tears dismayed.

There is indeed no topic which Robert Bridges has treated
more exquisitely and touchingly than certain phases of childhood, the poetry of childhood, the purity of childhood, the
pathos of childhood. I do not think that any one except
Patmore, and Patmore only in one poem, "The Toys," has
even approached him. Take this little poem for example,
on the death of a little boy. It is the father who is speaking.

ON A DEAD CHILD

Perfect little body, without fault or stain on thee,
  With promise of strength and manhood full and fair!
    Though cold and stark and bare,
The bloom and the charm of life doth awhile remain on thee.

Thy mother's treasure wert thou;—alas! no longer
  To visit her heart with wondrous joy, to be
    Thy father's pride;—ah, he
Must gather his faith together, and his strength make stronger.

To me, as I move thee now in the last duty,
  Dost thou with a turn or gesture anon respond;
    Startling my fancy fond
With a chance attitude of the head, a freak of beauty.

Thy hand clasps, as 'twas wont, my finger, and holds it:
  But the grasp is the clasp of Death, heartbreaking and stiff;
    Yet feels my hand as if
'Twas still thy will, thy pleasure and trust that enfolds it.

So I lay thee there, thy sunken eyelids closing,—
  Go lie thou there in thy coffin, thy last little bed;—
    Propping thy wise, sad head,
Thy firm, pale hands across thy chest disposing.

So quiet!—doth the change content thee?—Death, whithcr hath he
      taken thee?
   To a world, do I think, that rights the disaster of this?
      The vision of which I miss,
Who weep for the body, and wish but to warm thee and awaken thee?

Ah! little at best can all our hopes avail us
   To lift this sorrow, or cheer us, when in the dark
      Unwilling, alone we embark,
And the things we have seen, and have known and have heard of,
      fail us!

You will see the exquisiteness of this more fully after a
little explanation. The father is performing the last duty
to his little dead son: washing the body with his own hands,
closing the eyes, and placing the little corpse in the coffin,
rather than trust this work to any less loving hands. The
Western coffin, you must know, is long, and the body is
placed in it lying at full length as upon a bed, with a
little pillow to support the head. Then the hands are
closed upon the heart in the attitude of prayer. The poem
describes more than the feelings of a father, during these
tender offices. As he turns the little body to wash it, the
small head changes its position now and then, and the motion is so much like the pretty motions made by that little
head during life, that it is very difficult to believe there is
now no life there. In all modern English poetry there is
nothing more touching than the lines:

> Startling my fancy fond
> With a chance attitude of the head, a freak of beauty.

The word "freak" is incomparably beautiful in this line,
for it has a sense of playfulness; it means often a childish
fancy or whim or pretty mischievous action. The turning
of the dead head seems so like the motion of the living head
in play. Then as the hands were washed by the father, the
relaxed muscles caused the opened fingers to close upon the
father's finger, just as in other days when the two walked

about together, the little boy's hands were too small to hold the great hands of the father, and therefore clasped one finger only. Then observe the very effective use of two most simple adjectives to picture the face of the dead child —"wise" and "sad." Have you ever seen the face of a dead child? If you have, you will remember how its calmness gives one the suggestion of strange knowledge; the wise smile little, and fond fancy for thousands of years has looked into the faces of the unsmiling dead in search of some expression of supreme knowledge. Also there is an expression of sadness in the face of death, even in the faces of children asleep, although relaxation of muscles is the real explanation of the fact. All these fancies are very powerfully presented in the first five verses.

In the last two verses the sincerity of grief uniquely shows itself. "Where do you think the little life has gone?" the father asks. "Do you want me to say that I think it has gone to a happier world than this, to what you call Heaven? Ah, I must tell you the truth. I do not know; I doubt, I fear. When a grief like this comes to us, all our religious imaginations and hopes can serve us little."

You must read that over and over again to know the beauty of it. Here is another piece of very touching poetry about a boy, perhaps about the same boy who afterward died. It will require some explanation, for it is much deeper in a way than the previous piece. It is called "Pater Filio," meaning "the father to the son."

> Sense with keenest edge unusèd,
>   Yet unsteel'd by scathing fire;
> Lovely feet as yet unbruisèd
>   On the ways of dark desire;
> Sweetest hope that lookest smiling
> O'er the wilderness defiling!
>
> Why such beauty, to be blighted
>   By the swarm of foul destruction?

Why such innocence delighted,
    When sin stalks to thy seduction?
All the litanies e'er chaunted
Shall not keep thy faith undaunted.

.   .   .   .   .

Me too once unthinking Nature
    —Whence Love's timeless mockery took me,—
Fashion'd so divine a creature,
    Yea, and like a beast forsook me.
I forgave, but tell the measure
Of her crime in thee, my treasure.

The father is suffering the great pain of fathers when
he speaks thus, the pain of fearing for the future of his
child; and the mystery of things oppresses him, as it oppresses everybody who knows what it is to be afraid for
the sake of another. He wonders at the beautiful fresh
senses of the boy, "yet unsteeled by scathing fire"—that is,
not yet hardened by experience of pain. He admires the
beauty of the little feet tottering happily about; but in the
same moment dark thoughts come to him, for he remembers how blood-stained those little feet must yet become
on the ways of the world, in the streets of cities, in the
struggle of life. And he delights in the smile of the child,
full of hope that knows nothing of the great foul wilder-
ness of the world, in which envy and malice and passions
of many kinds make it difficult to remain either good or
hopeful. And he asks, "Why should a child be made so
beautiful, only to lose that beauty at a later day, through
sickness and grief and pain of a thousand kinds? Why
should a child come into the world so charmingly innocent
and joyful, only to lose that innocence and happiness later
on through the encountering of passion and temptation?
Why should a child believe so deeply in the gods and in
human nature? Later on, no matter how much he grieves,
the time will come when that faith in the powers unseen
must be sadly warped."

And lastly the father remembers his own childhood, thinking, "I too was once a divine little creature like that. Love, the eternal illusion, brought me into the world, and Nature made me as innocent and trustful as this little boy. Later on, however, the same Nature abandoned me, like the animal that forsakes her young as soon as they grow a little strong. I forgave Nature for that abandonment," the father says, turning to the child, "but it is only when I look at you, my treasure, that I understand how much I lost with the vanishing of my own childhood."

Nobody in the whole range of English literature has written anything more tender than that. It is out of the poet's heart.

One would expect, on reading delicacies of this kind, that the poet would express himself not less beautifully than tenderly in regard to woman. As a matter of fact, he certainly ranks next to Rossetti as a love poet, even in point of workmanship. I am also inclined to think, and I believe that critics will later recognise this, that his feeling in regard to the deeper and nobler qualities of love can only be compared to the work of Browning in the same direction. It has not Browning's force, nor the occasional sturdiness that approaches roughness. It is altogether softer and finer, and it has none of Browning's eccentricities. A collection of sonnets, fifty-nine in number, entitled "The Growth of Love" may very well be compared with Rossetti's sonnet-sequence, "The House of Life." But it is altogether unlike Rossetti's work; it deals with thought more than sensation, and with joy more than sorrow. But before we give an example of these, let me quote a little fancy of a very simple kind, that gives the character of Robert Bridges as a love poet quite as well as any long or elaborate poem could do.

> Long are the hours the sun is above,
> But when evening comes I go home to my love.
>
> I'm away the daylight hours and more,
> Yet she comes not down to open the door.

She does not meet me upon the stair,—
She sits in my chamber and waits for me there.

As I enter the room she does not move;
I always walk straight up to my love;

And she lets me take my wonted place
At her side, and gaze in her dear, dear face.

There as I sit, from her head thrown back
Her hair falls straight in a shadow black.

Aching and hot as my tired eyes be,
She is all that I wish to see.

And in my wearied and toil-dinned ear,
She says all things that I wish to hear.

Dusky and duskier grows the room,
Yet I see her best in the darker gloom.

When the winter eves are early and cold,
The firelight hours are a dream of gold.

And so I sit here night by night,
In rest and enjoyment of love's delight.

But a knock at the door, a step on the stair
Will startle, alas, my love from her chair.

If a stranger comes she will not stay:
At the first alarm she is off and away.

And he wonders, my guest, usurping her throne,
That I sit so much by myself alone.

You feel the mystery of the thing beginning at the second stanza, but not until you get to the sixth stanza do you begin to perceive it. This is not a living woman, but a ghost. The whole poetry of the composition is here. What does the poet mean? He has not told us anywhere, and it is better that he should not have told us, because we can imagine so many things, so many different circumstances, which the poem would equally well illustrate. Were this the fancy of a young man, we might say that the phantom love means the ideal wife, the unknown bride of the future, the beautiful dream that every young man makes for himself about a perfectly happy home. Again, we might suppose that the spirit bride is not really related at all to love in the common sense, but figures or symbolises only the devotion of the poet to poetry, in which case the spirit bride is art. But the poet is not a young man; he is an old country doctor, coming home late every night from visiting his patients, tired, weary, but with plenty of work to do in his private study. Who, then, may be the shadowy woman with the long black hair always waiting for him alone? Perhaps art, perhaps a memory, most likely the memory of a dead wife, and we may even imagine, the mother of the little boy about whose death the poet has so beautifully written elsewhere. I do not pretend to explain; I do not want to explain; I am only anxious to show you that this composition fulfils one of the finest conditions of poetry, by its suggestiveness. It leaves many questions to be answered in fancy, and all of them are beautiful.

Let me now take a little piece about the singing of the nightingale. I think you remember that I read to you, and commented upon Keats's poem about the nightingale. That is the greatest English poem, the most perfect, the most unapproachable of poems upon the nightingale. And after that, only a very, very skilful poet dare write seriously about the nightingale, for his work, if at all imperfect, must suffer terribly by comparison with the verses of Keats. But Robert Bridges has actually come very near to the height of Keats in a three stanza poem upon the same subject. The treatment of the theme is curiously different. The poem of Keats represents supreme delight, the delight which is so great that it becomes sad. The poem of Bridges is

slightly dark. The mystery of the bird song is the fact
that he chiefly considers; and he considers it in a way that
leaves you thinking a long time after the reading of the
verses. The suggestions of the composition, however, can
best be considered after we have read the verses.

NIGHTINGALES

Beautiful must be the mountains whence ye come,
And bright in the fruitful valleys the streams, wherefrom
      Ye learn your song:
Where are those starry woods? O might I wander there,
Among the flowers, which in that heavenly air
      Bloom the year long!

Nay, barren are those mountains and spent the streams:
Our song is the voice of desire, that haunts our dreams,
      A throe of the heart,
Whose pining visions dim, forbidden hopes profound,
No dying cadence nor long sigh can sound,
      For all our art.

Alone, aloud in the raptured ear of men
We pour our dark nocturnal secret; and then,
      As night is withdrawn
From these sweet-springing meads and bursting boughs of May,
Dream, while the innumerable choir of day
      Welcome the dawn.

Other poets, following the popular notion that birds are
happy when they sing, often speak of the nightingale as an
especially happy bird because of the extraordinary sweetness of its song. The Greek poets thought otherwise; to
them it seemed that the song of the birds was the cry of
infinite sorrow and regret, and one of the most horrible of
all the Greek myths is the story of Philomela, transformed
into a nightingale. Matthew Arnold, you may remember,
takes the Greek view. So in a way does Robert Bridges,
but there are other suggestions in his verse, purely human.
Paraphrased, the meaning is this (a man speaks first):

"When I listen to your song, I feel sure that the country from which you come must be very beautiful; and very sweet the warbling music of the stream, whose sound may have taught you how to sing. O how much I wish that I could go to your wonderful world, your tropical world, where summer never dies, and where flowers are all the year in bloom." But the birds answer: "You are in error. Desolate is the country from which we come; and in that country the mountains are naked and barren, and the rivers are dried up. If we sing, it is because of the pain that we feel in our hearts, the pain of great desire for happier things. But that which we desire without knowing it by sight, that which we hope for in vain, these are more beautiful than any song of ours can express. Skilful we are, but not skilful enough to utter all that we feel. At night we sing, trying to speak our secret of pain to men; but when all the other birds awake and salute the sun with happy song, while all the flowers open their leaves to the light, then we do not sing, but dream on in silence and shadow."

Is there not in this beautiful verse the suggestion of the condition of the soul in the artist and the poet, in those whose works are beautiful or seem beautiful, not because of joy, but because of pain—the pain of larger knowledge and deeper perception? I think it is particularly this that makes the superior beauty of the stanzas. You soon find yourself thinking, not about the nightingale, but about the human heart and the human soul.

Here and there on almost every page of Bridges are to be found queer little beauties, little things that reveal the personality of the writer. Can you describe an April sky, and clouds in the sky, and the light and the colour of the day, all in two lines? It is not an easy thing to do; but there are two lines that seem to do it in a poem, which is the sixth of the fourth book:

> On high the hot sun smiles, and banks of cloud uptower
> In bulging heads that crowd for miles the dazzling South.

Notice the phrase "bulging heads." Nothing is so difficult to describe in words, as to form, than ordinary clouds, because the form is indefinite. Yet the great rounding masses do dimly suggest giant heads, not necessarily the heads of persons, much oftener heads of trees. The word "bulging" means not only a swelling outwards but a soft baggy kind of swelling. No other adjective in the English language could better express the roundish form here alluded to. And we know that they are white, simply by the poet's use of the word dazzling that completes the picture. But there is more to notice; the poet has called these clouds banks of cloud, and has spoken of them as crowding the sky for miles. Remember that a bank of clouds always implies masses of cloud joined together below. Now on a beautiful clear day you must have often noticed in the sky that a clear space, straight as any line upon a map, marks off the lower part of the cloud. Between the horizon and this line there is only clear blue; then the clouds, all lined and joined together at the bottom, are all rounded, bulgy at the top. This is what the two lines which I have quoted picture to us.

In the simplest fancies, however, the same truth to Nature is observable, and comes to us in like surprises. Here is a little bit about a new moon shining on the sea at night.

> She lightens on the comb
>   Of leaden waves, that roar
> And thrust their hurried foam
>   Up on the dusky shore.
>
> Behind the Western bars
>   The shrouded day retreats,
> And unperceived the stars
>   Steal to their sovran seats.
>
> And whiter grows the foam,
>   The small moon lightens more;

And as I turn me home,
My shadow walks before.

You feel that this has been seen and felt, that it is not merely the imagination of a man sitting down to manufacture poetry at his desk. I imagine that you have not seen the word "comb" used of wave motion very often, though it is now coming more and more into poetical use. The comb of the wave is its crest, and the term is used just as we use the word comb in speaking of the crest of a cock. But there is also the verb "to comb"; and this refers especially to the curling over of the crest of the wave, just before it breaks, when the appearance of the crest-edge resembles that of wool being pulled through a comb (*kushi*). Thus the word gives us two distinct and picturesque ideas, whether used as noun or as adjective. Notice too the use of "leaden" in relation to the colour of waves where not touched by moonlight; the dull grey could not be better described by any other word. Also observe that as night advances, though the sea becomes dark, the form appears to become whiter and whiter. In a phosphorescent sea the foam lines appear very beautiful in darkness.

I shall quote but one more poem by Robert Bridges, choosing it merely to illustrate how modern things appear to this charming dreamer of old-fashioned dreams. One would think that he could not care much about such matters as machinery, telegraphs, railroads, steamships. But he has written a very fine sonnet about a steamship; and the curious thing is that this poem appears in the middle of a collection of love poems:

The fabled sea-snake, old Leviathan,
Or else what grisly beast of scaly chine
That champ'd the ocean-wrack and swash'd the brine,
Before the new and milder days of man,
Had never rib nor bray nor swindging fan

Like his iron swimmer of the Clyde or Tyne,
Late-born of golden seed to breed a line
Of offspring swifter and more huge of plan.

Straight is her going, for upon the sun
When once she hath look'd, her path and place are plain;
With tireless speed she smiteth one by one
The shuddering seas and foams along the main;
And her eased breath, when her wild race is run,
Roars through her nostrils like a hurricane.

While this is true to fact, it is also fine fancy; the only true way in which the practical and mechanical can appeal to the poet is in the sensation of life and power that it produces.

I think we have read together enough of Robert Bridges to excite some interest in such of his poetry as we have not read. But you will have perceived that this poet is in his own way quite different from other poets of the time, and that he cannot appeal to common-place minds. His poetry is like fine old wine, mild, mellowed wine, that only the delicate palate will be able to appreciate properly.

INDEX